Interpreting the Internet

Interpreting the Internet

*Feminist and Queer Counterpublics
in Latin America*

Elisabeth Jay Friedman

UNIVERSITY OF CALIFORNIA PRESS

University of California Press, one of the most
distinguished university presses in the United States,
enriches lives around the world by advancing scholarship
in the humanities, social sciences, and natural sciences. Its
activities are supported by the UC Press Foundation and
by philanthropic contributions from individuals and
institutions. For more information, visit www.ucpress.edu.

University of California Press
Oakland, California

Library of Congress Cataloging-in-Publication Data

Names: Friedman, Elisabeth J., author.
Title: Interpreting the Internet : feminist and queer
    counterpublics in Latin America / Elisabeth Jay
    Friedman.
Description: Oakland, California : University of
    California Press, [2017] | Includes bibliographical
    references and index.
Identifiers: LCCN 2016030570| ISBN 9780520284494
    (cloth : alk. paper) | ISBN 0520284496 (cloth : alk.
    paper) | ISBN 9780520284517 (pbk. : alk. paper) |
    ISBN 0520284518 (pbk. : alk. paper)
Subjects: LCSH: Internet and women—Latin America. |
    Internet—Social aspects—Latin America. | Sexual
    minorities—Latin America—Social life and customs. |
    Internet and activism—Latin America. | Feminism—
    Latin America. | At sign—Social aspects—Latin
    America.
Classification: LCC HQ1178 .F75 2017 | DDC 302.23
    /1—dc23
LC record available at https://lccn.loc.gov/2016030570

ClassifNumber   PubDate
DeweyNumber'—dc23   CatalogNumber

Manufactured in the United States of America

25   24   23   22   21   20   19   18   17   16
10   9   8   7   6   5   4   3   2   1

For my family
Kathryn, Annabel, and Arlo

Cambia lo superficial
Cambia también lo profundo
Cambia el modo de pensar
Cambia todo en este mundo

—Mercedes Sosa, "Todo Cambia"

What we see, we see
and seeing is changing
. . .

       I am an instrument in the shape
of a woman trying to translate pulsations
into images   for the relief of the body
and the reconstruction of the mind.

—Adrienne Rich, "Planetarium"

Contents

Illustrations

Acknowledgments

This book exists because activists in Argentina, Brazil, and Mexico took time away from the neighborhoods they were organizing, the magazines they were publishing, the campaigns they were coordinating, and many other pressing commitments to have a conversation (or two) with me about the internet. Seasoned veterans discussed the implications of connectivity to long-term trajectories; a younger generation described the creative ways they deployed social media. Several people went above and beyond to explain the context of what I was hearing: Mariana Pérez Ocaña and Erika Smith in Mexico; Gabriela Adelstein, Irene Ocampo, and Constanza Tabbush in Argentina; and Sonia Corrêa, Lisa Earl Castillo, and Magaly Pazello in Brazil. I am deeply grateful to everyone who spoke with me, whether or not their individual stories and ideas emerge in these pages, for what they taught me about how Latin American feminist and queer counterpublic organizations have interpreted the internet over time.

Many others helped me to develop my ideas, refine my analysis, and present my research. Lincoln Dahlberg and Radhika Gajjala were encouraging and insightful at the book's proposal stage. My manuscript reviewers, Sonia Alvarez and Jocelyn Olcott, pushed me to clarify my contributions through their close readings and well-honed perspectives on the region and its feminisms. They also shared contacts and archives that were fundamental for the project. I greatly appreciate their efforts on my behalf. I am indebted to Dorothy Kidd for all the useful citations, interesting suggestions, and thoroughly feminist collegiality she has directed my way. About thirty years ago, Karen Barad introduced me to the idea that society and science are co-constituted; although it has taken a while to sprout, I am thankful for the seed she planted. And in field sites, conference hotels, and email messages, Kathy Hochstetler has illustrated over and again that immense distances can be connected through solidaristic networks. These brilliant and committed scholars' own work and work ethic(s) have long inspired me; I am blessed to have such mentors, colleagues, and friends.

My loving family of origin has cheered me on through this project as they have with the rest of my life. My father, Martin Friedman, trained his finely focused grammarian's loupe on the introduction; my sister, Edith Friedman, offered insights and procured texts from the UC Berkeley library. And my brother, Max Friedman, was always ready with a reassuring word, a quick read, and excellent academic role modeling. Sadly, my stepmother, Elena Servi Burgess, did not live to see this book in print. But she celebrated the news that it would be published with reliably effusive pride.

I am thankful for the many opportunities to present material from this project, and the useful commentary I received on it, at venues including Amherst College, Duke University, Université Lille 3 CECILLE-Université Paris 13 CRIDAF, Universidad de Buenos Aires, and the University of San Francisco, as well as meetings of the American Sociological Association, the American Political Science Association, the Berkshire Conference on the History of Women, the International Studies Association, the Latin American Studies Association, and the Western Political Science Association.

For assistance with research, quiero agradecer a mi querida amiga Silvia Ostrovsky por los años de amistad, intercambios y apoyo durante mi trabajo de campo en Argentina. The ever-helpful librarians Pamela Graham of Columbia University and Carol Spector of the University of San Francisco answered my many questions and pointed me toward valuable resources. Research assistants Vanessa Barchfield, Janet Chavez, Alexa Gonzalez, Jennifer Holthaus, Adriana Lins de Albuquerque, and Angelica Miramontes contributed their diligence and perspectives at various points along this project's winding path. Dan Battle kindly spent hours scanning images. My initial fieldwork was made possible thanks to a 2001–2 Fulbright-Hays Faculty Research Abroad

Award administered through Columbia University. All subsequent field-work and research assistance was generously underwritten by the Faculty Development Fund of the University of San Francisco.

At UC Press, I deeply appreciate editor Kate Marshall's unflagging enthusiasm for the project and her faith in my ability to bring it to fruition. Her assistants Zuha Khan and Bradley Depew patiently fielded many queries. Glynnis Koike designed the perfect cover, Cindy Fulton shepherded the book through publication, and Andrew Frisardi provided painstaking and essential copyediting.

Kathryn Jay started on this adventure with me sixteen years ago, when she suggested that I find a research topic a little closer to home; at that point we still believed you could study the internet by going online. She then cheerfully and efficiently packed us up and moved us around Latin America so that I could carry out the field research that took us much farther from home, but closer to each other. A few years, a transcontinental move, and two children later, she stayed home to take care of them while I went off to learn about change over time. After making sure that I really wanted to write a book, she then made sure that what you are reading really is a book. A girl could not ask for a more collaborative life partner, or a more incisive, dedicated, and persevering editor. As I wrote, our amazing daughter Annabel Jay and awesome son Arlo Jay offered daily reminders of our wonderful life beyond the screen. This project started a while before they did, but their future, and my family's love, are what keep me moving forward. This book is dedicated to my favorite team, the Berkeley Jays.

This book draws on these previously published works:

"Feminism under Construction." *NACLA Report on the Americas* 47, no. 4 (2014–15): 20–24.

"ICT and Gender Equality Advocacy in Latin America: Impacts of a New 'Utility.'" *Feminist Media Studies* 3, no. 3 (2003): 356–60.

"Lesbians in (Cyber) Space: The Politics of the Internet in Latin American On- and Off-line Communities." *Media, Culture, and Society* 29, no. 5 (Fall 2007): 790–811.

"The Politics of Information and Communication Technology Use among Latin American Gender Equality Organizations." *Knowledge, Technology, and Policy* 18, no. 2 (2005): 30–40.

"The Reality of Virtual Reality: The Internet's Impact within Gender Equality Advocacy Communities in Latin America." *Latin American Politics and Society* 47, no. 3 (2005): 1–34.

"Seeking Rights from the Left: Gender and Sexuality in Latin America." In *Women's Movements in the Global Era,* edited by Amrita Basu, 285–314. Boulder, CO: Westview Press, 2010.

Introduction

Interpreting the Internet: A Feminist
Sociomaterial Approach

In 2016, internet-fueled protest is everywhere. Across South Africa, students have used social media to spark mass protests and ignite a national debate on the right to education, shutting down universities in the process. Black Lives Matter activists in the United States have created hashtags and used "Black Twitter" to reveal the devastating impact of systemic, institutional racism on black and brown bodies. On Facebook and Twitter, immigration advocates circulate pictures, stories, and petitions, seeking just treatment for those whose homes are battle zones in declared and undeclared wars. Around the world, people rely on the internet to decry injustice and demand change.

But there was a time, not very long ago, when digital natives had yet to be born and activist communities were going online for the first, and second, and hundredth time, learning as they went. As they explored this new technology, which emerged simultaneously as a tool to wield and as a place to engage with each other and the world around them, users made and remade the internet in their own image(s).

This book is the story of that mutual development and its impact in a dynamic and complex context: Latin American feminist and queer communities.[1] Whether defying the Catholic Church's defense of heterosexual marriage and rejection of abortion, calling out neoliberal profiteers for their exploitation of working women and men, or demanding that democratic legislators and voters live up to their constitutions' declarations of equality and freedom, these diverse communities embrace a

FIGURE 1. International Women's Day commemorative stamp, Mexico (March 8, 1999). Reprinted from Servicio Postal Mexicano.

wide-ranging repertoire of means to confront deep-seated regional hierarchies. For the last two decades, a range of internet-based applications has changed, and sometimes enhanced, this repertoire of activism.

When I first started to wonder about the internet's impact on Latin American feminist activists and organizations in particular, I noticed a striking trend. As the technology spread across the region in the early 1990s, a new use for the typographical "@" symbol cropped up everywhere I looked. Even as activists began to share their *correo* (short for *dirección de correo electrónico,* or email address) in order to increase their connections, they repurposed the all-important @. Instead of typing out the *o/a* used in Spanish words to indicate that both genders were intended—an awkward, but rhetorically crucial, feminist grammatical intervention—*niño/a* (child) became "niñ@"; *ingeniero/a* (engineer) became "ingenier@"; *político/a* (politician) became "politic@"; *ellos/as* (they) became "ell@s"; and so on. Spanish-speaking feminists interpreted the @ symbol as symbolic inclusion, a new solution to an old linguistic challenge.

This was far from the original intent. Ray Tomlinson, a U.S. programmer, established the symbol's use in email addresses to indicate the location of a user's server. The @, an accounting or commercial symbol meaning "at a rate of," was readily available on English-language keyboards, handily located above the 2. But @ was seldom needed by Spanish-speaking writers before the advent of email; traveling around Latin America in the early 2000s, I found that cybercafé computers often had a strip of paper glued to their keyboards with instructions on how to type the crucial symbol by using a complex combination of keys.

As the use of email spread across their region, Latin American feminists had good reasons to memorize that combination. The symbol's use in email would enable them to further a regional specialty: extensive networking. But they had also found a symbol which looked to their gender-sensitive eyes like an *a* embedded inside an *o*. The @ wasn't originally intended for feminist use, but that is how they interpreted it in their own vernacular. Because activists were seeking ways to challenge gender-based exclusion, they found what they were looking for literally embedded in the internet.

What I noticed during the initial popularization of the internet among feminist activists illustrated what another decade of observation and conversations would finally teach me. In asking "What is the internet's impact on Latin American feminist communities?" I had been considering only half of the topic. In addition to wondering what the technology was doing to them, I needed to consider what they were doing to the technology. I needed to ask, "How have the internet and feminism changed each other?" Eventually, I came to realize that the internet's significance is determined through use; in this case, the diverse ways in which activists in Latin America have incorporated the internet over time.

This book makes two original contributions to our understanding of the intertwined nature of the internet and society. Empirically, it offers the first in-depth exploration of the way Latin American feminist and some queer communities have interpreted the internet to support their "counterpublics." Counterpublics are the places, spaces, or means through which those pushed to societies' margins develop their identities, construct communities, and formulate strategies for transforming wider publics. Latin American feminist and queer communities, and their regional networks, long predate the internet, but they have always relied on the circulation of alternative media. The internet has both enhanced and complicated their preexisting practices. Encouraged by a global network of women and men determined to make an internet accessible to all, feminists and LGBT activists have changed—and been changed by—this web connecting all they do. Other regions and other activists have had similar experiences, but Latin America was uniquely positioned to take advantage of the early internet. In no other region of the Global South were so many "early adopting" technically skilled organizations ready and eager to get such deeply regionally connected counterpublics online. This book also considers what has happened over time, as the internet has become entrenched in activist practice.

Conceptually, this book addresses some of our central preoccupations about the internet: Does it change everything? Fall short of fulfilling its promise? Mirror preexisting experience? Does it shift our perceptions, weaken or strengthen our attachments, stimulate or restrict our participation? Around the world, development planners, venture capitalists, teachers, parents, community organizers, elected officials, and even terrorists ponder these questions. Every day, a burgeoning array of news sources, whether digital versions of traditional media or our own Facebook and Twitter feeds, offer reflections, prognostications, or critiques of our digital lives. We are wrestling with the implications of the internet. How can we grasp them? This question consumes change-seekers. Because the two major attributes of the internet—its facilitation of communications and its information distribution—are essential to the work of counterpublics, it seems ideally suited to their endeavors. But how is it helping the lives beyond the screens?

Through an exploration of Latin American feminist and queer, principally lesbian feminist, counterpublics, I advance three interrelated arguments about the nature of the internet and its potential for producing social and political transformation. First, as is true of all technologies, the development of the internet, from creation to deployment, is influenced by social contexts, variable over time and place. Second, the internet in itself offers no guarantee of transformation; as Faith Wilding and María Hernándes of the cyberfeminist collective SubRosa warn, "it is foolish to believe that major social, economic, and political issues can be addressed by throwing technology at them."[2] Instead, my third contribution is to argue that the internet's potential depends on the consciousness and creativity with which activists translate it into their own contexts, through adopting, sharing, and deploying it.

In our 2012 interview, Carlos Alvarez, a founder of Wamani, a Buenos Aires–based internet provider and civic capacity-building organization, attested to the importance of context when he cautioned me that "technological spaces are never different from society."[3] But the argument that technology's significance depends on use reaches beyond that deterministic equivalence: it tells us, in the words of media studies scholar Liesbet van Zoonen, to take into account not only contexts, but "practices of usage."[4] As different people and communities interact with the internet over time, they alter its meaning and (re)shape its structure. Following social theorists Saskia Sassen and Robert Latham,[5] I call this approach to understanding technology's meaning to society "sociomaterial": it incorporates the material practices of technology, or local attempts at interpreting global forces, along with the contexts in which such practices are embedded.

I did not begin this study with a sociomaterial perspective. Instead, I started off in a straightforward social science way: I had a factor, internet technology, whose impact on a political phenomenon, gender- and sexuality-based organizing, I wanted to study. I designed a comparative study of this subject in Argentina, Brazil, and Mexico, and went to talk to over a hundred feminist, women's,[6] and LGBT counterpublic organizations, individual activists, and socially motivated computer technicians in 2001–2. I completed a round of research within a framework that held subject and object as separately intelligible. Using these organizations as the primary example, I published research that examined the internet's impact on civil society in new democracies. I wrote another piece exploring whether the internet had enabled lesbians to address major challenges to their sexuality-based organizing. In this work I advanced claims about the ways in which this technology could assist civic organizations in promoting democratization and diversity. I based these conclusions on the common assumption that we can treat technology and society as two separate phenomena—so that we can look at how one factor affects the other.

Since writing those first publications, however, I have become convinced that, like other technologies, the ever-evolving internet is "constitutively entangled" with society.[7] As scholars who study science and technology have shown, technology is inseparable from its environment. But this doesn't mean that society determines technology or is determined by it. Rather, they are intimately related parts of a whole—what has been called an "assemblage" or a "network of actants"[8]—that takes its shape from the relations among humans and nonhuman elements. We normally think and talk about people and technologies as separate from one another, making it difficult to conceive of, conceptualize, and express this relationship. But if we want to grasp the implications of a technology that each day becomes more profoundly integrated into our lives, we must understand the internet and ourselves as parts of an interconnected web.

In retrospect, I can see why my early research separated technology from society. In my interviews, I heard activists trying to come to grips with something new. They could easily remember life before the internet. Indeed, some of them mainly lived a pre-internet life when I arrived to ask nosy questions about email traffic and website design. But because I followed some activists and organizations over the course of a decade or more, I saw the gradual interpenetration of activism and technology, and realized that, even at the beginning, the processes had interlocked. Talking to and watching Latin American feminists and queer activists as they interpreted the internet through their practices forced me to reject the idea of either techno-causality or social determination. A "cause and effect" model could not capture the mutual and dynamic unfolding between the internet and activism. To understand the meaning of the internet to activist communities meant seeing both sides as an integrated whole.

This sociomaterial approach differs from early feminist theories of the internet, which understood the internet as separate from, and inherently useful to, women. "Cyberfeminists" proposed that the internet ideally suited women's agency, given its fluid, horizontal, relational nature, and its availability in multiple sites.[9] Such views assumed that both the internet and women had a given, and fixed, nature, largely ignoring the social construction of the technology and of gender itself. They also neglected the many women who could not access the new technology, or who were effectively embedded within the "integrated circuit" through their work on the assembly lines of digital devices.[10]

The next generation of researchers proved more skeptical. They warned that internet technology, like all technology, incorporated dominant ideas about how technology should work—and for whom.[11] But they still saw society and technology as separable.

Other scholars have refuted essentialist assumptions about machines and their integration into women's lives. They emphasize "the medium as well as the embodied experience of and with the medium."[12] Instead of seeing women and technologies as separate from one another, "as if there was such a thing as a body or a world unmarked and unmediated by technologies,"[13] they see them as intertwined. The feminist sociomaterial perspective I use in this book acknowledges the shifting entanglements of individuals, including their positions in gender, race, class, and sexual hierarchies, with a technology laced with utopian fantasies and mined by persistent inequalities.

WHY LOOK AT LATIN AMERICAN FEMINIST
AND QUEER COUNTERPUBLICS?

This book traces the evolution of Latin American feminist and queer counterpublics, from close to the beginning of the internet through the advent of social media, to show how on- and offline worlds have merged and what that demonstrates about the social relations of technology. Such insights could come from focusing on many different communities. But Latin American feminist and queer counterpublics are ideal sites for the evaluation of global trends in digitally enhanced activism. Like activists in other world regions, they have responded to exclusionary social hierarchies and political institutions, as well as exploitative economic models, by constructing counterpublics at local and national levels. But nowhere else have activists developed such a vibrant *regional* community in response to shared challenges, communicating through the widely shared language of Spanish, as well as Portuguese in the case of Brazil.[14] Moreover, these communities are committed to inclusion. Latin American feminists have valiantly, though not always successfully, attempted to work across deep-seated divisions of ideology, geography, class, ethnicity, race, sexuality, and even gender itself. Since the 1980s, LGBT communities have also organized to demand that their lives and rights be recognized by states and societies. These counterpublics have seized the opportunities seemingly afforded by the internet, in many cases becoming early adopters. Building on their histories of struggle, they have incorporated new technologies to strengthen their communities and achieve world-renowned successes in political representation, legal reform, and identity recognition.

Feminists' mere existence, let alone their goals, have long stirred controversy in Latin American societies.[15] Powerful politicians and threatened patriarchs have belittled, ignored, and punished them for their outspokenness. Pastors have railed, and rallied their followers, against them. Hierarchies that subordinate women and LGBT people structure Latin American society and politics, contributing to a set of norms that cross national boundaries. The historic dominance of the Catholic Church has embedded traditional Catholic ideals in society. In particular, patriarchal heteronormativity, or the privileging of male power and heterosexual gender relations, anchors social, political, and even economic institutions. This has made it difficult for women to challenge Catholic gender roles, particularly women's primary identification as devout mothers. In fact, in the first half of the twentieth century, political parties judged whether to support women's suffrage on the basis of party leaders' perceptions of women's fidelity to the interests, if not the instructions, of the Catholic Church. Until the late twentieth century, LGBT communities also faced denigration because their sexuality or gender identity seemed to violate the social order.

Gender and sexuality are far from being the only social relations of power structuring this region. Although *mestizaje* or racial mixing is a hallmark of Latin American countries, racial hierarchies generally privilege people with lighter skin over those with darker, presumed to be a sign of African heritage or indigenous ancestry. Such hierarchies overlap perniciously with those of class; Latin America is notorious for having the worst economic inequality in the world. School systems, economic opportunities, urban development and the like reflect these relations of power. The region's social rankings relegate poor Afro-Latin and indigenous women to the bottom, and generally stack the deck against those without gender, racial, sexual, or class privilege.

Not surprisingly, political organization has most often reinforced social hierarchies. Pendulum swings between authoritarian and democratic politics, with periodic attempts at revolutionary transformation, have alternately repressed and opened space for citizen incorporation. Paradoxically, women's political inclusion has not always tracked larger shifts. During the worst periods of political repression in the 1970s and 1980s, Latin American military and military-backed governments, under the banners of national security and anticommunism, often violently repressed all manner of social organizing. But from Argentina to Guatemala, mothers emerged as the backbone of opposition movements as they denounced that their sons and daughters had been kidnapped, tortured, and murdered by their governments.[16] However, with the return of democratic politics, women found themselves sidelined and their demands for full participation in political life and leadership positions brushed aside. This has also been true in more radical contexts: despite having leading roles in revolutionary struggles in Cuba and Nicaragua, radical women were subsequently organized in support of the state, rather than allowed to defend their own interests.[17] And early LGBT activists faced similar demands and challenges.[18] Although they were stalwart members of leftist parties, their sexuality was judged as taboo, contrary to "revolutionary morality." This attitude was reflected in the homophobic policies and practices of the early revolutionary regimes in Cuba and Nicaragua. Access to Latin American political institutions was limited on the basis of gender and sexuality.

Often but not always in tandem with political transitions, shifting regional models have also conditioned opportunities on the basis of gender. The neoliberal export orientation of the late twentieth century led to the creation of jobs disproportionately filled by women, such as in the manufacturing, processing, or assembly plants known as *maquiladoras*.[19] But as public social service provision weakened or disappeared under the neoliberal dictate of "shrinking the state," low-income women took up the slack in expanded responsibilities for family and community survival.[20] Even after left-leaning governments rose to power in the early twenty-first century's "pink tide," antipoverty programs continued to rely heavily on women to ensure their families' well-being.[21] Both market-oriented and state-led economic models have been based on the exploitation of women's productive and reproductive labor.

To confront the shifting, multiple, and overlapping sources of repression, marginalization, and dependence that they have faced, women have constructed a wide array of historical and contemporary counterpublics. Unlike the male-dominated institutions in wider society, these are communities where women could develop and share their own strategies for social change. A century ago, educated women circulated their ideas in their own journals, held feminist literary salons, and, eventually, built suffrage organizations.[22] By the 1970s, women in left-wing parties and movements debated whether to withdraw from or engage with these male-dominated efforts. Some chose to create feminist organizations as a platform from which to critique capitalist patriarchy and strategize to achieve women's liberation and equality with men. Others opted to engage in "double militancy," fighting from the inside to put gender issues on the agenda. Despite their differences, all agreed that their natural constituency were the poor and working-class, and often the indigenous or Afro-descendant, women who made up the majority of female Latin Americans. However, they were not waiting to be recruited. Instead, many were fighting their own battles, whether for improved state services or in defense of their cultures, families and communities against repressive regimes. They often did so by claiming, instead of rejecting, their traditional roles as mothers. Over the next twenty years, self-identified women's organizations and movements grew in strength and numbers, informed by—but always in uneasy tension with—the feminist ideals and organizing principles of middle- and upper-class white and *mestiza* women.[23] Throughout the twentieth century, Latin American women created a variety of counterpublics that reflected their distinct interests.

The region-wide transitions to liberal democracy and neoliberal economics beginning in the 1980s spurred activists to develop—and debate—new approaches to women's empowerment. Some feminists with educational and class privilege formed nongovernmental organizations (NGOs) whose aim was to influence state policies on issues such as economic development, violence against women, and the promotion of women's political leadership.[24] But the autonomy of these NGOs could be curtailed by the priorities of their funding agencies, whether these were international philanthropies or governmental ministries. Moreover, feminists in NGOs began working with state bureaucracies just as they were beginning to shed their responsibilities for social welfare and economic growth as demanded by neoliberal models. As a result, feminists who chose not to engage with state institutions criticized those who did as being a "gender technocracy" in support of "global neoliberal patriarchy" by teaching poor and working-class women how to cope with, rather than oppose, austerity measures.[25] The division between the self-proclaimed *autonomas* (autonomous ones), who continued to work in grassroots organizing, and those they identified as *institucionalizadas* (institutionalized ones), who sought change through formal institutions, marked a painful rending of feminist energies.

But despite their many differences, feminist and women's organizations have maintained contact, not only coming together in local and national counterpublics, but also expanding and developing regional counterpublics through which to contemplate their common challenges and to debate solutions. One of the most notable spaces for counterpublic work is the Latin American and Caribbean Feminist *Encuentros* (encounters) that began in 1981. These unique regional meetings provide multiple ways for activists to interact around a shifting agenda of regional preoccupations, becoming "key transnational arenas where Latin America–specific feminist identities and strategies have been constituted and contested."[26] In turn, these meetings have nurtured and inspired thematic and identitarian networks focused on issues such as reproductive rights, Afro-Latin identity, and lesbian feminism. Through these opportunities, broadcast by alternative media, women have created productive confluences, whether around gender-specific issues such as violence against women, or more general challenges such as the detrimental impact of exploitative economic development on their families, communities, and ancestral lands. Coalition building has emerged as a central strategy, as it enables collaboration without demanding comprehensive political alignment. Considerably prior to the internet's arrival, Latin American feminist communities developed and expanded their identities and strategies for change. They were poised to take advantage of a technology in many ways geared toward enhancing networks.

Queer activists have joined feminists in seeking their own liberation and acceptance. Faced with social denigration, rejection, and outright repression by many of the same forces as feminists, they also seized the opportunity of democratization to build counterpublics.[27] Often marginalized in both gay male-dominated and straight-feminist arenas, lesbian feminists began independent organizing by the 1980s, often forming the most radical of feminist groups.[28] The HIV/AIDS crisis of the late 1980s resulted in some rapprochement between mixed-gender groups and lesbian feminists, as well as more state support for LGBT efforts. Transgender people have also established their own organizations and collaborated in more general LGBT efforts. Pride parades, the most outward manifestation of queer counterpublics, have reached epic proportions in places like São Paulo, Brazil, the home to the world's largest parade; given rise to anti-assimilation countermarches by more radical activists in Buenos Aires, Argentina; and include a yearly thousands-strong lesbian march through the center of Mexico City. Thanks to the growth and development of their counterpublics, LGBT and feminist activists were able to develop coalitions around issues of gender and sexuality.[29] As the internet spread across the region, they eagerly incorporated it to undergird their efforts.

Although their internet access now depends on the commercialization that has helped to make Latin America the developing world region with the highest percentage of internet users,[30] some in these communities were early adopters. Given the many forms of exclusion they faced, they had already built alternative means of communication and organization and were eager for new tools to support their counterpublic work. Such tools were extended to them by progressive technology activists such as the men and women of the international Association for Progressive Communications, whose goal was to democratize digital access and provide internet training across the developing world. Latin America was a central hub of this activity. From the early 1990s, these technologists made it possible for activists to incorporate the resources of the internet in order to achieve their goals for social change.

Through their increasingly internet-enhanced coalitions, the region's vibrant, deeply networked counterpublics have achieved world-renowned policy gains. Although reproductive autonomy remains largely out of reach, with abortion restricted or prohibited nearly everywhere, feminist demands for candidate quota legislation have translated into the highest regional average of women in national parliaments, currently at 27 percent.[31] Thanks to collaborative, intensive lobbying, Latin America leads the world in regional and national legislation outlawing violence against women.[32] Savvy strategizing by LGBT organizations has also been remarkably effective.[33] A majority of Latin American countries now ban discrimination on the basis of sexual orientation, and a third do so on the basis of gender identity or expression. Same-sex marriage has been legislated in Mexico City, Uruguay, and Argentina, and several countries have approved some of the most progressive gender-identity recognition policies anywhere in the world. Drawing on their history, their diversity, and their ability to work on a national and even regional scale, feminists and queers in Latin America have demanded and received recognition and support from varied sources of power.

WHY COUNTERPUBLICS?

Given the internet's potential for enhancing gender- and sexuality-based activism, a study of Latin American feminist and queer counterpublics provides an excellent opportunity to consider the interconnection of technology and society. But why focus on feminist and queer counterpublics, rather than their actions in the shared space of the so-called "public sphere"?

From its beginnings, users and analysts alike declared the internet the ideal arena for widespread, egalitarian participation, a sphere of unfettered exchange made possible by its (relatively) low cost and widespread availability. Cyberoptimists channeled social theorist Jürgen Habermas' utopian vision of a universal public sphere, free from the effects of societal inequalities, where every individual has the same standing to express herself and be heard.[34] Habermas modeled his vision of this ideal on nineteenth-century European civic society, where vigorous debate took place in public squares and coffeehouses and was widely transmitted by a vibrant print culture.[35] Many have hoped that, in the move from "coffeehouse to . . . cyber café,"[36] the internet could (re)construct the Habermasian ideal by providing both a place and a means for free expression, agenda-setting, debate, and discussion outside formal political channels, that would create a truly public opinion.[37] The kinds of conversations made possible through internet-based technology would form, even if slowly, the conditions for the emergence of a public sphere.[38]

As this book shows, inclusive, widespread access and participation was, in fact, a goal of the early developers of the internet. But it has evolved to reflect real-world hierarchies instead of fundamentally changing the dynamics of public communication. Some of those hierarchies are embedded in the institutions of the state and the market. States can put up "digital gates," ranging from basic filtering or blocking techniques to real-time surveillance.[39] Corporations seeking to commodify users' information have enclosed the so-called "internet commons"[40] by offering a devil's bargain: trading access to global networks for individual privacy.[41] In the Global South, private owners who have purchased formerly state-run telecommunications have often concentrated telephone coverage and services in wealthy and urban areas. Neither the state nor the market is invested in open access.

Other hierarchies embedded in the internet reflect seemingly inescapable social relations of power. Internet-based technology has (re)produced and (re)configured offline inequalities: as gender and communications scholar Jenny Sundén argued about the early internet, the "material body marked by gender, race and class not only forms the physical ground for the cyberspace traveler, but is also clearly introduced and reproduced in the new electronic space it inhabits."[42] Racial inequalities permeate the online, just as they do the offline, world. The powerful idea of a "digital divide," a phrase often used to evoke global inequalities in internet use, was first introduced in a 1995 study discussing the limitations that African Americans faced in accessing the technology. Communications scholar Jessie Daniels argues that such a notion takes "whiteness as normative,"[43] putting racial minorities on the "wrong side" of the divide. Development practitioners borrowed the concept to reference how predominantly poor, darker-skinned people around the world were also stuck across a chasm, implicitly or explicitly suggesting their need for rescue by wealthier, whiter digital natives. Deeply raced understandings of power are also implanted deep in hardware—such as "master and slave" devices (where the "master" has control over the actions of the "slave")—as well as in software, including the "white hand pointer" used by some applications.[44] Race and media analyst Lisa Nakamura's work shows that while users can produce new race-based meaning through the visual culture of the internet, from Instant Messenger icons to YouTube videos, these applications remain embedded in broader racial hierarchies.[45] Since every point of the technological trajectory, from development through distribution, reflects such hierarchies, substantial obstacles remain to achieving the internet's promise of becoming a sphere of participation open to all.

Not only race, but also economic relations power the internet. The development and distribution of the physical infrastructure that brings us the internet embed worker exploitation, as does much of the content we see. Those who make chips, screens, mice, hard drives, smart phones, and the like labor under difficult circumstances, and are often forbidden to organize for better working conditions.[46] The information age also depends on "produser" (producer-user) collaboration[47]—that is, unpaid contribution of both data and analysis through social media—whether through reviews on product websites or volunteer writers on sports, politics, and activist Facebook pages, Twitter feeds, and blogs. Today's internet thrives because of low-cost, if not unpaid, labor.

Sexual relations of power also help to determine access to the internet. Again and again, proposed measures to regulate who can gain access to the internet, what they can see, and how they can do so reflect normative assumptions about sexuality. Powerful decision makers use the excuse of protecting children against sexual predators in chat rooms and sexualized content on websites and blogs to insist on state control over sexuality-related resources. They find support for this interpretation of the internet from influential conservative, often religious organizations,[48] who share their understanding of and goals for society. While there is a real need to guard against sexual predators online, queer people can find their issues or interests blocked by heterosexist screening algorithms and politicians who rely on patriarchal and heteronormative narratives to determine what is appropriate for social circulation.[49]

Not only state control, but also market forces pose obstacles to the internet-mediated expressions of queer identity. Jan Moolman, the senior project coordinator for the international internet-focused Women's Rights Programme, argues that "one of the biggest transformative powers of the internet was the potential to be free from having . . . identity regulated, including gender identity and sexuality."[50] But identity exploration is not profitable for firms seeking to extract revenue from personal information, as illustrated by Facebook's insistence that transpeople use their legal, rather than chosen, names.[51] For those for whom "coming out" online is not an option, or who wish to choose their own online identities, anonymity or pseudonymity is a benefit challenged by identity commodification.

Finally, women and queers face serious aggression online, where threats and harassment have even led to physical assault. Individuals and groups attempt to exert control over girls, women, and queers, using a barrage of digital means to hound them about the way they look, the stories they tell, and the genders they subvert. Misogynistic hackers—or others seeking to shame or humiliate—break into accounts and steal intimate photos and videos. Those brave enough to explore issues of gender and sexuality online, whether through advocacy or research, face targeted abuse. Brutal harassment, ranging from sexist, homophobic, or transphobic comments to death threats, have forced some to back away from their public work or even to go into hiding.[52] And recipients of virtual abuse have even killed themselves to stop the all-too-real pain.[53] The internet can be a very dangerous neighborhood.

The deep-seated inequalities that permeate every aspect of the digital world make it a difficult and often discriminatory arena for public interaction, yet the internet still holds great potential for alternative counterpublics. Critical theorist Nancy Fraser articulated this concept in a critique of Habermas's ideal model of the public sphere: nineteenth-century European civic society. Though Habermas presented it as a place that invited universal participation and free expression, Fraser argued instead that the public sphere was where materialistic, conventional middle-class men could entrench their own power. She concluded that only under conditions of full equality could such an egalitarian sphere exist. Living in a world that clearly failed to provide such conditions, "members of subordinated social groups—women, workers, peoples of color, and gays and lesbians—have repeatedly found it advantageous to constitute alternative publics"[54] because these counterpublics enable community empowerment outside wider publics.

Fraser singled out gender inequality as a motivation for, and illustration of, counterpublic construction. She pointed to the "late-twentieth century U.S. feminist" community, which generated a wide range of artistic, academic, and political production through which they conceived and circulated language that captured women's experience of subordination, from "sexism" to "the double shift." Using their own tools, women built their own communities and created pathways to broader publics.[55] Although Fraser's illustration of the U.S. feminist counterpublic suggests that they are a national phenomenon, they are not limited to the national level. They exist wherever people meet to contest their subordination through individual and community growth. This book focuses on national and transnational (particularly regional) counterpublics, but these in turn depend on efforts at the local level. Latin American feminists and queer activists have long histories of carving out spaces in which they come together to figure out who they are, what they stand for, and how they can stand together to face their common sources of oppression. They are exceptionally experienced counterpublic constructors.

Why focus on counterpublics instead of social movements, the more familiar term for sustained collective challenges to the social order? Both counterpublics and social movements are vehicles through which those who have recognized their exclusion seek to challenge it. But while social movements forcibly assert their dreams, desires, and demands in wider publics and challenge those with power, counterpublics serve as arenas for internal development and debate, where movement participants articulate their identities, build their communities, and hone their strategies. Counterpublics undergird movements' emergence and expansion, as "spaces of withdrawal and regroupment" as well as "training grounds for agitational activities directed towards wider publics."[56] As such, they are the places to look in order to see how social transformation happens from the inside out.

As for what to look at inside counterpublics, alternative media is fundamental. Although Fraser's conceptualization predated the popularization of the internet, she argued that the currency, so to speak, of counterpublics is communication: in her words, these are "discursive" arenas. To articulate their ideas, members of counterpublics rely on what media theorist Clemencia Rodríguez calls "citizens' media," the "communication spaces where citizens can learn to manipulate their own languages, codes, signs, and symbols, empowering them to name the world in their own terms."[57] The internet offers one such communicative space: sociologist Ann Travers makes the case that feminists and other progressives "occupy public space in a way that is unprecedented offline," given the new ways they can construct "parallel publics."[58] Offline, as Fraser described, women create separate spaces where they build their skills, confidence, and solidarity. Online, feminists also construct their own alternatives to the exclusionary public sphere. This is particularly important for women who may be unable to access the (physical) public, due to social or physical constraints, meaning that the internet can augment or transform the way activists engage the world on their own terms. Since the late 1990s, the internet has increasingly become the primary communications conduit of feminist and queer counterpublics. As I will show, activists have widened their counterpublics through the internet in ways that have brought them new resources and ideas as well as new sources of discord and inequality.

The internet holds the potential for buttressing the three central characteristics of a counterpublic, according to media studies theorist Lincoln Dahlberg: building identities, creating community based on new ways of thinking, and strategizing for change. First, the internet provides a space where people who cannot be heard (or, I would add, seen) in wider publics come together to explore who they are. Second, its "interactivity and reach" helps communities dispersed in time and space to articulate alternative discourses. Finally, the internet enables counterpublics to contest dominant, mainstream beliefs.[59] Given these contributions, existing counterpublics have integrated the internet, even as new counterpublics have cropped up largely within its confines. Jac sm Kee, a prominent feminist internet policy advocate, affirmed the internet's potential for those "who've had difficulty accessing spaces in general" because it provides a space to "articulate a sense of self. Like who am I in this space? Who am I in relation to you? Who are we in relation to this larger world that we are occupying, and who do we want to be?"[60] The internet simultaneously becomes a counterpublic space and a means for a counterpublic development when it enables people to explore who they are, who else shares their values, and what it is that "we want to be" to larger publics.

INTERPRETING INTERNET PRACTICES IN LATIN AMERICAN COUNTERPUBLICS

Effective integration of the internet by counterpublics depends heavily on social contexts. Dahlberg reminds us that technology is both "socially constituted and constituting," thus requiring "mutual constitution analysis."[61] Although careful observers of technology argue that this has ever been the case, the extensive spread of internet-based media makes it a prime area in which to see and explain—to interpret—how society and technology affect one another.

Because the social and material cannot be separated, they must be examined together. To do that with respect to Latin American feminist and queer counterpublics, I am inspired by a sociomaterial approach called "information ecology analysis," as conceptualized by Bonnie Nardi and Vicki O'Day.[62] This analysis focuses on the interactions among the people, values, practices, and technology of a given environment. Its central insight is to show that the values of social communities inform technological practices, rather than practices emerging from static technological attributes that somehow inevitably guide users to a predetermined end. This approach centers the preexisting social environment—where the values are formed—incorporating why communities do what they do with technology, as well as how they do it. As in the ecologies of the natural world, technological developments are facilitated or mediated by those who make up an influential "keystone species." These are the people who have an outsized impact on their communities due to their ability to introduce new information technologies to their communities.

Counterpublics shape their own information ecologies. As Nardi and O'Day explain, an ecology is a "lively . . . intensely social place" where technology and human relationships evolve together under the guidance of a keystone species. As a result, the participants in the ecology "construct the identities of their technologies through the rhythms and patterns of their use."[63] This approach underscores the importance of context to counterpublics' interpretation of technologies such as the internet. A given interpretation cannot be predicted from the internet's "affordances," like its low cost and rapid transmission from one to many. Instead, the technology's attributes evolve depending on the values and practices of a given community. In other words, the internet offers *contextual* affordances. Technological advances affect and mold counterpublic work, but users also shape the medium in unexpected and creative ways.

One of my contributions to the study of practice is not only to analyze the counterpublics I have learned from, but also to take into account how they change over time. Because I was able to talk to activists near the dawn of their time online, I observed a unique period. The experimental early days of technology feature utopian dreams and messy practicalities.[64] This introductory period is a "special historical occasion," according to media theorist Carolyn Marvin, "when patterns anchored in older media that have provided the stable currency of social exchange are reexamined, challenged, and defended."[65] This reexamination can be hard to access once the new media has become part of the communicative fabric. In addition to capturing the early experimentation, I was able to interview many of the same people up to a decade later, tracking what had happened to their dreams and practicalities as the internet permeated their lives and work. Although an ever-accelerating explosion of and prognostication about internet-based technology makes it impossible to analyze every new dynamic, chronicling the evolution of practices from near their beginning may offer insight into their future. It also offers the opportunity to consider whether new generations of technology bring fundamental changes.

To understand these activists' internet practices and their changes over time, I have followed the multi-sited feminist sociomaterial methods advocated by Kristine Blair, Radhika Gajjala, and Christine Tulley, who argue that to understand the way women use the internet, ethnographic work must be done in "online and off-line" spaces, taking into account the relevant political, economic and social contexts in which technology has, or has not, become available.[66] While those studying "purely" online phenomena are at pains to justify their work as effectively embodied, that is, still anchored to offline phenomena and people,[67] the place where I focus, at the intersection of activism and technology, is rooted in offline experience. Many of the counterpublic organizations I study preexisted the internet, and they flourish or fade in real time. To interpret their experiences with the technology, I traveled to talk to them in Latin America, while also following their digital trails across the web and social media.

Although I focus in this book on regional communities, given the many parallels in feminist and queer reality across Latin America, these are, of course, grounded in national experiences. In particular, I have observed practices within feminist and queer counterpublics in Argentina, Brazil, and Mexico. I chose these three countries because of the ways that technology and activist communities developed there. They had the greatest numbers of internet users in the region when I began my study at the beginning of the 2000s.[68] And underneath those numbers was a little-known history of the internet: in all three, social justice-oriented technicians attempted to ensure that some people on society's margins would be in the center of this new media environment. Moreover, a long history of discrimination had inspired feminists to create activist counterpublics, from the earliest production and distribution of periodicals by and for women in the nineteenth century through the tumultuous years of late twentieth-century democratization and beyond. Building alongside feminist activism, queer counterpublics were becoming more visible toward the end of the century. The intersection of the internet and counterpublics provided a complex landscape to survey. I went to talk to activists, particularly those inside the organizations that form the counterpublic architecture, about what it looked like on the ground.

In order to grasp the relevance of email, distribution lists, websites, Facebook pages, and other applications to these organizations, I conducted 125 interviews with feminist, women's, and LGBT advocates, along with the technicians who facilitated their access to digital platforms, in workplaces, cafés, or other public spaces, and in homes. Sometimes we would sit next to their computers, as they patiently put off answering an avalanche of email, or in later years, not-so-surreptitiously checked texts on their smart phones. In my early visits I was generally received by the director or founder of an organization; a decade later I was often directed to the staff member tasked with responsibility for social media. My initial collection of interviews (conducted in 2001–2) was divided evenly: thirty-two in Mexico and thirty-four each in Argentina and Brazil. I began all the interviews with the same set of survey questions, although my interviewees often shared their most profound insights during the digressions prompted by open-ended questions. To explore changes over time, particularly with respect to the rise of social media, I returned to the (offline) field sites between 2009 and 2013 for follow-up interviews with a quarter of the original interviewees. The early and later interviews helped me to estimate the extent to which the internet was changing, and being reinterpreted by, the organizations and people who made counterpublics possible.

Given the vast array of people working to contest gender- or sexuality-based inequality in these countries—living in small villages and capital cities, organized in collectives and nongovernmental organizations, relying on their own resources and external support—I sought to capture that heterogeneity. Because technologies map over preexisting sources of inequality such as class and race, I could not rely only on prominent groups located in capital cities if I hoped to gain a broad picture of internet interaction. I had to visit a wide variety of organizations. To find them, I relied on my own and colleagues' contacts; listings from the internet service providers run by community-minded technicians; and "snowball sampling," that is, asking interviewees for references to others with whom I should talk. Relying on two essential criteria for selection—that my interviewees had an email address and a focus on gender or sexuality in their counterpublic work—I cast a wide net.

This approach provided me with a highly diverse set of observations in terms of geographic location, years of experience, scope, and resources. The interviewees not only represented three different countries, but twenty-one different cities. In each country, I spoke with activists working in the major cities (Mexico City, Buenos Aires, Rio de Janeiro, and São Paulo), and in smaller cities or towns (such as Comitán, Jujuy, and Olinda). Forty percent of the organizations had been active for ten years or less; 49 percent between eleven and twenty years; and 11 percent between twenty-one and forty years. Fifty-five percent had fewer than ten staff members; 22 percent between eleven and twenty; and 12 percent between twenty-one and fifty. Three groups had between sixty-four and four hundred members. In addition, seven networks brought together between 8 and 215 groups. Forty-two of the groups received financial support from their own governments and six from other national funders; forty-one from U.S. foundations and twelve from U.S. nonprofits; thirty-four from European governments and organizations; thirteen from UNrelated organizations or agencies; and six from the Inter-American Development Bank.[69] Eleven had no funding at all, and only two received membership dues. Other sources of income included payment for services or publications and personal resources (i.e., salary from other employment). Although it would have been impossible to select a set of interviewees that would provide an exact mirror of the extremely varied landscape of counterpublic organizations in the three countries, the various axes of diversity in my sample helped to make it representative.

While the organizations' objectives varied widely, all focused in some way on the feminist goal to contest and transform gender-based relations of power and/or the related queer goal to contest and transform those based on sexuality. Of course, this is quite a broad category! In my sampling, it included these among other subjects: women's rights and leadership; reproductive and sexual health and rights; violence against women and intrafamilial violence; women's access to microcredit and small business development; feminist communications, feminist theory, and cyberfeminism; Afro-Brazilian women, indigenous women, and racism; lesbianism, homosexuality, and sexuality; and paternity, masculinity, and sexism. To achieve their goals, the groups carried out a diverse array of activities, ranging from consciousness raising, to consulting, to political advocacy. They ran bookstores, community centers, and archives, and provided services, training, and evaluation. They also wrote and distributed research and analysis in print and electronic form. The organizations worked at various political levels: 23 percent identified as local organizations, 15 percent as functioning at the state level, 16 percent at the national level, 16 percent at both local and national levels, 21 percent at national and international levels, and 9 percent at all three. That they pursued a wide range of goals, employed a great variety of actions, and occupied a swath of the political spectrum enabled me to gain insight into the diverse character of regional counterpublic activity.

Although the interviews are my primary source of data and analysis, I also studied online evidence in order to enhance my understanding of counterpublics' interaction with the internet. Besides listening to people's stories, I looked at what they were writing on websites and distribution lists, blogs, and Facebook posts. And sometimes, I found myself scanning the bounced-back email messages, broken hyperlinks, missing websites, and stalled social media efforts where digital trails disappeared. Because internet technology gains its meaning through use, its departure also tells a story worth listening to.

BOOK ORGANIZATION

This book interprets how Latin American feminist and queer counterpublics have changed and been changed by the internet. I approach this mutual constituitive analysis by incorporating the contexts in which these counterpublics have developed, which are often regional and global as well as local and national. I start by grounding the account of this mutual development in the rich history of Latin American feminist counterpublics, and explain how they have been nurtured by long-standing alternative media production. I then move up to the global level to tell the little-known story of how women and men with a vision of an internet open to all invented and shared technology in order to create counterpublic construction and impact. With both the regional counterpublic and global technological context in place, I move on to analyze what the encounter with and development of that technology has meant for Latin American feminist and some queer counterpublic organizations. I then narrow the focus to consider an application that has been a fundamental part of the regional digital architecture, the distribution list, and its meaning to Argentine feminists. The final chapter explores the ramifications of internet incorporation for privacy and visibility in Latin American lesbian feminist communities. Together, these chapters constitute a complex sociomaterial analysis of the ways in which counterpublics have built identity, created community, and struggled for social transformation before, during, and after the inception of the internet.

Chapter 1 traces the historical outlines of Latin American feminist counterpublics. Through their publications and face-to-face meetings, activists during the late nineteenth and early twentieth century, and their extraregional allies, developed strategies to name and claim women's rights long before the advent of the internet. Their work served as a model for the explosion of activism beginning in the 1970s, when new regional publications enriched and inspired an unprecedented, and globally unreplicated, counterpublic space, that of the Latin American and Caribbean feminist "encounters." The chapter then profiles two global communication projects in which Latin American counterpublics were embedded, and ends with an analysis of the very first computer-mediated project to promote women's rights at an international venue.

Chapter 2 turns to the story of how social justice-oriented web enthusiasts built the internet as we know it today—a network of networks—because they wanted to ensure access for progressive communities around the world. Their extension of the internet to activists and advocates while the internet itself was taking shape presents a seemingly unique case in the history of technology. Those seeking to change the world were offered a place at the front of the line by a keystone species looking to transform society through technology. Within this global project, feminist communication activists carved out a space for women's organizing, providing the material basis for their work. From their early efforts to today, such activists have contested the gendering of internet technology as the province of men. In doing so, they have also subverted the West's domination over the internet by opening spaces for women from the Global South, particularly Latin America, to create their own counterpublics.

Chapter 3 returns to Latin America to explore how the architects of today's vibrant counterpublics—feminist, women's, and queer organizations in Argentina, Mexico, and Brazil—have integrated the internet to support their goals of inclusion, community building, and strategizing for social change. It focuses on the early encounters between counterpublic organizations and internet applications to capture that "special historical occasion" of experimentation, exultation, and confusion, but also incorporates the advent of social media. Activists have struggled to confront how class, ethnic, and racial inequalities, as well as workloads, are exacerbated by a new technology. Nevertheless, they have linked chains of access across their own digital divides; built community on the basis of low-cost services; and made an impact on national and international politics using and transforming a range of applications.

Chapter 4 takes a deeper look at the way in which a particular community of activists transformed a particular internet application, the distribution list, into a vibrant online counterpublic. It profiles one of the region's longest-lasting national feminist lists: RIMA, the Red Informativa de Mujeres de Argentina (Women's Information Network of Argentina). Large and diverse, it has boasted up to fifteen hundred subscribers; has included members from every Argentine province, all South American countries, and beyond; and incorporates women from many walks of life who espouse different political ideologies. The chapter analyzes how the values of RIMA's information ecology, which were developed through preexisting national feminist counterpublic spaces, inform their online practices. Together, "Rimeras" have built a counterpublic that encourages personal and community growth, enables debates, and undergirds campaigns for social change. Through their contested moderation, evolving list policies, and negotiated user demands, they have fashioned a digital counterpublic.

Chapter 5 turns to regional counterpublics that count as members some of RIMA's constituents, but have their own distinct dynamics: that of lesbian feminism. As is true of the RIMA ecology, Latin American lesbian feminist internet practices reflect their own circumstances and values. These have led them to focus their counterpublic work with internet applications on privacy and visibility. They need a place for their private life, to find each other and build community away from the threat of violence and rejection that still, despite significant changes in their legal status, characterizes their daily existence. Yet they also need support for lesbian visibility, to confront exclusion, bringing the fact of their existence and their demands for the worlds in which they want to live to larger publics. In doing so, they have also reinterpreted internet applications toward their own ends, such as through the innovative project of a blog-based archive of lesbian history. They have integrated the internet in order to turn it into a space of private grappling with public issues as well as a platform on which to articulate private issues to heighten public awareness.

In chapters 2 through 5 I deepen the sociomaterial analysis by exploring the three constituent layers of the internet: physical, logical, and content. The physical layer refers to the hardware through which people access the internet—computers, phones, or other devices—in addition to other elements of material access, such as cables, modems, wireless transmitters, and servers. The logical layer contains software, operating systems, "apps," and so on, or the various "ways of translating human meaning into something that machines can transmit, store, or compute."[70] Finally, the content layer is just that: the content that people transmit through the physical layer by means of the logical layer.

I use this disaggregation to show that the weaving together of society and technology happens in all three layers. Most social studies of the internet tend to focus on the physical layer, for example the issue of the digital divide, or the ways in which traditional sources of inequality, such as class and gender, can lead to uneven access to the "tools." Some examine the content layer, such as the transmission of racist hate speech, pornography, and "slut shaming." Yet the logical layer, programmed by human hands, also reflects distinct goals, values, and biases. Will software be available to anyone (open source) or protected by copyright (proprietary)? Are assumed audiences wide or narrow? What might people want their avatars to look like or be able to do? What kinds of boundaries are embedded in interactive applications? Social hierarchies are not the only values embedded in the distinct layers; so are democratic aspirations. And these values change through user appropriation and re-signification. Latin American feminist and queer counterpublics, and the larger counterpublics in which they are embedded, demonstrate such adoption and meaning-making in their own contexts.

Why the "internet," Rather Than the "Internet"?

Although it is just now (2016) becoming widely accepted, the choice I have made throughout this book to write internet with a lower-case *i* merits a brief explanation. I am following in others' footsteps. Back in 2002, Joseph Turow, a professor at the Annenberg School of Communication at the University of Pennsylvania, drew the attention of the *New York Times* for his decision to drop the upper-case *I* in his book on families and the internet. Well over a decade ago, he argued that "it's part of the everyday universe," common as air and water. And because it was already so common, he believed it was not "private" or "brand-name": "at least philosophically, [it] should not be owned by anyone."[71] Although he did not convince the U.S. newspaper of record to change its house style, other publications have changed theirs. In 2004, the magazine *Wired* dropped the upper case *I* in order "to put into perspective what the internet is: another medium for delivering and receiving information." However, it hastened to offer historical perspective on this most recently developed medium: "That it transformed human communication is beyond dispute. But no more so than moveable type did in its day. Or the radio. Or television."[72] Given its centrality to communication, the internet should no longer be regarded as a proper noun. Indeed, as this book was sent to the press, the Associated Press announced that "internet" had become a generic term, and that the AP, too, would no longer write it with the capital letter.

Hewing to the *Wired* side, this book considers the internet to be a medium of communication, like the radio or television. After all, my central argument is that the internet is inseparable from social processes—like the radio, television, or, for that matter, moveable type. But, like Turow, I acknowledge that the extent to which it has become embedded in daily life provides yet another reason to deprive it of its capital letter, even as I insist that its definition is open to interpretation.

CHAPTER I

Conceiving Latin American Feminist Counterpublics

On December 6, 1873, the founder of *O Sexo Feminino* and girls' educator, Dona Francisca Senhorinha da Motta Diniz, wrote an editorial in her three-month-old, path-breaking Brazilian women's periodical. In this editorial, also entitled "O sexo feminino," she informed men that women, given the opportunity, could be their intellectual equals: "We have intelligence equal to yours, and if your pride has triumphed it is because our intelligence has been left unused." She exhorted women to take up the arms her new endeavor provided: "From this day we wish to improve our minds; and for better or worse we will transmit our ideas in the press, and to this end we have *O Sexo Feminino;* a journal absolutely dedicated to our sex and written only by us. *Avante, minhas patricias!* [Onward, my countrywomen!] The pen will be our weapon."[1] Speaking to both the men whose minds she sought to change, and the women she hoped to inspire, Dona Diniz charged into the public sphere. But she did so fully aware that she would need her own vehicle to propel her and her countrywomen's ideas forward.

As the work of Diniz and many other members of the keystone species of editors and publishers over the next century demonstrated, by the time the internet spread across Latin America in the 1990s, feminists had over a hundred years of experience constructing alternative media to achieve their own goals. In historical counterpublics, women learned how to shape media to their own ends, absorb and contest international ideas, and strategize how to achieve impact and inclusion

Anno I.   Cidade da Campanha, 6 de Dezembro de 1873.   Num. 14.

O SEXO FEMININO

SEMANARIO DEDICADO AOS INTERESSES DA MULHER.

Assignaturas.

Por anno . . . . . 3$000
Por semestre . . . 2$500
Publica-se 1 vez por semana.

« E' pelo intermedio da mulher que a natureza escreve no coração do homem »

(AIMÉ MARTIN.)

Observação.

Toda a correspondencia será dirigida á D. Francisca Senhorinha da Motta Diniz.

PRINCIPAL REDACTORA—D. FRANCISCA S. DA M. DINIZ.—COLLABORADORAS, DIVERSAS.

O Sexo Feminino.

Quando tomámos a ardua tarefa de dirigir este jornal, dedicado tão sómente aos interesses do nosso deprimido sexo, não pensavamos nas difficuldades que haviamos de encontrar no cumprimento de nossa missão e conhecendo, que nos faltavão muitos dados para bem desempenharmos esta tão importante missão, rogámos ás nossas amaveis patricias nos quizessem coadjuvar com suas lucubrações, e com especialidade convidâmol-as para que nos dirigissem seus ensaios litterarios, e que estes tivessem por fim sustentar nossa grandiosa idéa. Por este pedido ficárão nossas patricias sabendo que não inseririamos em nosso jornal artigos alheios ao assumpto principal—a educação de nosso sexo e sua relvação na sociedade.

Teremos, pois, todo o cuidado em não só não nos afastar do plano, como em empregar todos os esforços que couber em nossas forças para enchel-o com artigos de interesse geral.

Em tal intento não deixaremos de apresentar extractos de algumas obras que se dirijão ao mesmo fim, isto é, á nossa illustração, e á nossa capacidade intellectual para receber as luzes que se nos quizerem dar. Transcreveremos algumas partes da historia antiga e moderna em que encontrarmos exemplos dignos de ser imitados, como por exemplo, as Cornelias, as Porcias e muitas outras que praticárão actos de valor e acções virtuosas, com especialidade as nossas amaveis patricias.

Se alguem nos sensurar de plagiarias, teremos valor para dizer-lhe em face:

E' a vós que é devida a nossa insufficiencia; intelligencia temos igual á vossa, e se o vosso orgulho tem triumphado é por causa do nosso descuido. Ergueremos de hoje emdiante a cabeça; e torto ou direito, bem ou mal, transmitiremos nossas idéas pela imprensa, e para esse fim temos o Sexo Feminino, jornal absolutamente dedicado ao nosso sexo e escripto só por nós.

Avante, pois, minhas patricias! a penna seja nossa arma.

Pedimos ás nossas collaboradoras que seus artigos sejão assignados,

Vantagens da educação moral.

A educação moral coròa e domina toda a educação do homem ; por ser ella quem fórma o caracter, quem nos ensina a dirigir-nos ; quem faz frutificar a edu-

FIGURE 2. Front page of *O Sexo Feminino* I, no. 14 (December 6, 1873). Reprinted from http://istoecampanha.blogspot.com.

in wider publics. Wielding pens, typewriters, printing presses, and, eventually, copiers and fax machines, these women laid down the foundations upon which late twentieth-century feminists would build their internet-enhanced communities.

Writing in their own and other periodicals, Latin American feminists of the late nineteenth and early twentieth centuries steadily amassed their written arsenal, as increasingly well-educated professionals sought to contribute their passion and perspectives to social reform. But because of their political disenfranchisement—women's suffrage would not begin until 1932, in Uruguay, and took until 1961, in Paraguay, to extend across the region—and subordinate legal and social status, members of this keystone species helped to construct counterpublics centered in the distribution of their own writing and reinforced by face-to-face meetings. From these communities, they participated in general movements to improve social welfare, and their own movements to improve women's status.[2] Given the limitations of a social system that left the vast majority of women and men at the bottom of a steep economic and racial hierarchy, the early counterpublics were largely inhabited by educated, lighter-skinned, middle-class and wealthy women. But their approach of using their own media to find each other, develop their ideas, and wrestle with the world around them would continue throughout the twentieth century.

Two international developments expanded these efforts in the 1970s. The UN Decade for Women (1975–85) and its three international conferences opened global opportunities for Latin American activists to engage with new ideas about how to confront their subordination. Simultaneously, they found their own countries' contexts converging. Military and military-backed governments unleashed a wave of fierce authoritarian repression to silence reformers and revolutionaries alike. Many governments also imposed an economic model rooted in fiscal austerity and free markets that displaced and impoverished millions of workers. In response, widespread movements mobilized to demand the protection of human rights and a transition to democracy.

To respond to these international opportunities and regional challenges, feminists built a powerful regional counterpublic. Its most tangible instance, the likes of which does not exist anywhere else, was the Latin American and Caribbean Feminist Encuentros, or encounter-based mass meetings. Begun in 1981 and continuing every two or three years afterward, the Encuentros have been a space of learning and solidarity, yet are always riven by profound disagreements over the methods and direction of women's activism. But again and again, activists from across the region have come together to have those debates, which have expanded with the explosion of feminist principles and perspectives spanning racial, ethnic, class, ideological, and geographical boundaries. Throughout, they have relied on their own media to circulate ideas before, during, and long after the participants have turned the outcomes of their workshops, panels, and protests into extensive lists of conclusions and demands. The propagation of the ideas and fierce discussions from the regional Encuentros has, in turn, nurtured and challenged national and local communities. Latin American feminist counterpublics have grown through regional cross-pollination.

Feminist counterpublics in Latin America have relied on two forms of communication: the distribution of alternative media and face-to-face national and transnational opportunities to connect and strategize for change. These endeavors inspire each other. This chapter does not present an exhaustive exploration of either feminist media or regional organizing, focusing instead on illustrative examples and pivotal inter-sections. It begins with the founding of the first women's publications and transnational networks, and then profiles several alternative media projects created during the regional upsurge of feminist energies starting in the late 1970s. Just as their feminist descendants would incorporate and transform internet-based technologies based on their goals and val-ues, these foremothers' previous alternative media strategies reflected their own objectives and ideas. As community media scholar Caroline Mitchell argues with respect to women's radio production, "feminist val-ues tend to be central to both the production process and the content of what is produced."[3] Although focused on different elements of counter-public construction from different ideological perspectives, all of these projects encouraged regional solidarity. Such solidarity also spurred and supported the exceptional counterpublic space of the Encuentros.

The final section profiles three relevant international endeavors to connect women through alternative media, two of which directly influ-enced Latin American feminist counterpublics. The third was the first attempt to use a computer-based network to promote international women's rights: "Hotline International," meant to broaden participa-tion in the United Nation's 1975 World Conference of the International Women's Year in Mexico City. This venture was not specifically directed by or at Latin Americans, and in fact effectively ignored the "heated confrontations"[4] over class, sexuality, development, and politics among the diverse conference participants. Nevertheless, it offers a glimpse into the early problems and potential of computer-mediated communica-tions for women's rights work prior to their expansion in the 1990s.

CONSTRUCTING COUNTERPUBLIC COMMUNICATIONS

In the nineteenth century (and even before), educated women of means created journals, such as Brazil's *O Sexo Feminino, La Mujer* (Chile), and *El Aguila Mexicana* (Mexico), that were foundational for early feminist counterpublics because they offered a platform through which women could discuss, debate, and publicize ideas largely absent in the male-dominated media. Due to their founders' lack of resources, the publications were often short-lived. But as their descendants would do decades later, these publishers, editors, and writers refused to allow scarcity to dictate outcome as they moved from one masthead to another in search of a venue.[5] The historical record attests to their persistence: over two hundred women's magazines were published in Latin America before 1979.[6] Across the region, the first generation of a feminist keystone species built the communications infrastructure for their counterpublics.

Although internationally connected, initial attempts at counterpublic communications interpreted ideas from the Global North through the reality of local and national environments. Activists eagerly read international feminist writings as they contemplated their own pathways toward improving women's status and rights in Latin America, and among them a "transnational, often multilingual network of print culture blossomed."[7] Thus, the participants in this "transnational" conversation spoke in regional accents, with publications demonstrating collaborative cross-fertilization of ideas across Latin American countries. As in later periods, editors and writers often carried these ideas across borders along with their suitcases. Women such as the nineteenth-century Argentine writer Juana Manuela Gorriti, who spent much of her adult life in Peru, practiced journalism in more than one country; Gorriti herself founded both an Argentine and a Peruvian newspaper. Immersed in the realities around them, their feminist attention to circumstance was evident in the subjects they addressed—and how they addressed them.

As with feminist production in the United States and Europe, Latin American women's "literary-journalistic" activity blurred the "cherished boundaries" between a masculinized public and feminized private sphere: women wrote about domestic issues as well as their status in social, economic, and political life.[8] They did so following their own set of priorities, driven by what historian Francesca Miller has termed their "different mission" from that of men.[9] They focused on reforming legal and social conditions that impinged upon their ability, if not duty, to fulfill their roles as wives and mothers. Education, employment conditions, and social status, particularly women's rights within marriage and divorce, topped their agendas,[10] as "they expanded the definition of motherhood to include devotion to the pen."[11] However, crusaders like Diniz did not only focus on women's conditions; she herself used her pulpit to condemn Brazilian slavery. As times changed, writers and publishers followed suit. The over fifty feminist periodicals of the 1920s and

1930s—along with feminist contributions to other publications—reveal writers profoundly influenced by the politics of the day, including the growing anarchist, socialist, and conservative movements.[12] Counterpublic communications reflected shifting contexts.

Even when focused on improvement from within traditional gender roles, women writers' violation of those "cherished boundaries" between their private lives and the male-dominated sphere of public expression struck a nerve. Their public activity elicited negative, often satirical, reactions from male journalists. One Argentine publisher even went so far as to distribute a fake women's magazine for the sole purpose of slandering *La Aljaba,* a feminist publication from 1830.[13] Such reactions illuminated the importance of creating and maintaining counterpublics. Those assumed, and thus often forced, to be on the periphery of public life needed alternative ways of acquiring, processing, and presenting information. The women's periodicals of Brazil and elsewhere offered "mutual support and intellectual interchange"[14] fundamental to counterpublic construction, even as they sought wider audiences for their ideas.

Face-to-face exchange nurtured and reflected the production of counterpublic communications. Some of this took place at *tertulias* or salons, where writers such as Gorriti would host discussions of literature, women's emancipation, and other issues of social reform. Through personal visits, others acted "as 'godmothers' to one another's organizations."[15] They also sought to draw attention to feminist issues in regional scientific congresses, an effort culminating in the first regional feminist meeting: the International Feminist Congress, held in Buenos Aires in 1910. As with the publication of feminist periodicals, this presaged the explosion of regional and global opportunities feminists created in the late twentieth century.

Organizing in Latin America and reaching across the north/south divide, this generation of activists sought to bring the perspectives nurtured in their counterpublics into wider spheres of influence. For example, working together, organizations such as the Alianza Femenina Cubana (Cuban Feminine Alliance), the Consejo Feminista Mexicano (Mexican Feminist Council), and the National Woman's Party of the United States successfully pressured nascent Pan-American organizations to consider an Equal Rights Treaty in 1928 and to establish the Inter-American Commission of Women, a specialized agency of the Organization of American States responsible "for hemispheric policy on women's rights and gender-related issues."[16] This unique intergovernmental agency gave feminists an insider position from which to influence regional governance. And advocates also were active at the international organizations of the League of Nations and United Nations.[17] Both at the national and international levels, early Latin American feminist counterpublics supported the public-facing efforts of their members.

FEMINIST COUNTERPUBLIC COMMUNICATION AFTER THE 1970S

With the resurgence of feminist activism in the late 1970s, a new generation of the keystone species learned to support a diversifying set of counterpublics by producing and distributing their own publications. Between 1980 and 1990, this generation founded another two hundred women's magazines, many of which were outspokenly feminist, located in nearly every Latin American country.[18] Instead of the brief lifespans of earlier publications, these had staying power, finding an eager audience in women across the region who were coming to feminist consciousness in local and national counterpublics. Moreover, new women's organizations, including some that produced regular publications, were committed to sharing their information in order to nurture feminist community and/or reach larger publics.[19] Magazines including the influential *fem,* widely distributed *mujer/fempress,* and news service CIMAC circulated feminist perspectives on issues ranging from violence against women, to sexuality, to economic development. Both regional realities and international opportunities heavily influenced the construction of this communications infrastructure for local, national, and regional counterpublics.

Although Latin American feminists had begun to organize regionally by the middle of the twentieth century, their regional orientation took off with the traumatic dislocations of the 1970s. Waves of authoritarian repression, neoliberal economic models that increased inequality, and ongoing struggles against patriarchal and homophobic social mores showed many that they had much in common—as difficult as building alliances across class, race, ethnicity, sexuality, and geography would prove to be. As *fem*'s foundational documents argued, "the struggle of women cannot be conceived as an issue delinked from the struggle of the oppressed for a better world."[20] Latin American feminists understood their efforts as being joined to other work for social and political transformation.

But when progressive women sought to take part in the region-wide struggles against inequality, whether through socialist parties, guerilla organizations, or leftist movements, many became deeply frustrated with the subordination of women's to workers' liberation in both theory and practice. Women frequently found their ideas and actions slighted by left male leadership.[21] One outlet for their frustration was paradoxically created by the impact of political displacement. Those fleeing the fierce authoritarianism of military- and military-backed governments in the 1970s and 1980s traveled to Mexico or Europe, where they were exposed to other feminist ideas. There, some joined alternative media outlets, where they sought to draw attention to their home countries.[22] As with earlier generations, shared political experiences encouraged regional feminisms, which were reflected in regional and international periodicals.

At the same time, the UN Decade for Women (1975–85), with its three global conferences, increased the transnational connections of Latin American counterpublics beyond anything they had experienced in the first half of the century. The location of the United Nations' 1975 International Women's Year conference in Mexico City inspired discussion of feminism across the region, and especially in Mexico.[23] Moving on to the World Conference of the United Nations Decade for Women (1980), and culminating (for that time) at the World Conference to Review and Appraise the Achievements of the UN Decade for Women (1985), these conferences provided some political "shade" for Latin American feminist organizing. Even the authoritarian governments that restricted political activity in general sought international recognition through their lip service to women's rights issues (if not their fulfillment). When their governments came together to negotiate positions on women's rights and status at the official conferences, feminists sought to articulate their own positions and fought for space at the table. In nongovernmental forums linked to official processes, they participated in strategy sessions and debates with women from around the world. Participants brought home ideas and tactics to their national and local counterpublics, but those who could not attend still could engage by reading accounts and analysis in feminist media outlets.[24]

Inspired by a feminism that was beginning to take into account not only gender subordination but also the cross-cutting impact of other social hierarchies, the editors and writers of this period confronted the dominant portrayal of women in the Latin American mass media. They objected to profiles and pictures of women as middle class or wealthy, light-skinned, and conforming to the commodified gender norms of eager, happy consumers. Adriana Santa Cruz and Viviana Erazo, founders of *mujer/fempress,* critiqued what they named the "Transnational Feminine Model," circulating in mainstream media, which "does not have a single physical or cultural characteristic that originates in one of the many cultures of the continent." Instead of reflecting the diverse racial, ethnic, and class positions of the region's women, this model presented "an essentially consumer woman who belongs to a socio-economic level to which, in this continent, less than 10% of women reach. The young, slender, Western and sexually 'irresistible' image is put forward as the possible dream of all women and a goal to fight for."[25] These feminist editors argued that such images had little to do with regional reality. Just as their forerunners had before, their goal was to counter such images with their own pictures.

Latin American feminists increased the numbers and stability of their publications by taking advantage of then-new technologies, "especially the ubiquitous Xerox machine."[26] The technology itself was not responsible for the expansion of feminism's reach; feminists adapted it to their local settings. In the widely available copying machines they found a means through which they could sidestep mass media outlets dominated by men and often subject to political control.[27] Some publications also used a graphic format to reach women with low literacy, and many media activists turned to community radio to transmit their research and opinions where journals did not circulate or could not be read.[28] As with the internet, women incorporated these technologies and adjusted them to serve feminist goals: sharing perspectives on Latin American women's lives with regional audiences.

As the four examples below illustrate, alternative media outlets focused on distinct counterpublics and/or distinct elements of counterpublics. The three publications—*La Correa Feminista, fem,* and *mujer/fempress*—all enhanced the identity development and community building dimensions of counterpublics. But *La Correa Feminista* was intended to support the regional counterpublic of radical feminists, and less concerned with strategizing for public impact. *Fem* had an academic, as well as activist, feminist audience in mind, and encouraged action in wider publics. *Mujer/fempress* also covered all three counterpublic functions, while seeking to place its articles in the mass media. Finally, CIMAC, a women's news service still active today, concentrates on the circulation of feminist production in wider publics. Whether reaching local, national, or regional audiences, all of these efforts distributed information and analysis that framed women's issues within broader regional contexts.

La Correa Feminista, active in the 1990s, focused on the nearly free distribution of radical, anarchist, or socialist feminist writings in order to stimulate the identity and community aspects of a militant regional counterpublic. The editors published theoretical reflections, essay collections, photojournalism, and reports on feminist meetings; their influential collection *Feminismos cómplices: Gestos para una cultura tendenciosamente diferente* (Feminist Accomplices: Gestures for a Tendentiously Different Culture; 1993) became a loadstar for grassroots-oriented, politically independent feminists across the region. The publishers increased their impact by effectively bartering the majority of each press run for other printed material from feminist and women's organizations, or giving copies to those with no means to pay or material to offer.[29] Through their largely volunteer efforts, they brought together a regional counterpublic of producers and readers known as autonomous feminists.

The influential publication *fem* sought to inform activist struggle with academic research, deepening Mexican feminism while bringing it into a transnational dialogue. Taking on one subject at a time, the initial editorial board of scholars, journalists, and community organizers contributed their distinct perspectives to issues such as abortion, feminism, women and science, domestic workers, maternity, young women, and peasant women.[30] They published a range of feminist views, from liberal to radical, from abroad as well as inside the region. The January 1985 issue on women and violence illustrates their approach. It included the articles on state torture, rape in the Soviet Union and the Mexican court system, feminist nonviolence, and translations of eco-feminist Susan Griffin, lesbian feminist poet Adrienne Rich, and radical feminist theologian Mary Daly, all from the United States.[31] As with earlier counterparts, this feminist publication drew ideas, and increasingly translated key feminist texts, from the United States and Europe. And here again, it selectively adapted them to its readers' contexts.[32] *Fem*'s editors and writers were more than a mirror for other women's ideas; they broadcast their own feminist fusion.

Reaching out to Mexican women and around the region, these members of the keystone species enabled the three central elements of a counterpublic. They contributed to identity formation. Letters to the editor in the late 1980s from women far from the dynamic feminist activities of the major cities, particularly Mexico City, attested to how energizing it was to read coverage of women's successes and their participation in contemporary politics.[33] In addition, *fem* fostered what would become a central characteristic of Latin American feminist counterpublics: thoughtful and passionate debate incorporating distinct perspectives. For example, writers offered multiple interpretations of sexuality politics rather than hewing to a party line.[34] This exploration connected directly to the third task of counterpublics: strategizing about ways to make an impact on broader publics. In this case, writers offered "pragmatic assessment of what concessions the feminist movement might expect to wring from the male-dominated state." In their pages was to be found not only the initial discussions about sexual violence legislation, such as the criminalization of rape and incest, but also reform proposals themselves.[35] *Fem*'s articles offered insights for feminist counterpublic construction and impact.

Mujer/fempress, the most widely circulated feminist magazine in Latin America in the 1980s and 1990s, focused on generating original reporting from across the region to support feminist counterpublics, and was more dedicated to reaching a wider audience than either of the other two publications. The founders, Adriana Santa Cruz and Viviana Erazo, two Chilean exiles from the Pinochet dictatorship (1973–88), brought their regional solidarity orientation from the organization where they got their start, the Instituto Latinoamericano de Estudios Transnacionales (Latin American Institute of Transnational Studies; ILET). According to Erazo: "We thought it was fundamental to create a magazine that would transcend the local, that would be able to be a Latin American magazine, . . . that would have another discourse, the discourse of women, what they were really living, feeling and what they were struggling for in that moment."[36] Santa Cruz made clear that Latin American women needed to build more solidarity to achieve their goals: "Whether working out of universities, churches, institutions, international organisations or governments, women in research, in activism, in politics, and in the media, badly needed to come closer in order to be effective."[37] The editors modeled this collaborative approach with a team of contributors who spanned fourteen countries and a territory—Puerto Rico, where many felt as much, if not more, affinity with the Latin American and Caribbean region as with the United States. Each contributor was expected to generate one substantial piece of reporting on her location, in addition to shorter notes, each month. Face-to-face meetings at the regional Encuentros reinforced their collaboration. Although *mujer/fempress* started with a modest run of two hundred Xeroxed copies, it soon became a full-fledged regional magazine, distributing five thousand printed copies by the mid-1990s, including an annual edition in Portuguese to reach Brazilian audiences.[38] In the pre-internet era, this magazine was one of the few ways activists across the region, as well as their extraregional supporters,[39] could stay up to date on developments outside of their countries.

Mujer/fempress made such an impression because it was central to the identity- and community-building aspects of counterpublics across

mujer/fempress

N°76

DICIEMBRE 87 — unidad de comunicación alternativa de la mujer

fempress

MEXICO
La búsqueda de una política
feminista
MEXICO
Hay mucho dentro y detrás de
cada una de las dos mil mujeres
MEXICO
Taxco 87: problemas
de la autogestión
BRASIL
Reconocimiento
del trabajo invisible
ECUADOR
Confiar en nosotras
PARAGUAY
La escritura del cuerpo
URUGUAY
Un triste triunfo machista
ARGENTINA
Develar la pesadilla

recortes

DOBLE JORNADA, México
Del amor a la necesidad
EL INDEPENDIENTE, España
El banquete misógino
de la política
EL NACIONAL, Venezuela
Es muy difícil negar
la paternidad
LA EPOCA, Chile
Mujer en el tercer milenio
MUJERES, Argentina
La mujer conquista
el derecho de votar
EL DIARIO, Paraguay
La mujer no quiere
que nadie mande por ella
COLOMBIA
La violencia de la sin razón.
de la sin alternativa

reseñas

Nuevas Publicaciones
Investigaciones

comunicándonos

Al reproducir artículos, cite
la fuente: **mujer/fempress**

FIGURE 3. Cover of regional feminist magazine *mujer/fempress*, no. 76 (December 1987). Reprinted from *mujer/fempress*. Photo reproduced by permission from *La Raíz y el Camino*, Mariana Yampolsky (Mexico: Fondo de Cultura Económica, 1985). All rights reserved © Fundación Cultural Mariana Yampolsky, A. C., Mexico. Scan by Dan Battle.

the region. Readers circulated articles among their communities: "organisations inform us on the way they xerox *Fempress* articles for a workshop; documentation centres write on the fact that our magazine is the one most requested . . . and indigenous groups let us know they are translating our materials into Aymara in order to reach Peruvian and Bolivian campesinos in their own language."[40] Besides circulating their own articles, editors used the last pages of each issue to alert readers to new publications of all kinds, further socializing potentially useful information. Through original articles written from and about the majority of Latin American countries, *mujer/fempress* reached organizations working on behalf of a wide array of communities.

But Fempress, the magazine's sponsoring organization, sought more than internal counterpublic development. It put considerable emphasis on a major goal of marginalized communities: making an impact on wider publics by convincing the mainstream media to take up counterpublic perspectives. As attested to above, the editors were well aware of the steep uphill climb this would be, given the stereotypical presentation of women in women's magazines and daily newspapers. In a 2014 interview, Puerto Rican correspondent Norma Valle explained that the editors hired feminist journalists who could not only draw on their political commitment and activist counterpublics, but also access mass media outlets, where they hoped to place articles. To educate mainstream journalists on feminist values, they also offered seminars on nonsexist publishing. To perform the essential "publicist" role of a counterpublic—"to disseminate one's discourse into ever widening areas,"[41] they circulated a free summary of the work published in the magazine to hundreds of newspapers; media outlets frequently picked up relevant articles. Valle's article on the 1989 Puerto Rican legislation against domestic violence, one of the first, and most advanced, laws in the region, republished hundreds of times, resulted in legislators from other countries contacting her for further details about its passage and function. Another article, on a female basketball player who successfully sued to play on a professional Puerto Rican team, was reprinted in sports sections throughout the region. Seeking to spread counterpublic ideas as widely as possible, Fempress did not limit itself to print journalism; the organization also circulated a ninety-minute radio service, which was broadcast by over 250 stations.[42] The magazine traveled to the highest decision makers, with legislators attesting to how articles spurred their policy making.[43] Fempress's strategy of outreach to the mainstream helped to change the context of Latin American women's lives.

To capitalize on the strategy of publicizing the ideas, perspectives, and demands of feminists to mainstream audiences, feminist journalists in Mexico altered the model of founding a publication: they established their own news service, documentation center, and training program. Veterans of the left Mexican newspaper *La Jornada,* who first came together to generate material for a regular newspaper supplement on women's issues, founded Comunicación e Información de la Mujer (Women's Communication and Information; CIMAC), in 1988. CIMAC took on the mainstream media in two ways: improving feminist organizations' capacity for media outreach, and "insur[ing] that journalists incorporate the human rights of women in their daily work" by providing the information and training they needed.[44]

CIMAC believed that the mainstream media could be convinced to broadcast the work of feminist counterpublics if appealed to from the outside and the inside. Sara Llovera, a central member of the keystone species as founder and former general coordinator of CIMAC, described this two-pronged approach in an interview. CIMAC helped women's organizations publicize their work through media-strategy training and publicity campaigns. Llovera explained that, if women were to "demand [their] own spaces, [they have] to know how to do it." To appeal to journalists, CIMAC made it as easy as possible to use their news, circulating their news service, CIMAC Noticias, by fax, mail, and broadcast-ready radio programs. Moreover, they built a network of journalists trained to understand the importance of women's rights, who could facilitate transmission from counterpublics to the wider public. And finally, they founded a documentation center to provide research resources for these journalists. CIMAC used an array of techniques to encourage media coverage of women's issues; determined to adapt to a new technological context, its efforts would continue online.

All of these initiatives required a serious commitment of resources, not only in staff time and energy, but also to publish and distribute the magazines and news service. But in general, feminist publishers sought to avoid the economic relations that produced traditional coverage of women's issues. Because of its dependence on advertising, mass media sold "what sells best, . . . violence, exploitative and abusive sex, and greed for power and consumer goods."[45] So *fem* did not take advertising for its first ten years; and instead of taking advertising, Fempress applied for foundation support. By 1995, the organization boasted a budget of $400,000, entirely underwritten by foreign assistance from European countries, private foundations, and the United Nations. CIMAC also depended on foundation support, as well as the income generated by its work with news and other organizations. Although much better funded than other projects, dependence on external support left them vulnerable. In the case of Fempress, the withdrawal of financial support when foundation attention shifted elsewhere, compounded by the challenges of negotiating the world of then-new internet technology, proved too difficult to overcome. *Mujer/fempress* stopped circulating in 2000.[46] In fact, all of the publications profiled here attempted some kind of online format, however brief; but only one, CIMAC, survived the digital transition. Financing, a long-standing contentious issue for feminists in the region, is one problem purportedly solved by the internet. But as their fate and that of other online initiatives will demonstrate, this solution is more complex, and more potentially costly, than initially assumed.

The alternative media feminists published and circulated prior to the widespread use of the internet attested that these communities supported their own development through their own means of communication. In different ways, the keystone species of editors and writers empowered their audiences to explore topics that the mass media overlooked or denigrated. These audiences, excited by the perspectives they read or heard, formed or reinforced the kinds of organizations profiled in the next chapters. The outward-directed efforts of Fempress and CIMAC attempted to ensure that some of their stories reached larger audiences.

REGIONALIZING FEMINIST ACTIVISM: THE ENCUENTROS

Building on the same regional solidarity that inspired *La Correa Feminista, fem, mujer/fempress,* and CIMAC, Latin American feminists, alongside their Caribbean counterparts, have established a regional counterpublic space like no other: the Latin American and Caribbean Feminist Encuentros. Only in Latin America has feminist commitment to regional solidarity resulted in such an undertaking. From its start in 1981, it has become a place where women could consider and articulate their own feminist identities; debate—often furiously—the meaning and goals of feminism; and strategize for transformation across the region. It has meaning beyond the face-to-face experiences of participants, as media outlets such as the ones above have been inspired by, and in turn, inspired, the interactions and results of the meetings. For two decades before the popularization of the internet, Latin American feminists assembled, debated, and disseminated at the regional level.

These regional meetings vividly illustrate a regional counterpublic in action: local organizing committees from Argentina, Brazil, Chile, Colombia, Costa Rica, the Dominican Republic, El Salvador, Mexico, and Peru have taken responsibility for organizing thirteen Encuentros. Each committee has chosen the major themes and decided how they will be discussed, in plenary sessions, workshops, and panels, through artistic displays and performances, and more. They have also been responsible for finding a locale and providing financing. As "critical forums" through which an ever-wider range of women has shared experiences of and debated strategies for addressing gender inequality,[47] these counterpublic spaces have reflected and influenced the development of the region's feminisms.

The tripling of attendance between the first and second Encuentros—from a mere 180 women in Bogotà, Colombia, in 1981, to 600 in Lima, Peru, in 1983—attests to the power of counterpublic communications. As word spread of this stimulating event, more women were determined to attend. The Encuentros grew to incorporate thousands of participants, with a high of 3,200 in San Bernadino, Argentina, in 1986. Reflecting the increasing identification with feminism as well as its diversification, those attending multiplied not only in number but also in terms of who they were and what they did. At the first Encuentro, mainly light-skinned, middle-class, and educated women representing twelve regional countries (and a few extraregional observers) attended. However, they manifest their diversity through the countries they represented and their occupations: participants included doctors, agricultural workers, staff at battered women's shelters, leaders of peasant organizations, and, of course, feminist journalists. Over fifteen hundred participants from every country in Latin America and the Spanish-speaking Caribbean managed to make their way to the fourth Encuentro, held in Taxco, Mexico, in 1987; in a striking development, hundreds of women from grassroots women's movements in Central America attended. Mexico seemed ideally located geographically for bringing together the many new participants who broadcast their entry into what seemed like a restricted community by chanting, "Todas somos feministas!" ("We are all feminists!") at the final plenary. But the region's media also played a key role, with "unprecedented advertising in the feminist press" a central factor in the Encuentro's growing numbers and impact.[48] Clearly, feminist press had arrived in feminist hands across the region.

In keeping with its counterpublic roles, every Encuentro has provided this expanding community multiple opportunities for self-reflection and

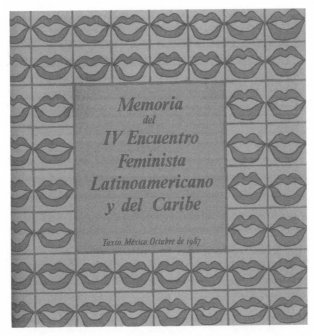

Memoria
del
IV Encuentro
Feminista
Latinoamericano
y del Caribe

Taxco. México. Octubre de 1987

FIGURE 4. Commemorative book of the fourth Latin American and Caribbean Feminist Encounter (Coordinadora del IV Encuentro Feminista Latinoamericano y del Caribe, October 1987). Reproduced by permission of Carolina Herrera, designer. Scan by Dan Battle.

political engagement. In artistic workshops and structured discussions, participants share their personal and political experiences. Those newly aware of patriarchal repression vent in intimate gatherings, while more jaded veterans of many years' conversations and campaigns retreat for savvy strategy sessions focused on lobbying policy makers. Friends reconnect and new relationships begin on shuttle buses, in registration lines, over lunch, and during drum circles. The Encuentro is a place for the region's feminists and feminisms to come together.

But this is no protected enclave. As feminisms have diversified across the region, debates over identity and strategy have grown apace. At early Encuentros, women deeply committed to left politics debated whether it was more effective, or even ethical, to create feminist groups separate from political parties and movements. With the growth of urban grassroots movements, low-income women insisted that the middle-class feminist founders of the Encuentros take into account many women's difficult material conditions.[49] Afro-Latin and indigenous women soon drew attention to the intersection of the issues of race, ethnicity, class, and gender.[50] By the end of the 1990s, Caribbean women, sensitive to the politics of language, challenged the hegemonic dominance of Spanish as the *lengua materna* (mother tongue) of the Encuentros.[51] Challenging as they may be to experience, these and other examples of dissent and debate have been inspiring to the region's activists and organizations. They, too, help to build communities seeking to recruit, honor, and engage a highly diverse membership.

The feminist press continued to be a key transmission belt for information before the Encuentros as well as reflection on their process, debates, and conclusions—which would then influence the next Encuentro. For example, in December 1987, *mujer/fempress* considered the problems of self-financing for the previous Encuentro. In 1993 *fem* published an article titled "The Disagreement [*Desencuentro*] of the Feminist Encounters," by one of the regular contributors to *La Correa Feminista*.[52] This piece and others published by *La Correa* itself helped to provoke the painful debate at the seventh Encuentro in Cartagena, Chile, in 1996, over whether the professionalization of feminism through work in nonprofits and state agencies, as well as the previous years' focus on preparing for the last of the UN conferences on women in Beijing, inherently co-opted their activism. *Fem* also covered the conferences, in reports such as "The 9th Latin American and Caribbean Feminist Encuentro: Active Resistance to Neoliberal Globalization."[53] The regional counterpublic has depended on regional media.

Following the Encuentros's model, other meetings, bolstered by general and more thematically specific publications, have captured the diversification of regional feminisms. Afro-Latin and indigenous women, lesbian feminists, activists focused on health, the prevention of gender-based violence, and sustainable development have called their own periodic encounters to focus on their challenges and common strategies, establishing their own counterpublic arenas. Magazines such as *Mujer y Salud,* the Latin American and Caribbean women's health journal, sprang out of such organizational efforts, but the publications above also wrote about them, for example in *fem's* coverage of the Latin American and Caribbean Lesbian Feminist Encounter and Black Women's Encounter.[54] As described in chapter 4, countries such as Argentina "nationalized" the Encuentro idea, establishing their own vibrant feminist encounters, which would in turn inspire an online feminist media initiative. But these media were always reflective of, as well as influential on, the activism itself.

Mirroring the region's diversity and divisions, the counterpublic of the Encuentros has been far from harmonious. But it has provided a space for exchange across difference, exchange that could lead to discursive and organizational innovation. As sociologist Millie Thayer explains: "It offered an arena in which battles could be waged and conflicts at least partially adjudicated. It was also a productive space, in which new discourses were generated and refined, and collaborations fostered."[55] Regional feminisms progressed through this opportunity. Beyond the meetings themselves, the wide circulation of Encuentro documents, debates, and personal experiences strengthened local and national counterpublics, as well as those focused on specific regional issues.

THE TRANSNATIONAL CONTEXT OF LATIN AMERICAN COUNTERPUBLIC COMMUNICATIONS, OFF- AND ONLINE

As with earlier efforts, the regional effervescence of women's rights advocacy in the late twentieth century happened within a larger transnational context. Latin American feminists drew on, and in turn shaped, transnational projects to connect women's rights activists around the world through alternative media circuits. Two of these initiatives illustrate differences in political location and orientation: the UN conference-linked International Women's Tribune Centre (IWTC), an information and communication clearinghouse formerly located across from the United Nations headquarters in New York, and Isis International, a research-based clearinghouse and publication aimed at strengthening grassroots women's activism in the Global South, with offices in Chile and the Philippines. As Alice Gittler, a former program associate with IWTC, argued, "Even before the word networking became synonymous with the Internet, women's information-exchange strategies facilitated, and, to a large extent, made possible the growth of an international movement."[56] The media were diverse, and would continue to be relevant even as the internet took off: "Popular theatre and radio listening groups, wall newspapers and women's wire services, fax trees and newsletters have informed, mobilized and built a global network of women activists. New information tools have joined rather than supplanted this media mix."[57] Long before the internet, Latin American feminist counterpublics benefited from the inception of global communication networks to support and connect local and national activist communities.

Although neither one of these initiatives used computers to communicate as far back as the 1970s and 1980s, another effort focused on the UN conference process did: Hotline International, intended to connect advocates who could not attend the 1975 International Women's Year (IWY) conference in Mexico City to their contacts on the ground. Hotline International suggested the potential of a proto-internet network, even as it was significantly limited in size and scope. Taken together, these three efforts reveal the transnational communications groundwork in place before the advent of the internet.

IWTC's founders sought to follow up on the energies released after the IWY conference. They included Mildred Persinger, the convener of the nongovernmental IWY Tribune, which hosted six thousand women in a parallel set of meetings during the official conference. In 1977, she and other IWY participants, such as the future executive director of IWTC, Anne Walker, established the IWTC in order to sustain the international ties from that dramatic encounter.[58] Such powerful members of the keystone species made IWTC a key player in the creation and expansion of global women's rights–oriented communication.

Although located in the Global North, this initiative responded to the demands of activists from the Global South, who most keenly felt the need for more connection. Because the convening organization for the IWY Tribune, the NGO IWY committee, based in New York, was "deluged with requests for information, support, finance, and technical assistance" from Tribune participants,[59] the IWTC focused on linking women, NGOs, governments, and the United Nations with an emphasis on the situation of women in the Global South. Their publication *The Tribune*, started as a modest cut-and-paste newsletter featuring the post-IWY updates IWTC staff received from around the world, became a major source of information about women's organizing. They also assembled regional resource kits. As the Latin American media outlets had for their region, these efforts helped national women's counterpublics assimilate the information and analysis circulating globally.

The IWTC continued to capitalize on the opportunities presented by the other UN Decade for Women conferences, establishing on-site resource sharing and networking hubs including Vivencia! at the 1980 Mid-Decade conference in Copenhagen. Under Colombian Vicky Mejia's coordination, the space became a key point of contact for Latin American women who gathered to share experiences and insights.[60] Afterward, IWTC's *Tribune* continued to provide connective tissue, circulating news about the flourishing networks formed during the conference.[61] During

The International Women's Tribune Centre (IWTC), a not-for-profit, non-governmental international women's organisation, is part of a worldwide women's movement given enormous impetus by the UN Decade for Women, 1976-1985. It was set up in 1976 following the International Women's Year non-governmental meeting (IWY Tribune) held in Mexico City, 1975.

INTERNATIONAL WOMEN'S TRIBUNE CENTRE
777 UNITED NATIONS PLAZA
NEW YORK, NY 10017, USA
Telephone: (1-212) 687-8633
Fax: (1-212) 661 2704
E-Mail: IWTC aigc org.
Cable: TRIBCEN

 PRINTED ON RECYCLED PAPER   IWTC IS WHEELCHAAIR ACCESSIBLE

Design: Laurel Douglas
Illustration: Laurel Douglas, Grace Jung and Anne S. Walker.

FIGURE 5. International Women's Tribune Centre pamphlet. Reproduced by permission of Anne S. Walker. Design by Laurel Douglas. Illustration by Laurel Douglas, Grace Jung, and Anne S. Walker.

the UN World Conferences of the 1990s, IWTC would take on a similar role helping to coordinate global efforts to strategize and lobby governments. It sought not only to ensure that the information generated at the conferences got into the hands of local and national counterpublics, but also to channel women's demands to conference attendees. The Tribune Centre used information to make the spaces opened by the UN conferences into an ever more effective target for activists.

In contrast to IWTC, Marilee Karl, Jane Cottingham, and Judy Sid-dens, who were working from Rome and Geneva to support progressive international communication in the 1970s, founded Isis as a feminist information documentation center and publisher focused on connecting women outside of government-sponsored opportunities like the UN con-ferences. They were inspired by the 1976 First International Tribunal on Crimes against Women in Brussels, where two thousand women came together of their own accord, rather than under the aegis of govern-ments, to publicize the brutal as well as the subtle ways in which women around the world suffered from violence, and to strategize about how to end it.[62] Isis responded to the low-quality coverage of the Tribunal in the mass media by producing its own coverage in the first issue of their *Women's International Bulletin*.[63] Isis's mission became providing oppor-tunities for women from the Global North and South to "shar[e] their ideas and experiences internationally, without the distortion of the male-dominated transnational-controlled press."[64] This direct communication was needed "so that women could recognize their situation and fight to change it."[65] Isis founders also established a center to collect women's media and research in order to counter commercial media's portrayal of women's rights activism. Inspired by women's autonomous transna-tional activism, Isis strengthened women's alternative media.

The circulation of Isis's *Women's International Bulletin* demon-strated how activists could leverage even modest publication runs to undergird their counterpublics. Peruvian activist Ana Maria Portugal, who helped bring Isis International to Latin America, described the *Bul-letin* as forming part of a burgeoning women's alternative media: "newsletters, mimeographed pamphlets, silk-screened posters, and so on, produced in small quantities and distributed by and among the ear-liest feminist groups."[66] Like these other media, the *Bulletin*'s impact was larger than its small numbers: they were "recirculated among new groups and information from them was reproduced in the alternative media of the South and North."[67] Passed hand to hand from group to group, women's alternative media reinforced transnational networks and local and national counterpublics, again long before the develop-ment of a technology that would ease such transmission.

Although Isis was headquartered in Europe, its founders realized that work for women in the Global South would be better undertaken from within their own regions.[68] Because Latin American women's groups were active in both providing and asking for information, Isis opened an office in Chile in the mid-1980s, run by two returning Chilean exiles who had worked in Isis's headquarters. Among other duties, the office took on the coordination of two of the networks nurtured by the regional Encuentros, focused on women's health and violence against women. To solidify these networks, Isis-Chile published their newsletters and analysis.

This office also put out two other magazines that served their regional audience. Following in the footsteps of other regional publications in reinforcing the counterpublic space of the Encuentros, the first number of *Ediciones de las Mujeres,* distributed in 1984, focused on the second Encuentro, which had taken place in Peru the year before. Published until 2002, its thirty-three numbers took up subjects ranging from health to women factory workers to masculinities. From 1996 to 2002, Isis also issued twenty-five numbers of *Perspectivas,* which focused on analyzing current issues for women's movements.[69] Isis's publications met a similar fate to those described above: with the withdrawal of foundation support early in the twenty-first century, all of them had to close.

Although IWTC and Isis carried out their media-based networking years before the popularization of the internet, another initiative attempted to use computer-mediated communication to enhance women's international rights advocacy. Hotline International was a computer-based network that allowed a group of U.S. advocates who could not attend the IWY conference in Mexico City to participate remotely. Organizers described it as "a limited time, action program operating on the dates of international conferences to enable interested NGOs and individuals to receive information, participate in decision making and to plan action strategy." What was unique about the initiative was its means of transmission: "All this to be accomplished without having to be physically present at the site of the conference. . . . And if someone asks you why you aren't in Mexico at the conference, you can say I am at the conference via the HOTLINE."[70] Although limited in time, scope, and participation, the Hotline offered the first experience of presence-at-a-distance in women's rights advocacy by attempting the blur lines separating physical and remote participation. And, as feminists from Latin America would experience with the internet, they adapted the technology to suit their own ends: in this case, attempting to influence elites at the official conference.

Hotline International had a distinct orientation from the more grassroots-oriented global communications networks assisted by IWTC and Isis, or those taken up two decades later at the 1995 Fourth World Conference in Beijing. Glen and Mildred Leet, a New York-based couple dedicated to fostering NGO participation in UN global conferences, became the keystone species for introducing computer-mediated communication to their community. In this case, it was largely limited to a preexisting group of U.S. middle-class and high-profile women's organizations with experience lobbying at the United Nations. But because the Hotline brought together a focus on global networking with the first use of an internet (although not the internet), its history offers an understanding of the initial difficulties with such networking, and a basis for comparing for how subsequent projects addressed them. Moreover, although the Hotline largely enabled discussions among women and men who were already part of the conference-lobbying process, it also facilitated the emergence of alternative perspectives.

Two decades before the widespread dissemination of the internet, these proponents understood the potential of computer-mediated communication for transnational civic participation. As they enthused about the Hotline, "This could lead to the development of an important capability through which NGOs can take a more active role in significant meetings. IT [Information Technology] can be a breakthrough by applying technology in a new way to enhance communications for global action."[71] The Leets had already begun to experiment with IT during other UN conferences of the 1970s, including the Human Environment Conference (1972), World Food Conference (1974), and Population Conference (1974). They helped to set up computer networks that were connected by telephone, enabling those in New York, Washington, and San Francisco to participate by receiving daily briefings and sharing their ideas.

As with IWTC, they believed that conferences could inspire work beyond the immediate goal of influencing governments. They sought to have "conferences serve as launch pads rather than splash downs to keep interest and action at a high level." The technological metaphor of space exploration, gleaming behind this conceptualization, reflected their sense that modern technology could provide answers to thorny global problems. However, the limitations of such technology, the "phone booths of our global environment,"[72] manifest in their descriptions of how people could join: all that was needed was access to a computer terminal— available at "universities and corporations"—that could communicate via phone lines at the relatively affordable rate of fifty cents per minute.[73] In the mid-1970s, the population with that kind of access was far from global, making this a restricted, Northern initiative.

Despite their international aspirations for the Hotline, the Leets were not able to get the funding and organization in place for widespread distribution across countries or communities.[74] Instead, they set up what they called "focal points," an individual or group with access to a computer terminal, in ten U.S. cities and Vancouver, British Columbia. The choice of focal points, in large urban and almost exclusively U.S. cities, necessarily limited the reach of this endeavor. The two IWY satellite conferences, where Hotline International participants discussed the information they had received from Mexico City and formulated collective responses, included around three hundred people in Philadelphia, with another fifty-three people from forty-nine organizations in New York. Many of those organizations, a set of mainly well-established NGOs, also had representatives in Mexico.[75] Although it did connect people across the Rio Grande, the Hotline did not succeed in widening participation far beyond already established networks.

Organizers' desire for the Hotline to be a "global town hall" connecting people, rather than machines, was reflected in their instructors to users, or what would become known to the next generation's internet users as "netiquettes." They entreated the participants to put the date on their missives, and consider using Greenwich time "to develop the sense of talking world wide at a specified instant." They also asked that everyone give their name on their entries to give "a people feeling, and not a computer machine feeling."[76] But the "people feeling" in this virtual meeting place was to be elevated by the technological interface. A summary of the "special features" of this mechanism for communication make clear that the town hall was intended to maintain a certain tone: "A typed input results in a more carefully considered response. There is less likelihood of an emotional one"; "New form of communication at conferences: absence of voice and body and facial movements and expressions creates a different quality to the communications."[77] The Leets believed that computer mediation would not only widen communications, but also bestow a kind of rationality they prized.

The rudimentary development of IT at this stage, made plain by multiple instructions from the keystone species about how to "code" contributions, manage virtual conversations, and deal with bad weather, meant that even those who had computer access depended on older technologies, like telephone calls and mail, to assist computer-mediated communications. There was no attempt to digitize the Hotline's archival legacy: the Leets were anxious to distribute physical copies (which they also hoped to sell to recoup some of their costs). Their instructions to participants reflected their intention to distribute the archive: organizers warned that nothing shared across the Hotline could be confidential, and exhorted participants to cite their sources.[78] The futuristic

Hotline International was embedded in its present reality in more than one way, as technological development did not match organizer goals.

However, this endeavor was quite plugged in politically, to use a technological metaphor of the times. One of the primary boosters was no less than Margaret Mead, at the time the president of the American Association for the Advancement of Science, who, in her "hearty congratulations" to the team, called their use of computer communications an "important break through."[79] The list of Hotline International "friends" in Mexico City,[80] from whom staffers solicited reports on a session, commentary on the NGOs' role, resolutions that need reinforcement from the United States, or help placing "special attention memos" from the Hotline in delegate mailboxes,[81] were well-known women's rights advocates, including Gloria Steinem and the secretary-general of the Tribune itself, Helvi Sipila. The Hotline implored Sipila to incorporate their voices: "Call on us, the NGO's, to help you as you seek equality, development and peace for humanity and for women. . . . Call on us—through our IWY Hotline we are listening."[82] Another major Hotline International booster was Esther Hymer, the international relations director of the National Federation of Business and Professional Women and a central figure in NGO representation to the United Nations. She affirmed the importance of the Hotline's work in networking and representation: "We feel that you are with us and we are here to advance your interests."[83] Even Senator Charles Percy congratulated their initiative and used what he termed this "creative and imaginative use of modern technology" to transmit his remarks.[84] At the conclusion of the conference, Hotline International staff sent letters congratulating Sipla and Ms. Mildred Marcy, IWY director for the U.S. State Department, on the conference's success, and offered them copies of the entire Hotline communications. They thanked Marcy in particular for "encouragement and assistance."[85] Thus, even as Hotline International organizers enthused that "the technology is at hand for a continuous town meeting of the world,"[86] it reinforced a preexisting network of high-profile, U.S.-based advocates.

Reflecting its limited participation and aspirations to influence high-level decision makers, Hotline International proceeded from an understanding of the role of information provision different from that of the transnational feminist efforts of groups such as Isis. Isis insisted that theirs was a political act: "We realize that the information we need to prioritize, document, file, and distribute is not neutral. It is directly related to the changes we want to bring about to achieve women's full

```
10.34.01 >PRINT IWY DC005

                                                                    015

   IWY ENTRY 015, FILE IWY DC005.  MESSAGE TO MRS. HELVI L. SIPILA,
   UNITED NATIONS ASSISTANT SECRETARY-GENERAL FOR SOCIAL DEVELOPMENT
   AND HUMANITARIAN AFFAIRS, AND SECRETARY-GENERAL OF THE INTERNATIONAL
   WOMEN'S YEAR, AND THE IWY CONFERENCE IN MEXICO CITY.

   (THE MEXICO CITY FOCAL POINT OF THE NGO "HOTLINE TO MEXICO CITY"
   COMPUTER-AIDED CONFERENCING SYSTEM, WHICH IS UNDER THE OVER-ALL
   COORDINATION OF MILDRED ROBBINS LEET, GLEN LEET, AND MARGARET
   MEAD OF THE NORTH AMERICAN COMMITTEE OF NON-GOVERNMENT ORGANIZATIONS
   CONCERNED WITH THE GLOBAL ENVIRONMENT, IS REQUESTED TO DELIVER
   THE FOLLOWING MESSAGE TO MRS. SIPILA.)


   ON BEHALF OF THE NON-GOVERNMENT ORGANIZATIONS FOCAL POINTS BECOMING
   DISTRIBUTED AROUND OUR WORLD, AND OUR INTERNATIONAL WOMEN'S YEAR "HOTLINE
   TO MEXICO CITY" COMPUTER-AIDED CONFERENCING SYSTEM, MAY I GREET YOU AS
   YOU PREPARE TO DELIVER YOUR REMARKS FOR THE OPENING OF THE CONFERENCE
   ON THE MORNING OF JUNE 19 1975.  MANY OF US WHO CANNOT BE WITH YOU IN
   MEXICO CITY ARE WITH YOU IN SPIRIT, AND IN GROWING NUMBERS ARE SHARING
   YOUR EXPERIENCES AND STANDING BY AS RESOURCES TO ASK QUESTIONS AND
   SUGGEST ANSWERS THROUGH THE TECHNOLOGY OF COMPUTER-AIDED COMMUNICATION.
   CALL ON US, THE NGO'S, TO HELP YOU AS YOU SEEK EQUALITY, DEVELOPMENT,
   AND PEACE FOR HUMANITY AND FOR WOMEN, THE "MOST UNDER-DEVELOPED OF ALL
   HUMAN RESOURCES, BECAUSE OF LACK OF OPPORTUNITY TO PLAY AN EQUAL PART
   WITH MEN IN ALL AREAS OF LIFE, AND BECAUSE OF THE STEREOTYPING OF MALE
   AND FEMALE ROLES", AS YOU HAVE STATED.  (PRESS RELEASE, IWY/23, 16 JUNE
   1975, UN OFFICE OF PUBLIC INFORMATION.)  CALL ON US - - THROUGH
   OUR IWY HOTLINE WE ARE LISTENING.
   WE WOULD WELCOME A STATEMENT FROM YOU FOR THE IWY HOTLINE AND OUR
   NGO HOTLINE CONFERENCES WORLDWIDE.
          .  .      .CARL C. CLARK, TECHNICAL ASSISTANT TO KIT GAGE, COORDINATOR
                    OF THE NGO DC FOCAL POINT, TRANSMITTED
                    197506180100 UNIVERSAL (GREENWICH) TIME.
                    VAYA CON LAS MUJERES!
```

FIGURE 6. Hotline International message of support to the secretary general of the IWY conference, Helvi Sipila (1975). Reprinted from International Women's Year Records, National Archives and Records Administration, Record Group 220, Schlesinger Library, Radcliffe Institute, Harvard University. Photo by Jocelyn Olcott.

participation in society."[87] In contrast, the Hotline "rested on the liberal distinction between information and ideology, assuming that more thorough dissemination of information would lead reasonable people to draw similar conclusions."[88] Intent informed technology use, even when organizers insisted otherwise.

The Hotline's approach, so embedded in the U.S. framework for public deliberation that it harkened back to the Puritan governance model of the town hall, had at its core an assumption that every voice could be heard, despite its limited reach to a small number of Northern participants. However, although they designed its question and answer relay with conference participants to ensure "a broad spectrum of points of view and a wide diversity of issues, comments and criticisms may be brought to bear on the conference held in Mexico City,"[89] organizers believed that those voices should sing in harmony for greatest impact, suggesting: "We [should take] all the resources of the women's organizations from the garden clubs to the professsional [sic] women['s] clubs to the mothers['] clubs and the park bureaus and [stand] firmly together, with one voice saying: no more money no more programs until women have a voice in setting national and international priorities."[90] While many women might have been interested in such a shift of priorities, the organization of women's energies through garden and professional clubs reveals the Hotline's assumption of middle- and upper-class women's protagonism. But, as the repeated failures "to distill the tumult of conflicts and encounters into unified statements of purpose" at the NGO forum revealed, those priorities were considerably different from country to country, and between the Global North and South. Rather than harmony, the voices of "radical heterogeneity" were raised outside of the official conference walls.[91] IWY historian Jocelyn Olcott finds the Hotline's attempt to incorporate more voices into IWY deliberations tainted by the same brush that Nancy Fraser used to critique Habermas: the assumption that the public sphere can ever be a "space of zero degree culture . . . as to accommodate with perfect neutrality . . . interventions expressive of any and every cultural ethos."[92] The Hotline was using computer-based communications to promote women's rights, but not to strengthen counterpublics.

Although it sought harmony, the Hotline itself was not always in tune. Its one international partner, the focal point in Vancouver, pointed out that different national situations should be taken into account. Staff there reported a low turnout for their face-to-face meeting, in part because of "limited preparation time and budgetary restrictions"—the same reasons the Hotline organizers gave for the limited reach outside of the United States. But they went on to describe the Canadian politics at work: women's groups felt as if their government had mishandled their issues, from equal employment to abortion, refused to spend IWY funds on their priorities, and did not allow them to appoint their own delegates. Even the Canadian IWY slogan, "why not," was felt to be "tasteless and condescending."[93] The politics on display here told a different story than the main Hotline narrative. Here were organizations that had a strong critique of their government's appropriation of the IWY opportunity. And because of their experience, they fostered a different aspiration for the Hotline, one that would wait a generation to be realized. They thought that computer-mediated communications should be used for horizontal exchange among women's organizations. To that end, they suggested that the Hotline put itself at the service of women's rights activists by pulling together a catalog of existing women's organizations and programs. They offered the Vancouver listings for a starting point.[94] In Canada, these women were ready to rely on computer-based communications to build counterpublic community.

On the ground in Mexico City, dissonance was also heard. After the Hotline reproduced Senator Percy's praise for their efforts and his remarks on development assistance for third world women,[95] the reporter summarized the reactions in the room: "The entire meeting seemed to focus on letting Senator Percy know that aid should be channeled through NGOs that work on the Grass-root level."[96] The Leets themselves eventually became convinced of this perspective, going on to become trailblazers in the area of microcredit loans in the Global South.

CONCLUSION

The history of Latin American feminist counterpublics shows that, considerably prior to the advent of the internet, this was a region in which women were determined to build communities where they could collectively address their subordinate status. They refused to accept inaccurate portrayals of their reality in the mass media, using their own publications to offer each other, and the wider world, a picture of the obstacles in their way and their many ideas for change.

This was also a region where, again long before the internet, increasingly diverse feminist communities relied on alternative media to construct regional solidarity with room for dissent. The keystone species of feminist publishers and writers demonstrated a regional sensibility as they supported different elements of counterpublics, from identity building to influencing mass media coverage of women's issues. The globally unique manifestation of regional feminist activism was the Encuentros. These gatherings were an opportunity for women from many different countries to reflect, debate, and celebrate together as they learned who they were in the world and how they wanted to change it. This most tangible example of a regional counterpublic in turn nurtured other spaces for connection and deliberation.

Regional counterpublics benefited from solidarity. But in what might seem a paradoxical development, they also grew through disagreement. Through their media, and in the classrooms, beachfront patios, hotel meeting rooms, and other locations of the Encuentros, feminists aired deep differences in identity and strategy. While difficult to experience, these opportunities for exchange enabled Latin American feminists to constantly and productively redefine themselves in the face of often-shared sources of oppression with distinct manifestations in women's lives. The diffusion of regional meetings' dynamics and conclusions through regional media rippled across local and national counterpublics, transforming their conversations and enhancing their activist repertoires. Latin America was a region ready for a technology of connection and diffusion.

It was also one that was already firmly embedded in global communication networks focused on the empowerment of local, national, and regional counterpublics. Initiatives such as the International Women's Tribune Centre and Isis International demonstrated distinct ways of circumventing "the distortion of the male-dominated transnational-controlled press," to quote the latter. Whether sharing women's UN-focused efforts or promoting more decentralized information exchange, the keystone species in these organizations also laid the groundwork upon which later transnational media endeavors would build.

As regional counterpublics and their transnational alliances developed largely without computer mediation, an experiment was underway in the first attempt to use computers to link women's rights proponents. Hotline International was an innovative step at the global level. Building on experiences outside of women's conferences, founders and organizers applied an infant technology to the goal of including more voices in the first UN conference on women. Limited in reach, the Hotline reinforced the elite nature of international negotiations even as it expanded participants beyond those who could physically attend the 1975 conference in Mexico City. In this way, the computer-mediated communications were bent to the perspectives of those who used it. It would take a feminist reorientation of global technology at a UN women's conference twenty years later to push forward the internet's potential for undergirding women's communications around the world—and its incorporation into Latin American feminist counterpublics.

CHAPTER 2

The Creation of "a Modern Weaving Machine"

Bringing Feminist Counterpublics Online

In 1992, long-time feminist activist Beatriz Cavazos moved from the stimulating metropolis of Mexico City to the more remote Yucatán for work. There, she felt isolated from the energetic counterpublics of home; besides expensive telephone calls, there was no way to keep up to date, and the local bookstores did not carry feminist books or magazines. Eager to resolve her communication and information conundrum, she reached out to a transborder activist from the United States, Erika Smith. Erika had become convinced that the emerging email technology could facilitate exchange between women organizing in the United States and Mexico—and among Mexican feminists themselves.[1]

When Smith and Cavazos began to collaborate, they found themselves in the midst of an ambitious transnational campaign to encourage feminist and women's organizations to get online. In preparation for the 1995 UN Fourth World Conference on Women in Beijing, the Women's Networking Support Programme (WNSP) of the Association for Progressive Communications (APC), the international organization of nonprofit computer networks dedicated to supporting progressive counterpublics and movements, spread the gospel of the internet across the Global South and eastern Europe. Effectively, they were attempting to create an exponentially expanded, and counterpublic-focused, version of Hotline International.

Smith and Cavazos joined the dedicated keystone species of the WNSP and started an online working group to prepare Mexican feminists for the Beijing conference, orienting their efforts in two directions. As staff at the Mexico City–based APC member, LaNeta, Smith traveled around the country explaining to women's organizations that, as clunky as the current modems might be, communicating using email and distribution lists would be cheaper and faster than the faxes they currently relied on. And, once online, they would be able to both receive immediate reports from the conference and share their own realities with the thousands of participants. The internet could be a boon to their counterpublic work.

Meanwhile, Cavazos and colleagues from other organizations founded Modemmujer, "modem woman." Although the scratchy static and beeping of a dial-up modem sounds archaic today, at the time the name invoked the cutting-edge cyborg of a woman empowered by the latest in technological connectivity. Modemmujer's initial project aimed to bring the conference proceedings to the growing numbers of women with access to the internet. Once the conference was underway, three attendees sent regular reports to Modemmujer, which in turn broadcast them to four hundred email addresses. The owners of those addresses then redistributed them to an even larger audience through a combination of new and old communication technologies, including "fax, local newspapers, and community radio."[2] That audience's responses were then "filtered back" to the team in Beijing, who used them to lobby the official Mexican delegation.[3] Repeated around the world, the work of women like Cavazos and Smith connected counterpublics to the enormous network of networks the internet was becoming, and, through it, to the Fourth World Conference on Women. This was the global town hall the Leets had predicted, brought into being by feminists intent on interpreting the internet to serve a vastly expanded number of participants.

Cavazos and Smith, who supported women's appropriation of internet technology from that point forward, were present at the inception of the digital enhancement of Mexican and transnational feminist and women's counterpublics. From their own experiences of activism, they appreciated the potential benefits that this new technology might bring. Their extension of the internet would help women's rights activists across Mexico expand and connect local counterpublics, reinforcing the networks nurtured by earlier generations. Along with other tech-savvy members of the keystone species elsewhere in Latin America and across the world, they would benefit from a transnational feminist network, the Women's Networking Support Programme.

The creation story of the Women's Programme inspires on its own, but it is embedded in a larger tale of the creation of the internet itself. In the 1980s, the social justice–oriented computer network builders who would eventually connect through APC established the internet as we know it today: a network of networks where, at least in theory, any device with access can connect to any other. Motivated by their progressive values, these technicians and administrators wanted to make sure activists and their organizations would benefit from this powerful technology even before its explosive commercial spread. It was within this framework of counterpublic empowerment that the WNSP carved out a space for women's exchange, providing the material basis for deliberation and debate. From their early attempts to today, they contested the gendering of the internet as the sole province of men. In doing so, they, like the broader APC, challenged the West's domination over the internet, by enabling those from the Global South, including Latin America, to expand their own counterpublics.

The women who took on this challenge, along with those involved in the building of a decentralized, globally connected internet, intervened in the debate over whether this technology is the appropriate medium to fight inequality and injustice. On the one side, proponents present the internet as a relatively available, low-cost technology ideally suited to the work of often underresourced counterpublics. On the other, skeptics see yet another "silver bullet" solution that ignores the deep-seated relations of power that structure both the technology itself and access to it. Both of these perspectives treat the internet—and people—as static and separate. But, as the stories of the WNSP and APC show, the impact of the internet, as with other technologies, follows from its use in a social context.

From a sociomaterial perspective, technology is inseparable from its social location; it is "a sociotechnical product—a seamless web or network combining artefacts, people, organisations, cultural meanings and knowledge."[4] This chapter demonstrates that the material work of women and men who literally connected people to each other through computers helped to create and maintain an internet that would be useful to counterpublics and their work to change broader publics. Not simply a diffusion of advanced technology from North to South, this outcome was a deliberate, transnational exchange of hardware, software, and knowledge in the service of social transformation.

This chapter demonstrates the interconnection of technology and society through two overlapping stories, both of which help to explain the creation of internet-enriched feminist counterpublics. First, it tells the creation story of the decentralized, extensive internet, including its spread across Latin America. Then, it investigates the parallel feminist effort to get the internet into the hands of women's rights activists. Throughout, it refers to the social construction of the three layers of internet technology: physical (such as computer hardware and internet servers), logical (the computer codes, software, and other elements that enable communication and information sharing), and content (what is transmitted across digital networks). As with other information ecologies, the values and goals of the keystone species guided how they built and shared each layer of the internet. Within these larger processes of internet construction and diffusion, Cavazos, Smith, and the other women of the WNSP helped Latin American feminist activists to bring their vibrant counterpublic construction online.

BUILDING AN ACCESSIBLE INTERNET: THE ASSOCIATION FOR PROGRESSIVE COMMUNICATIONS

Many scholars and activists have asserted that internet technology is the ideal tool or place for organizations and individuals to build local, national, and transnational counterpublics.[5] Once they invest in set-up costs, they have an inexpensive organizing tool with extensive, horizontal reach. The speed with which advocates can disseminate analysis assists with rapid replication of efforts[6]—an important attribute for groups with nonmainstream perspectives.

This description makes the internet seem as if it were the best possible device in the activist toolkit. Somehow a technology supposedly invented by the U.S. military turned out to be just what activists around the world needed! This mysterious conversion is usually taken for granted. But a closer look reveals that the early integration of technology into social justice communities was neither a foregone conclusion nor an inevitable development. Instead, it happened through the sometimes deliberate, sometimes fortuitous actions of those dedicated to expanding communication resources beyond the politically powerful, economically fortunate, and socially advantaged. Progressive computer engineers, programmers, and administrative staff delivered new technology to counterpublic builders. Whether inspired by liberal values of democracy and inclusion, or a commitment to uprooting deep-seated structures of inequality, these people actively influenced the internet's direction in order to enhance diverse forms of counterpublic construction. In Latin America, communities emerging out of the fiercely repres-

FIGURE 7. Association for Progressive Communications
(APC) logo. Courtesy of the Association for Progressive
Communications.

sive regimes of the 1970s and 1980s embraced these new opportunities
to enable their participation in emerging democracies.

An international network of NGOs (nongovernmental organizations),
the Association for Progressive Communications (APC) connected progressive internet service providers from around the world into a cohesive
system and then empowered those working for social justice to jump
online. Indeed, political scientist Peter Willetts places these NGOs at the
center of the internet's development, demonstrating how their values
influenced its construction. Because NGOs seek to transmit information
widely and inexpensively, the ones involved in APC's construction "were
inspired to construct a global public system."[7] Constructing this network
had a transcendental impact: it spurred the inception of the internet as we
know it today. These NGOs helped to make that internet by focusing on
its physical and logical layers, building code and distributing software
and even servers so that people around the world could communicate and
share their varied content.

The APC-based network connected computers to enable widespread
connectivity. In comparison, initial computer-mediated communications
networks were all "mononets," only able to exchange data with each
other rather than with any computer in any network. These state and
commercial systems reflected their governmental or market-based values
by restricting access to users who would advance their goals. The much-
discussed contributions of both the U.S. military and commercial enter-
prises were restricted in this way. In the 1950s and 1960s, Cold War
preoccupations, from the search for battlefield communications that
could continue even if headquarters were obliterated by a nuclear bomb,

to the space race with the Soviet Union, encouraged the Pentagon to invest in the field of computer science. The Department of Defense underwrote the expensive physical layer of massive computers at major research universities, and the physical and logical components of its ARPANET project enabled these computers to "talk" with each other. Although these advances also included the dividend of email accounts for university researchers, users were still in a limited network. In the 1980s, when commercial developers Compuserve and America Online created their own mononets, they reflected their profit-maximization goals by restricting email traffic to their own subscribers and charging for incoming email from other networks. These systems had limited value to people and organizations outside of these restricted arenas.

Cold War and capitalist interests seemed to be in control of early internet communications at the logical layer of software, and had a near monopoly on the physical layer in terms of server hardware. But they could not prevent the democratization of communications. Inspired by the spirit of 1960s openness, rather than Cold War control, distinct initiatives at the logical layer included "the poor man's ARPANET," when Duke University graduate students created a way for people with access to computers running Unix software to participate in the earliest distribution lists, "Usenet" online newsletters, and email exchange. The Berkeley Community Memory project sought to "liberate" computers in order to build community networks, and offered free computer time to the public.[8] In the late 1970s, hacker hobbyists began experimenting with home computers designed for Atari-like games. They devised the "bulletin board systems" (BBS) that allowed primarily local users to send messages, play games, and read news. By the mid-1980s, these local BBS could be connected through the FidoNet network, which enabled the transmission of email nationally and eventually internationally over telephone lines. These undertakings disrupted the restrictive models built by state and market forces.

But the establishment of a "network of networks," open to a much larger, global audience, came about because Latin American and African activists insisted on being included. Living in the Global South, they were well aware of the marginalization of their lives and demands, and understood the potential of communications technology to enhance their local and national counterpublic work and link it internationally. Thus, when they learned of the creation of decentralized computer-mediated communications, they pressured contacts in the Global North to extend their knowledge about computer-based communication.[9] For example, it was in response to their members from the Global South that the International Coalition for Development Action oversaw the creation of INTERDOC, a BBS network through which four thousand users could share information about computing, development, and human rights, as well as draw on the resources from the larger organizations' databases.[10] Activists from the Global South did not just insist on their inclusion, but also were involved in network construction: one of the inventors of INTERDOC, Mario Padrón, headed up a Peruvian NGO.[11] This pressure and invention meant that by the mid-1980s, some NGOs were able to communicate globally using computers. But these computers themselves were still in mononets that did not share a common logical layer.

Seeking to weave those mononets into a broader internet so that change-makers could communicate, progressive computer technicians and software designers built them the "most advanced networks" of the time.[12] Scott Weikart, formerly of Hewlett-Packard, believed that "there was a great need among non-profit organizations [for a data communications tool]," and sought to extend "sophisticated computing" to them.[13] In 1985, he and Mark Graham, another computer professional, established PeaceNet in San Francisco as a "civil server,"[14] an internet service provider (ISP) set up specifically for civil society access, in order to connect NGOs and individuals working for peace. Its sister EcoNet, begun by the Farallones Institute, a San Francisco organization focused on sustainable development, linked environmentalists. When Weikart and Graham co-founded the Institute for Global Communications (IGC) to tie together PeaceNet and EcoNet, they actively encouraged the use of email, mailing lists, electronic conferences, and news bulletins. As Weiker explained, "We looked for groups doing progressive work and asked them 'Could you use e-mail, conferencing or better communications?'"[15] At a time when the ability to use email and listservs was limited to those in academic, governmental, and commercial mononets,[16] this opening was a major victory for civil society organizations. Guided by their passion for peace, the environment, and democratizing communications, Weikart, Graham, and others made the internet into a more open space.

IGC's work led to the transformation of the internet, as they broke through mononet culture to create a "network of networks." In 1987, IGC intervened at the logical level when Weikart "cop[ied] all its [communications] software on a massive disk, [brought] it to London," and installed it on the computers of a similar organization in the U.K., Green-Net. This gift created the very "first public transatlantic computer link."[17] Such public-mindedness extended beyond this union: the link provided gateways to more than twenty networks located in academic and commercial arenas.[18] By 1988, people in over seventy countries could communicate through this civic endeavor, which kept expanding. IGC helped to establish yet more networks in the Global North and South by sharing free software and assisting with hardware configuration, thereby extending the logical and physical layers in the direction of globally connected activism. This was a boon in Latin America, where early civil servers such as Nicarao in Nicaragua and AlterNex in Brazil connected to IGC.[19] Latin Americans were included at the inception of the expanded internet.

IGC achieved its goal of consolidating a widespread network that could serve counterpublics around the world in 1990, when seven civil server organizations founded the Association for Progressive Communication (APC).[20] Well prior to the massification of the internet, some of these had up to ten thousand users.[21] Moreover, over half of APC's members were in the Global South, with many located in Latin America. APC's affiliates, which were not full members but still received significant support, also extended email capacity to the developing world, especially in Africa.[22] Between 1989 and 1995, APC was "the core of the internet,"[23] enabling people around the world using every type of computer to communicate. The APC connected those seeking to change the world by spreading the internet across it.

APC's Latin American civil servers led the region into networked connectivity at a propitious time: the late twentieth-century era of democratic transitions, and what such transformations potentially implied for civic inclusion. Brazil's AlterNex was not only the first nonacademic provider in all of Latin America, but became such even before the military left power.[24] It was housed at IBASE, an umbrella organization dedicated to strengthening human rights and development NGOs. At the time of AlterNex's founding, IBASE was in the thick of the opposition to authoritarian rule; in the new democracy, it would focus on bringing citizens into the policy-making process. As one of Brazil's most important and durable civic organizations, it was perfectly positioned to extend network access to a broad swath of Brazilian organizations. AlterNex was the brainchild of IBASE cofounder Carlos Alfonso. Inspired by INTERDOC, Alfonso and his colleagues managed to begin their own BBS system in the mid-1980s by connecting to the only public data network operating at that time in Brazil, run by the military-dominated government through the state telephone company. Although the company did not completely understand what AlterNex was doing, it knew enough to be suspicious, and periodically would cut off the telephone service upon which the BBS depended. But IBASE had enough clout to insist through channels that it be restored. In Brazil, those fighting for democracy had the internet on their side.

Alongside AlterNex, other Latin American civil servers got underway and linked across the region. AlterNex shared their connective model, as well as server hardware, with Uruguayan colleagues who themselves were just coming out of their own twelve-year-long civic-military dictatorship, so that they could also establish a civil server, Chasque.[25] In Nicaragua, a software collective brought the internet to the country in 1988, two years before the end of the Sandinista revolution, by opening up a channel to IGC. With the founding of Nicarao in 1989, the civil server helped the rest of Central America get online through research centers and organizations.[26] The Ecuadoran APC member, INTERCOM-Ecuanex, founded in 1991, was the sole provider of electronic mail in the country. Its very structure modeled democratic process, since it was run by its twenty-one user organizations.[27] Also in 1991, Mexico City's LaNeta, home to Erika Smith's efforts to get Mexican women and feminist organizations online and host to Modemmujer's website and email accounts, was established with a borrowed computer in the closet of another organization; it joined APC in 1993.[28] Mexican activists recognized its vanguard character. As María Eugenia Chávez, the communications coordinator of Salud Integral para la Mujer (Holistic Health for Women; SIPAM) remembered, "When it started not even the biggest telephone companies, ATT, Avantel, TelMex, not even the big media companies were using the internet. . . . And LaNeta was a vanguard, [an] innovative organization introduced internet into Mexico, and more than that, introduced it for civil organizations."[29] In 1992, with the help of AlterNex and Chasque, Wamani became the APC node in Buenos Aires. Both LaNeta and Wamani later sponsored branches outside the capital cities of their countries. Each APC member in Latin America contributed to Latin American counterpublics, and their contributions to Latin American democracy, through early adoption and diffusion of the internet.

Becoming APC members meant that Latin American civil servers linked to other NGOs around the world, strengthening global counterpublic bonds and their potential effectiveness. Activists used electronic conferences to share resources, whether in the form of knowledge, newsletters, action alerts or even fundraising appeals. Sheldon Annis describes one notable example of the power such networking had in its early days: "Within minutes of the assassination of Amazonian rubber tapper [and environmental activist] Chico Mendes [on December 22, 1988], word of his killing flew worldwide over the electronic web, sparking vigils, protests, demands for investigations, and prodding the news media to pick up the story."[30] This brutal killing became a symbol for the international environmental movement in large part because activists spread the word through newly powerful internet connections. APC enabled Latin American activists to participate in global counterpublics and to circulate their demands for social justice to wider publics.

Latin American civil servers made it possible for global, national, and local counterpublics to incorporate digital communications almost a decade before commercialized internet arrived in the region because they were part of the fabric of civic life. Carlos Alvarez, a founding member of Wamani in Argentina, explained that "there was a degree of trust among those who made up the network that required previous knowledge. . . . Not just anyone came and was a member of APC. They had to, in some way, show the capacity of articulation with local organizations."[31] The staff at Indeso Mujer, a women's rights group in Rosario, Argentina, initially heard of Nodo Tau, Wamani's local branch, through "social and organizational links" with the local progressive Christian community. They welcomed getting service through "a community organization, a social project" and saw working with Nodo Tau as "a way to support another organization like ours."[32] Sandra Infurna, librarian for the feminist research center CEPIA, described how AlterNex enabled her organization to participate in Brazil-wide work against violence against women, as they sent their publications across the country via email. It "brought the NGO world together," she testified. "It changed the way we work. A fantastic thing, it doesn't have a comparison. Really impressive!"[33] Activists also viewed LaNeta as a member of the broader community. "They were an NGO like us . . . many organizations solidaristically connected us to LaNeta," said Tania Robledo Banda of APIS—Fundación para la Equidad (Foundation for Equality) in Mexico City.[34] Mariana Pérez Ocaña, founder and publisher of the Mexican lesbian feminist magazine *LeSVOZ*, affirmed LaNeta's solidaristic approach when she mentioned that LaNeta would not cut off service when organizations were a few months late with their payment. Besides their path-breaking and solidaristic actions, these civil servers provided accessibility and service at low cost. But civil servers actions found such rapid acceptance because they were part of the community: like other organizations, their mission was to transform society. Their unique role was to use communications software and server hardware to bring about change.

The networking capacity of the global APC network became so effective that global leaders ended up relying upon it—through a Latin American civil server. A generation after Hotline International's pioneering computer-mediated communications at the UN conferences of the 1970s, Maurice Strong, the secretary general of the 1992 UN Conference on Environment and Development (UNCED), asked AlterNex to "design, implement, and operate" a computer network that would enable attendees and those connected to the network to access UNCED-related documents, exchange email, participate in electronic conferences, and receive a daily news bulletin. APC not only circulated conference-oriented materials globally, but it also set up four computer centers, one for official representatives, one for NGO members, one at their hotel, and one for the press. These centers linked to the APC network and through that to activist counterpublics around the world. The UNCED secretariat directed American media outlets to use APC networks to obtain conference materials, thereby recognizing the importance of the APC network in ensuring NGO participation in the official and parallel conference processes.[35] APC built on this success to provide computer communications at the 1993 UN World Conference on Human Rights, with its crowning achievement being to facilitate a Tibetan-led global pressure campaign to ensure the Dalai Lama's attendance.[36] Through its actions, APC nurtured global counterpublic communications that could oppose even a government notorious for its strict information controls, China.

Latin Americans seized the opportunity of the UN conference processes to insist on further democratization of the logical layer. Leaders of AlterNex demanded that, as part of the diplomatic agreement between the UN and the Brazilian government governing the UNCED conference procedures, AlterNex would be able to use the hitherto restricted communication language of the internet, TCP/IP, in order to facilitate electronic networking focused on the conference. Access to this key element of the logical layer was yet another step forward for global counterpublic communications, as it further eliminated traffic stops across the expanding network of the information superhighway.

With the commercialization of web access in the late 1990s, civil servers declined in importance in terms of their role in connectivity, forcing them to develop new keystone species roles within their communities. While groups that had come online thanks to the dedication of progressives with technical skills were grateful for their work, the higher speeds and, often, lower prices that telephone companies could provide were too good to pass up. Some, like Infurna's CEPIA, maintained an email address or a distribution list with their local APC member in solidarity with all that they had meant in the past. Others noted that retaining at least an email address with a civil server meant they could still count on technical assistance. But the overall decline in users provoked considerable soul searching across APC, as civil servers had to reconsider their central mission now that they were far from the only provider in town. Some transitioned to providing services beyond physical connectivity. Although AlterNex eventually commercialized, some of its founders began the Rede de Informações Para o Terceiro Setor (Information Network for the Third Sector or RITS) to provide limited internet services, civil society information, and policy advocacy. Wamani in Argentina turned to developing training modules on the internet and human rights. APC itself developed an active role in international communications policy, focused on communications rights.[37] Although it largely shifted away from direct service provision, this vanguard network continued to strive for social change through technological innovation.

But APC's original mission of providing community-oriented communications infrastructure remained relevant in some places. In 2011, LaNeta merged with a larger transnational, counterpublic-focused internet provider, the First of May/People's Network. With a hundred servers and a global presence, it resembles the early civil servers. The communiqué through which it informed the LaNeta community of their merger stated: "The left will not be able to win the battles that it has to fight if it doesn't develop its electronic communication capacities. Having a presence in Internet isn't enough, it is also necessary to create our own applications and make our infrastructure of networks and servers in Internet grow."[38] The People's Network saw the importance of orienting both the physical and logical layers toward the needs of their user base. In incorporating the projects, and some of the leadership, of LaNeta, this organization saw an opportunity to develop a bilingual presence, crucial to waging the social justice battles of the twenty-first century.[39] To take transnational action on issues such as environmental degradation, immigration, economic inequality, racism, and the like, border crossers needed to be able to communicate using all the resources at their disposal.

Whatever their ultimate fate, civil servers helped to create an internet in their own image by bringing together the efforts of change makers across the world. Of course, many strands came together to create the internet; NGOs were not single-handedly responsible for it. But they played a crucial role. According to Willetts, "they pioneered the creation of the Internet as a communications system to mobilize the general public to join social and political networks, and to take political action."[40] Other actors would have created a very different internet. If governments had taken the lead, the internet would have privileged national over international connections, with more financial and legal restrictions on cross-border networking and public use. If business had taken the lead, profit incentives would have dramatically affected access, with corporations trying to develop specific audiences through proprietary software and other technical barriers to networking. Many fewer people would have had access, and such access would have privileged the Global North and elites in the Global South.[41]

While governmental restrictions and corporate "fencing off" of the "internet commons" remains a real, if not entirely realized, threat today, the spirited defense of an open internet has much to do with those who "created the soul of the new network from the bottom up."[42] APC embodies this soulful construction by building a platform for counterpublics: "We help people get access to the internet where there is none or it is unaffordable, we help grassroots groups use the technology to develop their communities and further their rights, and we work to make sure that government policies related to information and communication serve the best interests of the general population, especially people living in developing countries."[43] Getting the internet to places and people without access; training with an eye to community building; and intervening to keep internet what it needs to be for general access: this orientation guided the construction of an internet for all.

FEMINISTS WEAVE THE WEB

As Tania Robledo Banda of APIS, Sandra Infurna of CEPIA, Mariana Pérez Ocaña of LeSVOZ, Noemi Chiarotti, Mabel Gabarra, and Susana Moncalvillo of Indeso Mujer, and María Eugenia Chávez of SIPAM testified, feminist and women's organizations took advantage of the APC network for their internet access. As a whole, they had help: a group of women working with and for APC members who were determined that women from around the world could enhance their counterpublics through digital means. These feminists understood the ways in which gender and other relations of power embed themselves throughout the "life trajectory" of technological artefacts—from design, to production, to distribution, to use.[44] To support their own work within male-dominated tech spaces as well as teach women how to incorporate technology according to their own goals, they started the Women's

Networking Support Programme in the early 1990s, soon becoming one of APC's "most successful and dynamic" programs.[45]

Like Hotline International in the 1970s, WNSP took advantage of the global opportunity of a UN conference process to promote computer-mediated communications for women's rights. But with very different actors, wider goals, and twenty years of internet expansion, this initiative proved to be a profoundly different encounter from the Hotline. It was much larger, more global, and more focused on what women could take away from the experience to nurture their own counterpublics, rather than primarily directed at influencing conference negotiations. Moreover, their work to examine how technology was affecting women and how women could shift technology continued through other means, such as development assessment and digitizing the global counterpublic campaign against violence against women. Their keystone species members in Latin America made sure the region was well represented in these efforts.

The genesis of the WNSP was the desire of women inside the APC network to coordinate their work to support women's organizing across the world. Working out of APC member organizations, or with the groups that used APC services, twenty "technicians, information workers, project managers, financial workers, coordinators, and executive directors from over fifteen countries" started a discussion list, apc.women, to help each other and their local and national women's organizations.[46] Without reliable financial or management support at their individual organizations, they shared their experiences as well as their technical and organizing expertise. Women technology workers used the internet to generate a space for their collaboration.

Although women within APC began to work in concert, they faced doubt from many directions. Colleagues and funders did not (yet) understand why it was important to ensure that women would not be excluded from this technology, as they had been from so many others. The WNSP also had to convince the activists themselves, who "were understandably reticent, wary, even suspicious" of using new communications technologies. A survey of early users demonstrated why: they faced considerable obstacles. While some of these were general to many organizations on the learning curve of internet adoption, such as "limited accessibility, time consuming, information overload," others seemed to reflect gender inequalities, such as "lack of privacy and security, potential fear of backlash or harassment, inappropriate use of information, skill deficiencies, lack of gender-sensitive training and support, and alienation." These kinds of obstacles were compounded for women from the Global South, who also protested the "language constraints . . . limited infrastructure . . . and the high costs of data transmission" with which they coped.[47] The early days seemed to confirm the worst of what some critical approaches to the study of gender and technology argue: that (capitalist, Western) patriarchal dominance of society dooms technology to be inappropriate, if not dangerous, for women, particularly those with few resources and/or located outside of the "developed" world.[48] But the women of APC confronted women's problems in order to make the internet into something that could enhance their counterpublics.

They steadily improved and distributed appropriate tools for women's organizing, first teaching each other and then branching outward. Building from their own success with the logical layer of apc.women as a platform for community building, they started newsgroups on health, violence, labor, environment, and development to connect activists across borders. They also encouraged women to start their own. In just four years, fifty newsgroups were underway, as women across the globe exploited the new platform for exchange. Aware that technology in itself does not empower, WNSP offered opportunities that would become a mainstay of their work: in-person workshops in the Global South to expand women's technical knowledge and skills. There, they could teach women what they needed to know to integrate the internet for their own ends.

Through regular communication, including surveys of their intended audience, and their own locations in many sites around the world, they largely avoided the problems of much transnational feminist outreach, where Northern feminists seek to transmit their values and know-how to dispossessed, helpless "victims" in the Global South.[49] Instead, they recognized women's preexisting counterpublics, such as the ones spanning Latin America, as well-honed sources of organizing experience. WNSP's goal was to enhance what was already present through contextually appropriate communication and information strategies.

The first major opportunity that they took advantage of to advance this goal was the 1995 Fourth World Conference on Women (FWCW), where seventeen thousand governmental representatives from 189 countries met in high-level discussions, while thirty thousand nongovernmental participants attended the parallel NGO Forum. Drawing on APC's successful provision of the communications infrastructure for earlier 1990s conferences, women within the APC network met with coordinators for NGO participation at the FWCW to discuss how to deploy electronic communications. In person and online, women in APC, activist media groups, and UN agency staff strategized with each other and consulted supportive male colleagues. In 1993, APC officially recognized WNSP, which immediately initiated a worldwide campaign to prepare local and national women's groups for "virtual" involvement in the FWCW. By the time of the conference, they had helped hundreds of organizations in over thirty countries, along with thousands of women around the world, gain access to preparatory information.[50] The WNSP prepared women to appropriate this global opportunity.

As a part of this global campaign, Latin American colleagues founded WNSP-LA (Latin America) in 1993. Initially coordinated through APC member INTERCOM-Ecuanex with the cooperation of the Agencia Latino Americana de Información (Latin American Information Agency, ALAI, an alternative media service focused on supporting social movements),[51] it offered women's organizations technical and strategic internet training, as well as introducing communications and media policy advocacy with a gender perspective. They worked in or with all the Latin American APC members: INTERCOM-Ecuanex in Ecuador, AlterNex in Brazil, Wamani in Argentina, LaNeta in Mexico, Colonodo in Colombia, Nicarao in Nicaragua, and Chasque in Uruguay. From their own experiences in their highly organized region, these women could see what an important contribution the internet could make to national and regional counterpublics. They were determined to help.

This type of horizontally organized leadership from around the world, including the Global South, was one of the many illustrations of how the Women's Programme transformed UN conference-focused electronic networking from the U.S.- and government-focused Hotline International. On the ground at the parallel NGO Forum in Huairou, China, forty women from twenty-five countries, who spoke eighteen languages, representing twelve APC members and seven affiliates, set up and ran an on-site computer lab. This team, the majority of whom were from the Global South, effectively constructed a civil server right at the forum. They also operated an auxiliary site at the official conference. The team had multiple roles to play to connect multiple on-site and off-site global audiences. Not least of these was to model what they hoped to teach the women who had gathered at Huairou. As the Women's Programme team oriented individuals and groups to email and word processing and also laid cables and fixed computers, Forum participants saw that women could master both the logical and physical layers of the internet. In the two decades since IWY, the advance of both the technology and feminist attention to it made the Beijing experience an ideal opportunity for women to instruct other women what computer-based communications could do for them and their communities.

Taking advantage of the remarkable opportunity for face-to-face exchange with women from around the world, the WNSP trained women to incorporate a new communications infrastructure into their own counterpublics. WNSP focused on providing new email accounts, a first at a UN conference. Staff members helped participants open seventeen hundred free email accounts, from which they sent and received sixty-two thousand email messages. By sharing their experiences and perspectives with contacts back home, they offered an alternative to official news sources. As one participant in the on-site organizing shared, "E-mail will never be the same. If it weren't for the ISP built from the ground up in China, we would have been at the mercy of the media and the government."[52] Women saw how the internet could help them with a central task of their own counterpublics, the formulation and distribution of information outside of governmental and mass media channels. Ironically, given the inadequate communications infrastructure at the official conference site in Beijing, WNSP staff also ended up supporting internet access for the media.

I had the good fortune to participate in the Beijing conference, where I saw the juxtapositions of the WNSP's dedicated work with the very different populations it assisted, under what turned out to be difficult conditions. Fairly late in the FWCW planning process, the Chinese government had unilaterally moved the NGO Forum from its original site across the street from the official conference in Beijing, to the city of Huairou, a forty-five-minute bus ride away. They wanted to avoid what they feared would be a staging ground for illegal mass protest, when women's rights activists from around the world would surely attempt to get the attention of the world's governments, and the world's media outlets. Although the kind of protest routinely staged at UN NGO fora is illegal in China, the government seemed especially concerned about the population attending this one. Rumor had it that Beijing police had stockpiled blankets to wrap up the naked lesbians they expected to run wild in the streets! Due to the late move, the Huairou site was still very much under construction when women arrived for the forum. Unfinished buildings stood in fields of construction-site dirt, which quickly became seas of mud underneath the unwelcome rain. Huge event tents billowed around rows of folding chairs, while tens of thousands of women attempted to find the hundreds of scheduled meetings, talks, and discussion groups scattered about the main area and neighboring streets. Wheelchair riders staged the first of the feared and forbidden protests when they could not maneuver themselves across the hastily thrown-down wooden and concrete pads that stood in for sidewalks across the mud. The lively forum was also an enormous mess.

It was under these conditions that the Women's Programme opened a door to the physical layer of the internet by setting up their on-site civil server. In a modest building, a few rooms were filled with rows of desks topped by boxy screens and keyboards. Cables snaked across the floor. On a typical afternoon a Mandarin-speaking Women's Programme volunteer would be teaching a small group of Chinese women how to use email on one side of the room, while two Brazilians attempted to access their messages on the other. Harried reporters demanded that busy staff members help them file stories by press deadlines. WNSP staff periodically participated in events and trainings next door at the "Once and Future Network Pavilion," run by veteran organizers with the International Women's Tribune Centre.[53] And forty-five minutes away, the team staffed the frenetic center they set up at the governmental conference. Although they prioritized NGO use, they were besieged by members of the media who did not have their own facility.[54] All over the Fourth World Conference on Women, the Women's Programme connected women, and men, to the hardware and software they needed to make a difference at and after the conference.

The team also provided the material basis of conference-focused activism by ensuring access to conference documents, and in some cases, to the conference itself. The WNSP team understood that they had a much wider audience than the people who had managed to get to China. Thus, they worked on the preparation, translation, and distribution of documents, and circulated a daily update bulletin (in English and Spanish) that included online summaries. Thirty-three thousand visitors accessed their local webpage, and a hundred thousand, the international one, during the month when the conference took place.[55] Finally, staff also participated in lobbying on media and gender at the official conference. They were determined to influence governments with their feminist perspectives on media accessibility, including the internet.

Both the Women's Programme itself and the exchanges it engendered succeeded in shaping the tangible outcome of UN conference processes: the final document. Developing this document is one the principal goals of a conference, since it is intended to summarize current understandings of and future solutions to the global challenges addressed at the meeting. In

Beijing, governmental representatives debated contentiously over the language of the Beijing Platform for Action (PFA), since it would become the road map for action on gender equality by members of civil society, governments, and multilateral institutions such as the United Nations. Many members of NGOs, well aware that their governments did not have adequate information and insight into women's lives, had traveled to Beijing to have an impact on this road map, and the WNSP and its allies on-site and around the world focused their attention on section J, "Women and the Media." Working through their "Political-Diplomatic" wing, the team helped to ensure that their emphasis on new information technology for women's empowerment, the need for gender-sensitive training, and the obligation to extend the internet and other communications technology to women would be found in section J.[56] It called on governments to facilitate the kinds of media development that WNSP knew to be crucial to counterpublics, by "encourag[ing] and recogniz[ing] women's media networks, including electronic networks and other new technologies of communication, as a means for the dissemination of information and analysis, including at the international level, and support[ing] women's groups active in all media work and systems of communications to that end."[57] Section J also exhorted NGOs and media associations to train women in internet technologies and to "facilitate the increased participation of women in communication, especially at the international level, in support of South-South and North-South dialogue among and between these organizations . . . to promote the human rights of women and equality between women and men."[58] Rhetorically, at least, governments had signed on to the Women's Programme's perspective. Technological advances were no longer seen as separate from feminist demands.

The experience at Beijing had a lasting effect on counterpublics. It "established computer networking as a powerful mechanism for women and women's groups across the globe."[59] The Women's Programme's campaign "marked the point where women's use . . . really took off" because organizations were able to download crucial documents, follow debates, and redistribute reports locally, whether by email or other mass media.[60] One participant noted the impact on national counterpublics, explaining that "the fact that there was relevant information, important to women activists not attending Beijing, allowed for new relationships to emerge purely via electronic mail."[61] This global experience reshaped internet integration when national organizations such as Beatriz Cavazos's Modemmujer used the conference to educate local groups and link them across the country. Feminists began to appropriate the physical,

UNITED NATIONS

*Fourth World
Conference
on Women
Beijing, China*
4-15 September 1995

Platform *for* **A**ction

Summary

Obstacles

Strategies

Actions

Media

Today, many women work in the media, but few have reached positions at decision-making levels. In most countries, the media continue to project a negative and degrading image of women and do not reflect women's diverse lives and contributions to society. Violent and degrading or pornographic media products in particular affect women negatively.

Everywhere the media have the potential to make a far greater contribution to the advancement of women. They can create self-regulatory mechanisms that can help eliminate gender-biased programming. Women can also be empowered by having greater skills, knowledge and access to information technology.

The Platform recommends action to:

■ *Increase women's participation in and access to expression and decision-making in and through the media and new technologies of communication; Governments should aim at gender balance through the appointment of women and men to all advisory, management, regulatory or monitoring bodies;*

■ *Promote a balanced and non-stereotyped portrayal of women in the media. The media organizations, NGOs and the private sector should promote the equal sharing of family responsibility and produce materials that portray diverse roles of women leaders;*

■ *Develop within mass media and advertising organizations professional guidelines and codes of conduct and other forms of self-regulation to promote the presentation of non-stereotyped images of women, consistent with freedom of expression.*

FIGURE 8. United Nations Fourth World Conference on Women *Platform for Action*, section J, "Women and the Media."

logical, and content layers of the internet to support their counterpublics by connecting activists and widely distributing relevant texts.

Latin Americans took on a leadership role during the Beijing process, as well as being major beneficiaries of it. INTERCOM-Ecuanex raised the money for and organized the Huairou lab, where Cristina Vasconi from Nicarao was the technical coordinator.[62] Women from five Latin American countries and four APC member networks were part of the team. They brought the region into regular electronic contact by capitalizing on regional counterpublic outlets. Women's information services that predated the internet, such as ALAI's Women's Programme in Ecuador and Isis International in Chile, along with WNSP-LA, developed regional distribution lists. The result was a significant increase in the flow of conference information in Spanish and Portuguese over previous UN conference processes. The information traveled along the preexisting pathways in Latin America's regional feminist counterpublic, reinforcing the ties that previous alternative media had put in place and giving activists more resources.

Activists felt the impact not only of the information flow but also of its method of transmission. From the Beijing process, "many women and women's organisations in the region learned about the importance of the Internet and its use in enhancing [their] work."[63] Many connected for the first time during the conference process. Moreover, they saw the benefits of being in regular electronic communication, discovering that it was "a very effective and efficient tool for organizing their work, agendas and plans."[64] But this tool was not inherently effective. A well-networked region absorbed network technology because it enhanced what was already there.

The experience of Modemmujer illustrates the way in which WNSP members supported the global impact and local expansion of Latin American feminist counterpublics before, during, and after Beijing. In 1992, Cavazos affirmed on apc.women that through the internet, local perspectives informed global organizing: "electronic networking is one part of a much broader overall strategy, in which we are working to promote transnational networking that is strongly rooted in local organizing, primarily the efforts of grassroots women."[65] Her affirmation shows the use of technology driven by "a much broader overall strategy," one that sought to enable women at the grassroots to gain access to an elite-oriented organizing and advocacy space.

The overall strategy of Modemmujer also included producing media for Mexican feminist counterpublics. The circulation and recirculation of reports from Modemmujer's eyewitnesses in Beijing linked those who attended to an ever-widening group of activists back home. These reports became the first feminist electronic bulletin in Mexico, establishing a model that Modemmujer used subsequently to distribute feminist information.[66] After the conference, its email distribution list eventually reached fifteen hundred subscribers. As this digital interface grew, its extension through other communication sources, from local newspapers to face-to-face meetings, was crucial for including those without direct access to the internet.

Similar to Mexico, organizing elsewhere in Latin America relied on a multimedia approach to integrating internet that combined old and new technology. As WNSP-LA coordinator Dafne Sabanes Plou affirmed, it was "not always necessary to have the latest computing equipment to do effective networking and information work."[67] After Beijing, many women's organizations continued to lack regular access, due to cost, a lack of training, language barriers, and, in some areas, no access to telephone lines. So WNSP-LA took reports on regional organizing and "repackaged these into abstracts, news and radio bulletins, articles, guides and pointers which were distributed to women's organizations in the region through e-mail, fax, post and walls."[68] As the next chapter will demonstrate, Latin American feminists took their regional context into account, attempting to contact women where they were through whichever resources were available to them.

WNSP continued to facilitate the communicative infrastructure of feminist counterpublics in Beijing's follow-up process by working with established alternative media initiatives. IWTC founder Anne Walker described how the collaborations among IWTC, the Isis networks, and WNSP became the glue holding together global mobilization against gender inequality.[69] IWTC and WNSP coordinated the WomenAction Coalition, focused on ensuring a nongovernmental perspective at the FWCW follow-up meeting, the UN's Beijing Plus Five Special Session in June, 2000. Their strategy included training women to run regional websites that featured NGO reports on women's status, monitor progress on the Beijing Platform for Action, and orient NGO participation in UN processes. The coalition worked closely with WomenWatch, the UN site dedicated to facilitating NGO participation. The coalition also ensured both timely reporting through the WomenAction 2000 website and its distribution to both alternative and mainstream press, through radio, web TV, newspapers, and streaming video. On site at the "Special Session," WomenAction reached out to women journalists and ran an internet café for NGOs.[70] All of these collaborations helped to ensure that NGO pressure could continue to influence governmental negotiations at UN conferences.

Beyond UN conferences, WNSP staff took advantage of other global opportunities to offer in-person support for women's counterpublics. In November 2008, the Women's Programme was invited to offer a Feminist

Tech Exchange (FTX) by the Association for Women's Rights in Development (AWID), at their forum in Capetown, South Africa. The Women's Programme had participated in a prior AWID meeting, in Bangkok, running an internet café. But this time, WNSP partnered with a South African member, WomensNet, and AWID staff to run a major preforum FTX in which a hundred women participated, and whose conclusions were presented to the two thousand participants of the forum. In this exchange, WNSP went beyond skills training to offer intended audiences a feminist perspective on technology use, including technology policy's differential impact on women and men. Margarita Salas, a coordinator of the AWID FTX and member of Sulá Batsú, an APC member organization in Costa Rica, argued that it was "strategic" to center women's issues and "the feminist practice of technology." Without those, she explained, training became the focus, with no time left for the discussion of communications policy and the reality of technology use in different contexts.[71] WNSP's strategy made technology relevant by helping women understand not only how to interact with it but the gendered politics of its development and diffusion.

More than a decade after Beijing, WNSP continued to nurture regional counterpublic construction in ways that responded to local and national needs. After the success of the first AWID FTX in South Africa, activists clamored to have similar opportunities closer to home, and the Women's Programme brought the initiative to more than ten countries. To kick it off, WNSP took immediate advantage of the main regional counterpublic event in Latin America, stretching scarce resources to offer a FTX at the eleventh Feminist Encuentro in Mexico City in 2009. There, WNSP sponsored a four-day experience for twenty-five activists "to get affirmation, share ideas, and take a more strategic and feminist look at tech use."[72] Activists with successful examples shared their knowledge. Documentary filmmaker Alejandra Novoa from Tepoztlán, Morelos, who worked with indigenous women to make their own videos, taught video techniques and learned alongside others, including Indira Mendoza from the Honduran lesbian feminist network Catrachas. Mendoza put that knowledge directly to use three months later, when feminist organizations played a vital role in protesting the June 2010 coup against Honduran president Manuel Zelaya, and its aftermath. By distributing via email video footage of the political repression that was not reported in the mainstream media, Honduran feminists were able to appeal for solidarity to their regional counterpublic and beyond. The strategic intervention of the FTXs made use of what is now called the "disruptive" capacities of the internet by enabling women to express themselves in all their diversity, and in the process, have an impact on the world around them.

Beyond training women to use a variety of resources at the logical level, WNSP has developed innovative applications to empower users to take action on issues of development and violence. In the early 2000s, they brought their feminist perspective to bear on the claim that the internet could provide an effective platform for economic and social development. To assess what the impact of internet-fueled development actually meant for gender relations, they worked with users in twenty-five countries from the developing world and eastern Europe to develop the Gender Evaluation Methodology (GEM).[73] The "GEM team" explained that this methodology "provides a means for determining whether ICTs [information and communication technologies] are really improving women's lives and gender relations as well as promoting positive change at the individual, institutional, community and broader social levels."[74] By 2008, over four hundred people from nearly forty countries had been trained how to apply GEM to understand the gendered dynamics of internet use in their own contexts. Organizations adapted GEM for areas including rural development, telecenters, and policy advocacy. GEM developers also undertook consultancies for institutions ranging from the UN Division for the Advancement of Women to the Cambodian Ministry of Commerce.[75] By designing their own application in consultation with counterpublic organizations from around the world, Women's Programme staff helped others take a close, critical look at the reality of internet engendering. Then, armed with gender-based evaluations of their own organizations, staff and members could shift the ways women and men learned about and deployed the technology.

As the WNSP examined the evaluations produced with GEM, they began to see a major discrepancy between the assumptions about the power of the internet and the reality of its use. As WNSP project manager Jan Moolman described their insight, "paternalistic development theory" offered a "gender-blind approach" that assumed access to technology would automatically translate into women's empowerment. But that was far from the case. Women and girls were often sidelined from computing, internet access, and the like, while boys and men were encouraged to explore them. Equally troubling, as the internet spread, chauvinists and predators used online spaces and interaction to demean women and threaten them with virtual and real violence. But, observed Moolman, "there was no connection or acknowledgement to the threats to women's online safety and security and the growth in technology-related VAW [violence against women]."[76] The Women's Programme was determined to make that connection and catalyze women's actions on online violence.

To do so, they collaborated with the global anti-gender-violence counterpublic established in the early 1990s, which insisted that violence against women be incorporated into more gender-neutral human rights frameworks and campaigns.[77] The most visible action of this counterpublic was the "16 Days of Activism against Gender-Based Violence" campaign, aimed to spark activism to end violence against women in all its many forms around the world. In creating the campaign, participants at the 1991 Women's Global Leadership Institute (sponsored by the Center for Women's Global Leadership at Rutgers University) chose the sixteen days from November 25, International Day against Violence against Women, to December 10, International Human Rights Day, to make the point that violence against women was an issue of human rights. The campaign spread around the world, with more than five thousand organizations in 187 countries participating by 2013.[78] In 2006, the WNSP expanded the reach and effectiveness of the campaign through Take Back the Tech Sixteen days of activism to end violence against women (TBTT), an initiative to connect offline and online endeavors.[79]

As its name suggests, Take Back the Tech harks back to an earlier model of women's antiviolence activism. Jac sm Kee, manager of the Women's Programme, explained that they deliberately used the antiviolence "take back the night" marches as a model.[80] She compared online space to the nighttime streets: "You're talking about spaces we need to use, to move, to occupy, but have become closed off to us because of violence! So we need to take it back! We need to change the infrastructure and the culture of this place." Just as women have sought to take back the night from potential perpetrators of violence, women had to learn to take back technology from those who would use it to harm them.

The WNSP designed the TBTT 16 Days campaign, along with other TBTT initiatives, to build on and reinforce the work of women's local and national antiviolence counterpublics. Its goal was to get women involved in strategizing against violence at the logical and content levels, "from use, creation, and development to the imagination of what it should and can be."[81] The 2016 TBTT website offers multiple arenas through which women from around the world can learn, teach, and take action against online violence. The global audience is hailed in three languages, English, French, and Spanish, and through the different images of activist women.

FIGURE 9 (*Left*). Women's Networking Support Programme's "Take Back the Tech" logo. Courtesy of the Association for Progressive Communications.

FIGURE 10 (*Right*). Women's Networking Support Programme's "Take Back the Tech" campaign material, Spanish visual: "Violence Silences: Document it. Defy it. Reclaim our right to express ourselves." Courtesy of the Association for Progressive Communications.

They are offered many resources. The "safety road map" explains various kinds of online violence, such as blackmail and cyberstalking, and links to a "toolkit" full of open-source and free applications through which users can protect their privacy when using computers and phones. Although this toolkit was not developed uniquely for women, the WNSP understands its audience can benefit from knowing about the tools. To address women's specific needs, the section on safety also hosts a page on "self-care," or ways that those who have been the objects of, or witness to, online violence can regain control by taking care of their mental and physical health. The "Map It" application allows anyone to report violence against women that involves the internet or internet-enabled devices such as cell phones. Turning data visualization software to feminist ends, the TBTT campaign converts these reports into a global map that makes visible the extent of abuse in different countries. Finally, there are multiple resources for campaigns against online violence, including stories about or by women who have experienced it. Through promoting innovation and strategy sharing among women's and feminist organizations across the world, the TBTT campaign illustrates how the internet can be reclaimed and reoriented to fight online violence.

Although the APC network has had to reevaluate its mission in the face of now widely available commercial internet access, the WNSP has continued to connect transnational feminist activists across local, national, and global counterpublics. Even as the modality of access has changed from "civil servers" to widespread commercial ISPs, and every layer of the technology has shifted, moving from desktops to laptops to cell phones; from telephone cables to fiberoptic cables and wifi; and from email and websites to Facebook and Twitter and texts, the continuing relevance of the Women's Programme reveals their commitment to integrating technology and action. Moolman explained that "the work of the Women's Programme is very consciously located within the women's movement; it is a significant point of departure for us."[82] Their past and more recent endeavors illustrate the deliberate steering of technology toward feminist goals.

The Women's Programme's feminist approach has been to facilitate counterpublic engagement with technology without imposing a vision of what that looks like. Valentina Pelizzer, cofacilitator of an FTX in Pakistan, reflected on the creative and political power of the "modern weaving machine" that enables women to express themselves and hear each other: "In this circle where imaginary get forged, computers are our modern weaving machine. We weave words, sounds and images. It is an individual as much as a collective process, it is existential and it is political. It is a challenge and an opportunity. It is a crossroad and a turning point."[83] The image of a "modern weaving machine" attests to the intertwining of technology and society, as a way to exhibit how "words, sounds and images" create an imaginary that includes women's specific experiences and offers them new ways to build lives free from violence. With direct attention to the reality of situated women's lives, the internet can be made to make this possible.

The success of the Women's Programme has meant its expansion beyond its original borders. It has boasted up to 175 members from more than fifty-five countries across the globe and a wide range of backgrounds.[84] It remains committed not only to hands-on training, but also to engendering global internet policy. Moreover, the Programme has moved into the intersection of sexual rights and the internet. All of this growth has resulted in a name change, from the "Women's Networking Support Programme" to the "Women's Rights Programme." Jac sm Kee recounted that after 2010 their "networking support," although still necessary, had become secondary to their main mission, creating opportunities where counterpublics and movements—for women's rights, queer rights, and communication rights—can connect. As she observed "now it's more about reaching out and bringing in—making more connections to different movements. In the early days, it's almost like you were the only feminist in the room! And in some spaces that is still true, but rather than saying I want to connect with the other feminists in this space, it's saying I want to bring the women's movement into the space. So that they can be part of the space and complicate it."[85] Being part of online space and complicating it: the Women's Rights Programme has enabled women to do this for themselves.

CONCLUSION

The history of the internet demonstrates the sociomaterial insight that the development of technology is inseparable from its context. As historian Roy Rosenzweig has argued, the ultimate impact of internet-related technologies—"whether the Net will foster democratic dialogue or centralized hierarchy, community or capitalism, or some mixture of both"—is deeply influenced by its dual origins in "both the 'closed world' of the Cold War and the open and decentralized world of the antiwar movement and the counterculture."[86]

His review of the histories of the "Net" demonstrated that, like all histories, many accounts contested the "official line." The story that rooted the internet's origins in the U.S. military-industrial complex and its Cold War preoccupations was incomplete. As Peter Willetts and others revealed through their work on the pathbreaking APC network, multiple actors and organizations contributed to making the internet. Even though both commercial and state interests have become embedded in the technology, those inspired by values of democracy and horizontality ensured that the internet would be a global network of networks.

The extension of the internet to activists at the moment when the internet itself was taking shape meant that those seeking to change the world were offered a place at the front of the line. Osvaldo León, the director of the Agencia Latino Americana de Información, explains that the academic and organizational sites in which the internet was "invented" made it "a decentralized, horizontal, open system," accessible to and reflective of alternative communities. As a result, those marginalized by deeply rooted social hierarchies "have been able to access a cutting-edge technology in full development and, therefore, even influence its direction."[87] This unprecedented access and influence was not circumstantial, but the result of a socially conscious project. Although much has changed since, in the beginning, the internet's physical and logical layers were designed to be not only open and accessible but also of use to those who sought to change the world through the content they sent across the web. The story told here reveals that the internet was not inherently "liberation technology,"[88] but deliberately oriented toward liberation.

Feminists from around the world who sought to promote women's access to the technology demonstrated their dedication to women's agency and empowerment. And their efforts also illustrate the sociomaterial understanding that that the internet's potential is determined within particular social contexts. Activists developed and distributed a "modern weaving machine" to enable counterpublic construction at the local, national, and transnational levels, ultimately bringing together those fighting against all forms of violence at UN World Conferences and around other issues in other transnational fora. Individuals like Erika Smith and Beatriz Cavazos extended these efforts to the fertile ground of Latin American feminism, where they would take deep root.

The APC Women's Programme, alongside other global women's initiatives with which it collaborated, offered opportunities to women from around the world that were nearly unimaginable to the first computer-based network for global women's rights, Hotline International. The Women's Programme brought together a global staff, enabling thousands of women to use computers onsite at UN conferences and distributing information across the world. Because of such efforts, women who could not be physically present could nevertheless take part in global conversations about women's rights at the end of the century. Moreover, the experiences, training, and analysis that the WNSP and others facilitated had a crucial impact on activists' work in their home communities. Finally, the impact of these counterpublic constructors was made clear in venues both large and small, from the Beijing Platform for Action to the stories women tell of their experiences when they "take back the tech." In their work with counterpublic communications, WNSP has sought to extend access to women in ways that enable them to fulfill their own objectives based on their own values.

The WNSP routed the internet directly to the doors of women's counterpublics. At the physical layer, members led the construction of an internet service provider at the Fourth World Conference on Women

apc WNSP
women's networking support programme

WWW.APCWOMEN.ORG
INFO@APCWOMEN.ORG
APC

THE ASSOCIATION FOR PROGRESSIVE COMMUNICATIONS WOMEN'S NETWORKING SUPPORT PROGRAMME

FEMINIST MIX WITH A TECH FIX

VIOLENCE AGAINST WOMEN AND ICTS

AS TECHNOLOGY HAS BECOME SMALLER AND LESS EXPENSIVE, INSTALLATION OF HIDDEN CAMERAS FACILITATE PEEPING AND SPYING. IMAGES OF WOMEN, RECORDED IN INTIMATE MOMENTS, WITHOUT THEIR KNOWLEDGE OR CONSENT, ARE BEING SOLD AS PORNOGRAPHY ON THE INTERNET. DOMESTIC VIOLENCE ABUSERS TAKE ADVANTAGE OF SPYWARE AND GLOBAL POSITIONING SYSTEMS TO TRACK AND CONTROL A PARTNER'S MOBILITY.

THE ROOT CAUSE OF VIOLENCE AGAINST WOMEN (VAW) LIES IN UNEQUAL POWER RELATIONS BETWEEN MEN AND WOMEN IN ALMOST ALL FACETS OF LIFE. THE FIELD OF ICT'S FACES THE SAME GENDER DISPARITY. VIOLENCE THAT HAPPENS IN PHYSICAL SPACES SUCH AS HOMES AND STREETS IS NOW ALSO TAKING PLACE IN DIGITAL SPACES.

RESEARCH ON THE INTERCONNECTION OF VIOLENCE AGAINST WOMEN AND ICTS, AND ON THE TRAFFICKING OF WOMEN IS AVAILABLE ON OUR WEBSITE. OUR TRAININGS PROMOTE THE USE OF ICTS TO COMBAT VIOLENCE AND ENSURE SECURE ONLINE COMMUNICATIONS.

TAKE BACK THE TECH!

THE APC WNSP CALLS ON ALL WHO USE ICT'S TO 'TAKE BACK THE TECH!' FROM NOVEMBER 25 TO DECEMBER 10 IN SUPPORT OF THE 16 DAYS OF ACTIVISM AGAINST VIOLENCE AGAINST WOMEN. THE CAMPAIGN AIMS TO RECLAIM TECHNOLOGY TO FIGHT AGAINST VAW WITH ANY ICT TOOL AT HAND - USING CELL PHONES, INSTANT MESSENGERS, BLOGS, WEBSITES, DIGITAL CAMERAS, EMAILS OR AUDIOCASTS.

CAPACITY-BUILDING IN EMERGING ICT TOOLS IS A CORNERSTONE OF THE CAMPAIGN WITH ACTIONS FEATURED THROUGHOUT THE SIXTEEN DAYS.

WWW.TAKEBACKTHETECH.NET

'TAKE BACK THE TECH! IS ABOUT LOOKING AT DIGITAL SPACES AS POLITICALLY RELEVANT. IT'S SETTING ASIDE SIXTEEN DAYS TO TAKE SIMPLE, CREATIVE YET CONCRETE ACTIONS TO ADDRESS VIOLENCE AGAINST WOMEN. IN THE PROCESS, KNOWLEDGE IS BUILT... FAMILIARISATION WITH TECHNOLOGY IS INSTILLED AND IMPORTANTLY, AN ATTITUDE ABOUT WOMEN'S RELATIONSHIP WITH TECHNOLOGY IS CHANGED.' - JAC SM KEE, CAMPAIGN COORDINATOR, MALAYSIA.

GENDER AND ICTS

THE POWER OF INFORMATION AND COMMUNICATION TECHNOLOGY (ICT) TOOLS AND PLATFORMS FOR ADVOCACY AND ORGANISING HAS LONG BEEN RECOGNISED BY WOMEN'S RIGHTS ACTIVISTS. ICT'S HAVE BEEN USED TO DOCUMENT ABUSES, REDEFINE HISTORY AND BUILD KNOWLEDGE. THEY HAVE HELPED DISSEMINATE INFORMATION, MOBILISE SUPPORT AND PRESSURE FOR CHANGE. NOW THEY ENABLE INTERNET USERS TO EASILY PUBLISH CONTENT, CONTROL THEIR OWN DATA AS WELL AS FORM DIGITAL COMMUNITIES - SHIFTING THE POWER DYNAMICS BETWEEN INFORMATION CREATORS, OWNERS AND USERS.

THE ASSOCIATION FOR PROGRESSIVE COMMUNICATIONS WOMEN'S NETWORKING SUPPORT PROGRAMME (APC WNSP) WANTS TO MAKE WOMEN TO USE ICTS TO STRENGTHEN

APC WNSP'S GENDER EVALUATION METHODOLOGY FOR INTERNET AND ICT INITIATIVES (GEM)

GEM IS THE ONLY EVALUATION TOOL THAT PROVIDES A SYSTEMATIC GUIDE TO INTEGRATING GENDER ANALYSIS AND PERSPECTIVES IN ICT PROJECTS. IT ASKS USERS TO CONSIDER IF AND HOW A PROJECT HAS TRANSFORMED GENDER RELATIONS. GEM PROVIDES A SUITE OF RESOURCES, INCLUDING A STEP-BY-STEP EVALUATION TOOL, DOCUMENTED EVALUATION FINDINGS, LINKS TO OTHER EVALUATION RESOURCES AND SUPPORT FROM FACILITATORS AND CONSULTANTS FROM AROUND THE WORLD.

THE APC WNSP HAS TRAINED MORE THAN 100 ICT PRACTITIONERS IN 36 COUNTRIES IN THE USE OF GEM. LESSONS LEARNED FROM THE EVALUATION EXPERIENCE HAVE LED TO INCREASED GENDER-PLANNING SKILLS. WWW.APCWOMEN.ORG/GEM

GEM IS AVAILABLE IN ENGLISH, SPANISH, FRENCH AND PORTUGUESE.

'APC WNSP HAS CHANGED MY LIFE. I HAVE BENEFITTED FROM THE VARIOUS TRAININGS THAT HAVE MADE ME GRASP THE POTENTIALS OF ICTS FOR WOMEN AND STRENGTHENED MY SKILLS BASE IN USING ICT'S. IT HAS ENABLED MY ORGANISATION TO PROFILE AND ACKNOWLEDGE IT'S WORK IN USING ICTS TO MAKE THE EFFECTS OF CONFLICT AND THE NEEDS OF WOMEN SURVIVORS OF ARMED

WOMEN'S TECHNICAL SKILLS BY ENHANCING INFORMED CHOICE AND USE OF TECHNOLOGY AMONG WOMEN'S ORGANISATIONS. TRAININGS RUN BY THE APC WNSP PROVIDE PRACTICAL, HANDS-ON SESSIONS FOCUSING ON WHAT WOMEN AND THEIR ORGANISATIONS NEED. THE APC WNSP SEES CAPACITY BUILDING AS ROOTED IN TECHNOLOGY PLANNING AND INSEPARABLE FROM THE POLITICAL ASPECTS OF TECHNOLOGY'S IMPLICATIONS FOR BUILDING INCLUSIVE RATHER THAN EXCLUSIVE SOCIETIES. IN THIS CONTEXT, THE APC WNSP IS A STRONG PROMOTER OF FREE AND OPEN SOURCE SOFTWARE AND COLLABORATIVE TOOLS THAT HELP GET WOMEN'S CONTENT AND VOICES PUBLISHED ON THE INTERNET, IN THEIR OWN LANGUAGES AND ON THEIR OWN TERMS.

WE AIM TO BUILD CAPACITY WITHIN WOMEN'S MOVEMENT'S IN THE CREATIVE AND STRATEGIC USE OF ICT'S SO THAT THEY CAN SHAPE TECHNOLOGY. THIS IN TURN GIVES WOMEN THE CHANCE TO EXPLORE THE CONVERGENCE BETWEEN ICT ISSUES AND WOMEN'S RIGHT'S AGENDAS. WE DEVELOP TOOLS AND RESOURCES FOR FOSTERING A GENDER ANALYSIS OF ICT PROJECTS AND POLICIES. WE IMPLEMENT INITIATIVES WITH OUR MEMBERS AND PARTNERS IN MANY COUNTRIES.

GENDER AND ICT POLICY ADVOCACY

IN 1995, THE APC WNSP LED ADVOCACY FOR INCLUDING ICT'S IN THE UN BEIJING PLATFORM FOR ACTION AT THE WORLD CONFERENCE ON WOMEN. ALMOST A DECADE LATER, THE COMBINED EFFORT OF MANY GENDER AND ICT ADVOCATES ENSURED COMMITMENT'S TO GENDER EQUALITY IN THE ACTION PLAN OF THE WORLD SUMMIT ON THE INFORMATION SOCIETY. THIS WAS DONE IN THE SPIRIT OF HARNESSING ICT'S FOR DEVELOPMENT. NOW, THE APC WNSP FOCUS IS ON NATIONAL AND REGIONAL ICT POLICY ADVOCACY AND COMMITMENTS, ESPECIALLY THROUGH IT'S POLICY MONITOR, GENDERIT.ORG.

'THE OPPORTUNITIES GIVEN BY APC WNSP ARE INVALUABLE IN TERMS OF RAISING THE AWARENESS OF WOMEN LEADERS ON THE BENEFITS OF TECHNOLOGICAL EMPOWERMENT. IT SHOWS WHAT COULD BE DONE ON-LINE. INSTANT INFORMATION SHARING, SUPPORT, CAMPAIGNING, LETTER-WRITING, RAPID MOBILISATION, EVEN SAVING LIVES...' - JIVKA GANEVA MARINOVA, GENDER EDUCATION, RESEARCH AND TECHNOLOGIES FOUNDATION (GERT), BULGARIA

GENDERIT.ORG

GENDERIT.ORG IS A TOOL FOR WOMEN'S MOVEMENT'S, ICT ADVOCATES AND POLICY MAKERS WHO WANT TO ENSURE THAT ICT POLICY MEETS WOMEN'S NEEDS AND DOES NOT INFRINGE ON THEIR RIGHTS. IT MAPS THE INTERSECTIONS BETWEEN WOMEN'S ISSUES, SUCH AS VIOLENCE AGAINST WOMEN AND ECONOMIC EMPOWERMENT, WITH ICT ISSUES. THE PORTAL HAS BEEN LABELED A TREASURE TROVE ON GENDER AND ICT FOR IT'S PRACTICAL TOOLS, GUIDELINES, ORIGINAL CONTENT AND GENDER ANALYSIS OF POLICY FRAMEWORKS.

WWW.GENDERIT.ORG WITH RESOURCES IN ENGLISH, SPANISH AND PORTUGUESE.

WWW.APCWOMEN.ORG

WOMEN'S NETWORKING SUPPORT PROGRAMME (APC WNSP)

INTERNET AND ICTS FOR SOCIAL CHANGE

THE APC WNSP IS AN INTERNATIONAL NETWORK OF INDIVIDUAL WOMEN AND WOMEN'S ORGANISATIONS PROMOTING GENDER EQUALITY IN THE DESIGN, IMPLEMENTATION, ACCESS AND USE OF INFORMATION AND COMMUNICATION TECHNOLOGIES (ICTS) AND IN THE POLICY DECISIONS AND FRAMEWORKS THAT REGULATE THEM.

WE ARE PART OF THE ASSOCIATION FOR PROGRESSIVE COMMUNICATIONS, AN INTERNATIONAL NETWORK OF CIVIL SOCIETY ORGANISATIONS DEDICATED TO EMPOWERING AND SUPPORTING THOSE WORKING FOR PEACE, HUMAN RIGHTS, DEVELOPMENT AND PROTECTION OF THE ENVIRONMENT THROUGH THE STRATEGIC USE OF ICTS.

FEMINIST MIX WITH A TECH FIX

THE APC WNSP IS MADE OF FEMINISTS AND ACTIVISTS WHO BELIEVE THAT ICTS HAVE A STRONG ROLE TO PLAY IN TRANSFORMING GENDER AND SOCIAL RELATIONS. IN OUR RANKS ARE TECHIES AND TRAINERS WHO HELP WOMEN'S ORGANISATIONS AND OTHER CIVIL SOCIETY GROUPS TAKE CONTROL OF THE TOOLS THEY USE TO ADVANCE THEIR MISSION AND ADVOCACIES. MORE THAN 175 WOMEN FROM 55 COUNTRIES - LIBRARIANS, PROGRAMMERS, JOURNALISTS, TRAINERS, DESIGNERS, SCHOLARS, RESEARCHERS, COMMUNICATORS - COME TOGETHER ONLINE TO WORK JOINTLY IN VARIOUS PROJECTS IN AFRICA, ASIA-PACIFIC, EUROPE AND LATIN AMERICA.

FIGURE 11. Women's Networking Support Programme brochure. Courtesy of the Association for Progressive Communications.

in Beijing. This literally brought the internet to the activists at the NGO Forum (as well as supporting the media's access). As a result, those who had gathered to insist that governments take their perspectives and demands into account brought the power of their counterpublics along with them. Over the course of the next decades, the Women's Programme stayed vigilant as the internet was twisted away from its emancipatory beginnings toward a space of gender exclusivity and aggression. But this keystone species followed in the footsteps of others who have refused the male domination of technology, and adapted the logical and content layers to ensure their contribution to feminist goals. At the logical level, the Programme sought to build or repurpose applications that individuals and counterpublics could use to fight against exclusion and violence.

From the beginning, Latin Americans were intimately involved in the creation of the APC and its Women's Programme, and thus in their attempts to build and broaden an inclusive internet. Whether pressing for the expansion of early networks to the Global South; providing the first national access to email; directing internet use at UN conferences; or offering context-appropriate training, a regional keystone species of internet proponents sought to get Latin American counterpublics online. The next chapter considers what that access has meant for Latin American feminist counterpublic organizations as they have taken matters into their own hands.

CHAPTER 3

Weaving the "Invisible Web"

Counterpublic Organizations
Interpret the Internet

In August 2010 I made a return visit to Defensa Jurídica y Educación Para Mujeres S.C. Vereda Themis (Vereda Themis Legal Defense and Education for Women), in Mexico City. Although I was happy to be received there again, I was not expecting to hear much of an "internet success story" from this organization. When I had visited eight years before, they had made scant use of online access, and they still had a minimal web presence. Their social media was a blog that served as little more than an electronic brochure, setting out their mission, services, and a few announcements. It had been dormant for over a year.

In the course of our conversation, Pilar Delgado, the coordinator of the legal area, described internet use at Vereda Themis much as I had suspected: staff email, the neglected blog, and a struggle to find good technical support. She also complained of the expense, not in terms of the price of being connected, but instead the cost of computer maintenance and web design. Faced with a choice between paying for a *paginita* (little [web] page) or a staff salary, the decision was obvious. They used the free blog.

But Delgado's frustration with technology went deeper. When she spoke of problems finding technical support, she blamed training, "which does not include our theme, gender perspective."[1] It was not enough to hire a reliable person with technical skills (although that in itself was difficult); they needed someone who understood their mission. By 2010, the internet had become an essential part of their organizational infrastructure. But the kind of gender-sensitive training provided by the APC Women's Programme a decade before was not as widely available as the now widely available internet, so groups like Delgado's were left fruitlessly searching for staff. Most often, they encountered male technicians uninterested in learning what feminist organizations, their staff and clients—in this case, domestic violence lawyers, counselors, and survivors—might want or need from their web pages, blogs, or other internet applications.

As we were wrapping up the interview, Delgado shared a very different experience. In a nonprofessional capacity, she participated in a Cuban solidarity counterpublic. One of their members had the time, resources, and technical savvy to channel contributions from over a thousand people into a vibrant web presence. "It's like this invisible web," Delgado effused. "You can't see it, but behind the website are all these people working together."[2] Outside of work, she had found the internet effectively woven into the fabric of her political activism.

As it turned out, my low expectations of my visit to Vereda Themis were unfounded. Pilar Delgado's astute observations about her professional and political experiences with the internet reflected two interlocking themes of its incorporation into Latin American feminist counterpublics. First, she testified to the shifting ways in which gender, along with other relations of power, inform internet use. Second, she referenced the expansion of the "invisible web"—that modern weaving machine through which counterpublics bring together communities and confront even the most intractable sources of injustice.

This chapter explores what happened in a region primed for networking technology when that web arrived, and then expanded. To begin, I explain the fieldwork through which I carried out my explorations. The region's grappling with new technology took place in big cities and remote locations, among large organizations and small collectives, as technology gained its meaning through use in the three countries I focus on: Argentina, Brazil, and Mexico. Thus, I draw from a wide range of feminist and some queer counterpublic experiences with the physical, logical, and content layers of the internet between 2001 and 2014, paying attention to the shifts over time from initial exposure to the advent of social media.

After discussing the fieldwork, I turn to each of the three counterpublic tasks—building identity, creating community, and strategizing for impact in wider publics—to interpret how internet has changed them, and been changed by them, over time. Counterpublic internet engagement has flourished, but not through a utopian unfolding of a fluid, horizontal, relational technology somehow ideally suited to feminist goals. Latin American feminists have struggled to confront preexisting divisions and manage new sources of communicational labor. Nevertheless, they have linked chains of access across their own digital divides; made low-cost access a foundation for ongoing community; and brought together effective, information-rich campaigns relying on older and more recent applications.

"THE ENCOUNTER IS RICHER THAN CONTACT BY EMAIL": FIELDWORK WITH LATIN AMERICAN GENDER EQUALITY ORGANIZATIONS

Why go to Latin America to study the meaning of internet use? Might it be more efficient—and, possibly, effective—to rely solely on online evidence to understand online interactions? After all, as this and the following chapters illustrate, websites and other online representations provide "an open space for self-representation to the rest of the world."[3] Indeed, lesbian feminist magazine *LeSVOZ* founder Mariana Pérez Ocaña emphasized the importance of her site when she explained, "Nobody's going to censor us, to tell us what we can and can't put on it. There it is, because we want it."[4] Nevertheless, feminist sociomaterial analysis requires a grounded examination of internet-based practice, or "how people creatively negotiate with and appropriate the structures of technologies."[5] Online spaces do not reveal the textures and complexities of people's varied experiences with the internet. That can only be found by listening to their stories of frustration, triumph, and everyday work with the technology. Even in an age of Skype and FaceTime, there is no substitute for a conversation with an activist, on her own ground, in order to understand her creative appropriation of and daily negotiations with the internet.

In suggesting the need to go beyond content analysis of websites and sending email questionnaires, I take my cue from my interviewees. When they received me in 2002, experienced activists Noemi Chiarotti, Mabel Gabarra, and Susana Moncalvillo, coordinators of Indeso Mujer, in Rosario, Argentina, argued:

> The meeting and in-person discussion are much richer. If not, why did you come to see us, if you could've send this [questionnaire] in an email?
> The encounter is richer than contact by email.
> Yes, always. The personal exchange develops creativity more, [and] thought.

Look, if you had sent all of this by email! One of us would have had to answer it!

And we'd be annoyed, because we don't like to answer them!

And also this way there is a give and take: we also learn. . . . It's a different thing![6]

As they made clear, a researcher could learn only so much online, especially if relying on the kindness of "virtual" strangers. Their objection that "one of us would have had to answer it," also suggests that long before the widespread distribution of social networking platforms and text message interfaces, electronic communication overload was a problem. Their straightforward complaint that "we'd be annoyed, because we don't like to answer them" could simply have referred to the increase in communication tasks email brought. But it could also be a critique of the assumption that feminists in Latin America have nothing better to do than respond to academics hoping to use an inexpensive shortcut for their data collection, especially given the power dynamics between feminist researchers from the Global North and their research subjects in the Global South. Sitting face-to-face with these women, who took the time to meet with me as a group, I heard that although email might have been an easier and cheaper way for me to communicate, to them it had a series of costs in time and effort. And I also heard that, in contrast, the conversation we were having was potentially valuable to all of us. It was a "different thing." Scratch the surface of a discussion of technology use, and multiple layers of meaning are revealed.

To construct my interpretation of the internet's meaning to Latin American counterpublics, I began my research in 2001–2 with one hundred individuals and organizations in Argentina, Brazil, and Mexico, where the internet was spreading rapidly in a context of vigorous feminist and queer activity. By that time, APC's Latin American members, including Wamani/Nodo Tau in Argentina, AlterNex in Brazil, and LaNeta in Mexico, alongside the Women's Programme, had made considerable inroads in getting counterpublics online. Moreover, these countries had the greatest numbers of internet users in the region.[7] They also boasted the largest numbers of internet hosts with specific country suffixes and had the greatest bandwidth, or capacity for internet traffic, in the region.[8] These indicators meant there would plenty of opportunities to hear about the internet. Moreover, long histories of gender-based discrimination had inspired significant Argentine, Brazilian, and Mexican feminist and queer advocacy efforts on their own behalf and for wider social change. And these efforts were already based on widespread alternative media production that enriched counterpublic activity. Here I could track what that history meant for this reality.

What I found was that at the start of the present century in Latin America, easy and extensive access was far from universal, but was increasingly important. About a third of the sample relied on free providers, few computers, and a single email address. While smaller, underfunded, and grassroots organizations tended not to have a website, the relatively large number of organizations with websites (or plans for them) showed how important this virtual presence had become as early as 2001. Still, most relied exclusively on email, not only for communication among organizations, but also to receive distribution lists. As I heard, these lists were a prime example of how, even in situations of limited access, activists could appropriate the technology.

I had an inkling that I should ask about this element of the logical layer from my own experience as a solidaristic researcher located in the United States. On a weekly, if not daily, basis, I received lists from Latin American contacts about feminist activity in individual countries, or more general news about counterpublic activity and political development in the region. But I had no idea what the email in-boxes of activists located in the region held. As it turned out, my interviewees mentioned receiving over 250 lists, on subjects ranging from Brazilian sex education to Latin American environmental movements to Colombian peace efforts. Some sent them; prominent lesbian feminist activist and academic Gloria Carreaga Pérez from Mexico City coordinated six lists that went to national, regional, and international audiences.[9] Lists helped to create and sustain ongoing counterpublic efforts within, across, and beyond Latin American countries, contributing to the expansion of an already-thriving regional identity and its extraregional connections.

Of course, list pathways through the region were circumscribed in different ways. In descending order of popularity, the five lists that traveled to all three countries were from Uruguay, Mexico, Guatemala, Ecuador, and Spain. Brazilian lists did not circulate much among groups in Mexico and Argentina, although Brazilians reported receiving about a fourth of their lists from other Latin American countries. Because at that point the internet was firmly rooted in text-based exchange, language—and the boundaries that language creates—had a real effect on its potential. On the one hand, communications from Spain were integrated into Latin American counterpublics; but on the other, the divide between Spanish and Portuguese speakers was reflected in communications flows.

Besides learning about the predominance of email and the importance of lists, I heard about what went on behind the public face of websites, which at the time were considered the pinnacle of internet applications. Here was a complex picture. Nearly all the organizations that did not yet have websites were interested in developing them; a few indicated that they were in the midst of a website design. They wanted to make the work they were doing visible—some to their own communities, others also to potential funders. As indicated by this chapter's opening story, those who already had them often used them as static electronic brochures because they could not find ongoing support for this new communications task. Lucia Javier and Jurema Werneck, co-coordinators of the Afro-Brazilian women's rights group Criola in Rio de Janeiro, explained that after they paid for an initial website it was updated once by a Canadian volunteer but that it no longer offered their most recent plans.[10] In Mexico, several groups credited LaNeta with helping them get websites up, but, like Criola, they did not have staff of their own who could design or update sites. However, larger and better-funded organizations were able to leverage resources for better presentations, often designed and maintained by a paid consultant rather than a staff member. In the early days of web development, resources mediated online representations. But there was much more to internet integration than the often-static websites revealed.

To examine how the organizations that focus on building counterpublics adopted and adapted to social media, I followed up the initial study by returning to the three countries between 2009 and 2013. My previous interviews had taught me not to assume that a given internet application would be interpreted as predicted by inventors, distributors, and commentators. I wondered what impact new applications were having on activist communities, and how the communities were altering the applications. How participatory was the so-called "participatory web" of social-networking sites, Wikis, blogs, and Skype? Would I see a shift from information retrieval to information creation, distribution, communication, and even modification of the applications used to interact with other users?

During my second round of field research in Argentina (June 2009 and June 2012), Mexico (August 2010 and June 2013), and Brazil (June 2012), I spoke with a quarter of the original organizations, complementing that with web-based analysis. I saw how groups combined newer technologies with earlier generation tools to achieve their counterpublic goals of inclusion, community creation and impact. Those with more resources at their disposal launched what they termed "cyberactivism," seeking to use applications such as Facebook and Twitter to incorporate new, often younger, populations and to lobby policy makers. For activists, social media offered new possibilities for interactions, but these possibilities were limited by other elements of activists' contexts, such as their access to material resources.

In the three sections below, I look at how each element of the counterpublic was transformed by, and in some cases reconfigured, internet applications. I do so by analyzing the ways in which the organizations undergirding counterpublics focused on developing identity, particularly with respect to expanding the people included; building community; and strategizing for impact in wider publics. Each section also tracks changes over time with the advent of social media. And I remain attentive to the internet layers at which engagement happens, whether physical, logical, or content-based.

"SOCIALIZING THE EMAIL": INTERNET AND COUNTERPUBLIC INCLUSION

When I asked Estelizabel Bezerra de Souza, the communications coordinator of Cunhã Coletivo Feminista (Feminist Collective), in João Pessoa, a Brazilian city in the northeastern state of Paraíba, what the internet meant to the organization's work in 2002, she compared it to a utility. "It's like water and electricity," she declared. "We can't even imagine how we survived without internet."[11] Yet in the same year I learned that the internet was part of basic survival for feminist NGOs in urban northeastern Brazil, I heard a very different story in rural northern Argentina. There, Nimia Ana Apasa, the secretary for law and land of the Consejo de Organizaciones Aborígenes de Jujuy (Council of Aboriginal Organizations of Jujuy), told me that she wanted to share "things that are going on in the rest of [South and North] America or the world that come to me via email" with the remote indigenous communities where she worked. When she traveled there, however, people were often dealing "with the emergency that the radio has stopped working, the emergency that a woman in labor had to get to town and there was no ambulance, or there were emergencies in school because the bus broke down and the teachers did not come." These crises took precedence, and she found it "very distant, very difficult to talk about other things. I take them pictures, newsletters from other indigenous peoples . . . but as you can see all this is very hard."[12] Like other utilities, the internet seemed to falter at the yawning gap created by long-standing sources of inequality.

This section examines what the incorporation of the internet has meant for the first element of counterpublics: building identity. It does so by focusing on the issue of inclusion, or incorporating new participants through digital means. In the early 2000s, the internet's uneven spread across the communities in which feminist organizing takes place reflected social hierarchies. While groups like Cunhã Coletiva Feminista quickly adapted to it for survival and success, others found preexisting obstacles nearly too great to surmount, as illustrated by the Consejo de Organizaciones Aborígenes de Jujuy. But technology is not destiny. As shown below, other organizations' deliberate appropriation of internet applications contributed to feminist goals of counterpublic expansion.

Almost a quarter (23 percent) of the organizations I spoke to attested that their outreach expanded in some way after they went online. Five specifically mentioned how international contacts reached out to them, with several discovering that students and domestic and foreign academics had become frequent "e-correspondents." Others noticed that it was easier to do local outreach to those with access to the internet. After they built a website, for example, an organization devoted to promoting breastfeeding located in Olinda, Brazil, found more middle-class people using their services, including online discussion fora; the largest AIDS organization in Salvador, Brazil, recruited more educated volunteers through their website.[13] In both cases, the internet provided an outlet for participation in progressive causes and expanded the geographical reach of NGOs. Organizations in Latin American counterpublics welcomed more allies and alliances through the spread of the internet.

Yet even as middle-class advocates, and their allies outside of Latin America, found the internet facilitating their communication and participation, these same advocates rarely used it with the low-income urban and rural communities in which they worked. I found a substantial digital divide mirroring class and racial/ethnic cleavages. Not one of the forty-eight organizations focused on disadvantaged communities, whether poor Afro-Brazilians, squatters in urban Argentina or indigenous Mexicans in rural areas, contacted them via email. Several described how their communications depended instead on regular mail or telephone, in some cases a community telephone, or a community radio. In urban Rio de Janeiro, Lucia Javier and Jurema Werneck Criola, did their outreach in person.[14] The staff of Rosario, Argentina's Indeso Mujer noted that the women's center they helped to coordinate "is in a zone of poor barrios, so there you can't take a computer because it would last two seconds."[15] In most poor urban areas, it was too dangerous to install the computers through which organizers could communicate with and provide resources to community members. It seemed as though the internet was not helping to expand their counterpublics, but further marginalizing their most marginal members.

Clearly, the physical layer of the internet proved to be a chasm in terms of access. As Edelmira Diaz, the coordinator of an Argentine network supporting peasant women, declared, "Peasant women do not use computers and many do not know that this technology exists."[16] Other activists pointed out that they worked in remote rural communities where "there isn't even electric light"—and "where there is no light, there is no telephone"—making computers and email out of the question. As with the distribution of other technologies, it was difficult to get computers and telephones into the hands of poor rural women; without them, they were also excluded from the expansion of participation.

Even when physical barriers could be overcome, the information available was not always relevant to remote communities. As Nimia Ana Apasa in Jujuy noted, the indigenous communities where she worked did not find what the internet offered of immediate use. If the structural barriers of poverty made access to the physical layer of internet rare in rural Latin America, the same barriers also made it difficult, though not impossible, to take advantage of the content layer in organizing rural women and men.

Within already established networks, uneven access to both physical and logical layers resulted in new forms of exclusion. Elba Muler de Fidel, a regional coordinator and the president of the national project committee of the Argentine chapter of the Asociación Mujeres de Negocio y Profesionales (Association of Business and Professional Women), explained that with email "the communications are much more fluid, but those who do not have it remain outside of everything. That is the drama. Before communication was more egalitarian. Now it is not egalitarian."[17] Despite the internet's horizontal design, it allowed for hierarchies of communication, in some cases creating them where they did not exist before. Limitations in access to computers, software, and information restricted counterpublic participation. These findings illustrated how the internet in itself offered no solution to deep-seated inequalities based on gender, class, race, geographical, or other privilege. At times it reinforced them.

To distribute the benefits of the internet required a deliberate politics of inclusion—an intervention at the physical, logical, and content layers. This politics resonated deeply, if differently, with many of the organizations with which I spoke. To mitigate technological hierarchies, if not dismantle them, several respondents gave examples of how they created "chains of access" connecting those who could not go online regularly to those who could. Often, this took the form of engaging with multiple communications technology, by this point a mainstay of Latin American feminist organizing. In 2002, Sara Llovera, the general coordinator of the CIMAC news agency in Mexico City, described how CIMAC's service—distributing news with a gender perspective—helped to counter the breach "between marginalization and disinformation and the enormous amount of information available on the technological superhighways." One person with a telephone and internet access in a small town could spread awareness through other local means, such as the radio. Sitting behind a desk covered in newspapers and topped by a PC, she explained that the feminist value of inclusion drove the impulse to link media sources: "The internet and newspapers live together. Maybe that's a feminist perspective, to believe in contacting everyone. In a world of disgraceful contrasts . . . [we need] community radio and videoconferencing at the same time."[18] CIMAC's insistence on reaching out to "everyone" meant operating across media platforms, integrating the internet as a link in a longer communications chain.

Llovera was not alone in her solution. Indeso Mujer, unable to provide direct access to the physical layer because of the insecurity of their urban work site, made sure the content traveled by other means. After staff gained access to the internet, they added a new section to the monthly newsletter they distributed in local women's centers in low-income neighborhoods. Called "socializing the email," this section covered events and materials that Indeso Mujer had received electronically. Grassroots groups also actively sought out the potential benefits of internet-linked communication, even if they were unable to go online themselves. Zildete Dos Santos Pereira, president of Mulheres do Alto das Pombas (Women of Alto das Pombas), an organization of Afro-Brazilian women in this low-income neighborhood in Salvador, explained that her organization relied on others, including her daughter and students at the local university, to send and receive email for them.[19] These varied efforts illustrate how activists bridged their own digital divides, extending hardware, software, and information along preexisting pathways of commitment.

Those without direct access nevertheless experienced the internet as mediated through others. Spurred by their own broader missions of inclusion, several organizations worked to shorten access chains to all three layers in order to mitigate this dependence. Five groups started to teach computing and email skills in poor, Afro-Brazilian, and indigenous communities, and among those living with HIV/AIDS. Their approaches varied from making sporadic computer access available at the organization's offices to running workshops on communications and media training. Luciana Siqueira Peregrino and Denise Arcoverde, the communications and executive coordinators of the Grupo Origem (Origin Group), based in Olinda, Brazil, combined breastfeeding promotion with computer training. They described their digital literacy training, where poor urban residents learned to operate computers, as still very much within their original mission. They were especially interested in teaching breastfeeding promoters skills, including web design, so that they could nurture their own organizations by earning income, communicating directly with international networks, and carrying out their own programs.[20] In northeastern Brazil, one of the poorest areas of the country, Grupo Origem sought to empower their community by extending access to all layers of the internet.

In a similar mode, Nilza Iraci, communications coordinator of Geledés—Instituto da Mulher Negra (Black Woman's Institute) in São Paulo, refused to accept that poverty and racism would exclude Afro-Brazilian women from this multilayer access. In 1999, she put together the first internet and media advocacy workshop for women in the city of Salvador, Bahia, thought to be the largest black city outside of Africa. In doing so, she had to convince the North American philanthropic community that access to internet mattered to black women's empowerment. She described having to win support from funders who objected that internet was a "luxury" for a population lacking basic health care and education.[21] She also had to convince black women that this resource could be useful to them, since there was a sense that "we are not going to advance because this technology was not made for us." To the outside world and the community itself, internet seemed irrelevant or inaccessible. Iraci knew it was relevant, and should be accessible to black women. As the story of the internet's creation testifies, the original internet was, in some way, made for them; but getting it into their hands was still an enormous challenge.

Iraci, like the staff of the APC Women's Programme, was determined to get her community appropriate access. She finally succeeded in convincing both grantors and community members to get on board, and around twenty women participated in a three-month training given at the Federal University, where four Afro-Brazilian women trainers

taught basic computer skills in a sophisticated lab. Vilma Reis, a sociologist and black women's movement activist who worked on the effort,
explained that their goal was to teach women technological skills in
order to alter the power relations within their organizations. As she
explained, "When you teach a woman to use internet, use fax, use everything . . . when she knows how to produce a document of her own, to
print, to make an electronic bulletin, to disseminate ideas from the [per-
spective] of the women inside the organizations, those organizations
take on another meaning." But she insisted that the hardware and software in themselves would not produce this outcome because "the technology in itself is nothing fantastic. Fantastic is you putting content in
the use of technology." Her team decided to focus on gender and race,
so that the women would learn how to wield the technology while
addressing issues "like sexism, homophobia, racial oppression, safe sex,
and also how to deal with the media."[22] By strengthening their ability to
counteract demeaning media portrayals of their communities through
their own alternative media production, Geledés made technology relevant to low-income Afro-Brazilian women's lives.

Learning how to put "content in the use of technology" created a
sense of empowerment among the participants. Iraci described how the
women "were delirious" when they started using the computers, and
sent and received their first email messages. At the end of the workshop,
women left with concrete access to the layers. In some cases, they
received a computer if their organizations did not have one. In all cases,
they designed a communications plan that would enable them to broadcast their own messages or organizational identities. They were ready to
wield technology on their world.

In the early 2000s, efforts to improve internet access were not limited
to feminists, and many other types of organizations developed digital literacy programs oriented to basic education or employment opportunities.
Although important, these were not inherently transformative, as Vilma
Reis emphasized. In contrast, the feminists above designed and imple-
mented projects to give women the power to take on central roles in their
organizations; to express their own thoughts; to reach broad audiences; to
analyze their socioeconomic and political contexts; and to resist misrepre-
sentation of their identities and communities. The internet can augment a
wide range of women's perspectives, but only when those perspectives are
taken into account. Technology in itself is "nothing fantastic."

When I returned to talk to organizations about how their work with
the internet had changed with advent of social media, I found that, in

some cases, the internet had been completely assimilated. In August 2010, Perla Vázquez, the general coordinator of Elige (Choose), a dynamic youth network for sexual and reproductive rights based in Mexico City, depicted how "the majority of [our] activities are via email, web, messenger. These are used daily."[23] In the middle class, Vázquez's generation had come of professional age using it. In June 2009, Edurne Cardenas, the twenty-nine-year-old coordinator of the Argentine chapter of the Comité de América Latina y el Caribe para la Defensa de los Derechos de la Mujer (Latin American and Caribbean Committee for the Defense of Women's Rights; CLADEM), declared herself "molded by the tool" of the internet: "I cannot imagine life, especially my work, without [it]."[24] My second round of interviews and website reviews revealed that many organizations had woven the internet into the fabric of their organizations.

But the spread of the internet—by 2013, reaching 43 percent, 56 percent, and 75 percent, respectively, of the Mexican, Brazilian, and Argentine population[25]—and its new applications still missed those on the "wrong" side of the digital divide, who had difficulty accessing the physical layer. Cardenas followed a reflection on the democratic nature of blogging ("The doors are open so that you can say what you want, anyone can open a blog") with a rumination on the literal distances rural women would have to cover in order to make use of a blog.[26] At an even more basic level, Indeso Mujer still did not use email to communicate with the women's center they help to run in a poor area of town, where it remained too risky to leave computers for fear of theft.[27]

Despite such difficulties, organizations attempted to fulfill their inclusive missions within a new technological context. When I visited Mexico City's pioneering feminist electronic network Modemmujer in 2010, I found that they had shifted from information provision to targeted training for those without regular access. A self-evaluation of their work had revealed that, as more women's rights organizations came online, "a moment came where there were many bulletins, a lot of information, and it filled our inboxes."[28] Rather than replicating alternative information circulation around the country and the region, they turned to where other needs were not being met.

Modemmujer, like organizations focused on digital empowerment in the earlier period, worked to provide low-income urban and rural women access to all three layers of the internet. Their innovation was at the logical level, where they designed interactive applications on topics ranging from citizen monitoring of governmental spending to ending violence against women. Their original software incorporated issue-focused

FIGURE 12. Modemmujer training application: "Gender Equity: Our Key against Violence." Courtesy of Modemmujer, Red Feminista de Comunicación Electrónica.

content into basic computer and internet literacy, all imbued with a feminist perspective that took into account the local realities of their clients. Beatriz Cavazos, Modemmujer's founder and director, explained that the typical design of the user interface, with its reliance on "desktops" full of "files," built in assumptions about users' exposure to office settings. Because their clients' work experiences were far from offices with desks and filing cabinets, Modemmujer staff designed new types of interfaces. For example, the Equidad de Género: Nuestro Llave contra la Violencia (Gender Equity: Our Key against Violence) program, in bright chartreuse with magenta figures, had users click on an old-fashioned keyhole to begin, and follow different key icons to learn about different issues related to gender-based violence. Aware that their target audience did not have computers at home, Modemmujer collaborated with local women's organizations and rented a cybercafé to carry out their day-long trainings. Each participant left with a DVD of the training program, and was put in touch with other opportunities to continue her work. Cavazos characterized the result: "This is citizen participation, this is having tools, this is transforming reality!" she exulted.[29] Modemmujer had intervened at the logical layer to expand women's access and knowledge.

Other initiatives built on the interactive web to capture younger audiences for their work. Veteran advocates like Mabel Bianco, founder and president of the Fundación para Estudio e Investigación de la Mujer (Foundation for the Education and Study of Women; FEIM), was eager to extol the virtues of social media for outreach. She described how their Red de Jóvenes por la Salud Sexual y Reproductiva (Youth Network for Sexual and Reproductive Health), which linked groups in twenty two of Argentina's twenty-three provinces, stayed in touch by text. FEIM gave them phone cards to cover their expenses.[30] Leticia Cuevas, executive coordinator of the Mexican Red por los Derechos Sexuales y Reproductivos (Network for Sexual and Reproductive Rights), emphasized that the online campaign she helped to create, "Tu Puedes Salvar Tu Vida" (You Can Save Your Life), was intended in great part to reach younger people through the use of *ciberactivismo,* or cyberactivism.[31] These veterans understood the need to go where younger people were, and communicate with them they way they communicated, in order to connect with them.

Feminist organizations not only reached out to younger audiences, but cultivated younger leadership to oversee the internet's new applications. In several of the 2009 and 2010 interviews, senior-level staff discussed bringing in younger people who were more directly involved in designing or implementing web strategies. Mariana Rios, who coordinated the redesign of the six-year-old website for Grupo de Información en Reprodución Elegida (Information Group on Reproductive Choice; GIRE), reflected, "a change in the logic of the website implies a change in the logic of the organization."[32] In GIRE's case, their goal of a more interactive page with associated Facebook and Twitter accounts resulted in hiring tech-savvy staff. Both Elsa Conde, a coordinator of the Mexican Campaña Nacional por el Derecho a Decidir (National Campaign for the Right to Decide), and Cuevas recognized the importance of finding these young people, with their unique profiles, including the Campaña Nacional's Lesley Ramírez: ("a lawyer, a feminist, and web savvy!" enthused Conde) and the Red por los Derechos Sexuales's Carlos Morales ("It is very difficult to find people like Carlos, who know about gender *and* technology," explained Cuevas).[33] Less positive experiences confirmed their good fortune. In the opening to this chapter, Pilar Delgado of Vereda Themis bemoaned the lack of qualified technical staff who also understood the "gender perspective" undergirding all of their work—and the intensive education it would take to train them in it.[34] As Graciela Selaimen, an expert on Brazilian civil society and the internet and coordinator of AlterNex's descendant, NUPEF Center for Research, Studies and Capacity Building, argued, hiring a communications technology staff person was a challenge with political implications. "It has to be someone who really knows your organization and its political speech because otherwise it's a crazy thing: a person representing an organization or feeding social networks that is not aware of the issues, who does not know the culture, who is not in tune with the political ideas," she warned, "it's dangerous."[35] As these experiences illustrate, expanding communications through social media could not be done by just anyone. It required a younger generation who understood feminism and technology.

Younger feminists were also aware of the need to upgrade their skills. While many could not "imagine life without the internet"—from communicating with their far-flung relatives, to reading the news, to carrying out research tasks for their organizations—these so-called "internet natives" were not automatic experts in online activism. Perla Vázquez of Elige affirmed the importance of training her staff in social media use, "because there is a myth around that young people can be like more cyberactivist because they have more access to the tools. But that doesn't signify that they use them daily for cyberactivism."[36] Luckily for Vázquez's organization, Erika Smith was available to give them, and other youth-focused organizations, the kind of context-appropriate training in which the APC Women's Programme specialized.

Deeply rooted divisions based on social and economic circumstance remain a primary feature of Latin American feminist counterpublics. But because the uneven distribution of the internet reproduces such divisions, some feminist organizations have focused on providing access to all layers of the technology to those currently marginalized from it. In the process, they have broadened the reach of their counterpublics. And some have reoriented the technology in the process, whether by creating new ways of gaining access or applications.

USING THE "DEMOCRATIC TOOL" OF THE INTERNET TO BUILD COMMUNITY

Cristina Zurutuza, a coordinator of the Argentine branch of CLADEM before Edurne Cardenas, explained how early internet integration reflected the CLADEM network's "political, not technological, ideology," a belief in participative, consultative democracy.[37] She described how early email use allowed national representatives to consult with their home branches directly during regional meetings, improving the group's ability to make decisions by consensus. Norma Sanchís of the Asociación Lola Mora, a Buenos Aires women's rights organization focused on regional and international collaboration, argued that before the internet, international contacts and even documents were concentrated in a few hands. But what she termed the "democratic tool" of the internet "allowed for many more women, many more NGOs to integrate into international and regional spaces, to exchange."[38] Although internet technology reinforced unequal relations of power, advocates already participating on national or international levels used the internet to democratize their counterpublic relations. They made the "tool" democratic.

This section explores the ways in which feminists took advantage of specific elements of the internet's logical layer, principally email, distribution lists, and websites, in order to enhance their preexisting counterpublic community building. In many ways, these applications were ideal for the kind of exchange activists already knew was vital to their communities. But organizations found themselves struggling to maintain community and accountability in the face of at-times overwhelming quantities of material and many new contacts. Moreover, internet access, as inexpensive as it was for many organizations, could not solve contentious resource issues.

Before the advent of the internet, Latin American feminists constructed counterpublics through alternative media, phone calls, faxes, and face-to-face meetings. Because activists often lacked local support or concentrated on issues that spanned geographical boundaries, multigroup and multisite coordination was crucial. So when the internet began to spread, feminists took advantage of its capacity for information distribution and rapid communications to dramatically improve earlier efforts. According to José Aguilar, the Mexico City–based coordinator of the reproductive rights and sex education network Red Democracia y Sexualidad (Democracy and Sexuality Network; DemySex), this national network of over 250 organizations and individuals used a distribution list not only to keep in regular contact, but also to circulate research, relevant news, and even the publicity from the right-wing, antichoice groups that opposed their efforts in the schools. This exchange "made us feel like a network," Aguilar shared.[39] Paula Viana, coordinator of the natural childbirth organization Curumim in Recife, Brazil, told me that although the 250-person Brazilian women's health network her group participated in, the Rede Nacional Feminista da Saúde Direitos Sexuais e Direitos Reprodutivos (National Feminist Network of Health Sexual Rights and Reproductive Rights, known as the Rede Nacional Feminista da Saúde), was not created online, the internet sustained it. "Before, everything had to be done by telephone and regular mail, some of this work would have been impossible, only by getting on an airplane, going up North, talking with those groups, coming back," she explained.[40] These demands were lightened in the late 1990s, when the network's communications team ran half-day workshops at their yearly meetings to train members on the internet. "It was incredible—use shot up from 25 to 100 percent in a year," remembered Jacira Melo, who headed up that initiative.[41] The internet made the Rede Nacional Feminista da Saúde's work much easier, becoming a "fundamental tool" for circulating information and staying in touch. Their coordination team, comprised of individuals from across the vast distances and developmental differences of northern and southern Brazil, made decisions about the network's campaigns via email, only meeting in person once a year. National networks strengthened counterpublic community ties through two elements of the logical layer: email and distribution lists.

Given the reach of the internet, activists also deployed it to construct or enter transnational networks. Sexuality Policy Watch (SPW), founded in 2002 as a network of researchers and activists from around the world coordinated by secretariats in Brazil and the United States, made internet their "main tool of work . . . because the way SPW operates being an English-speaking venture based in Brazil and speaking to the world is mainly through the web."[42] As Norma Sanchís put it, "As isolated groups, to integrate into global networks . . . this would have been impossible without internet."[43] While Latin American feminist counterpublics have been integrated in global networks since their inception, the internet's communication capillaries facilitated greater regional contributions to global initiatives.

Interactive websites provided new spaces for community building, albeit with different outcomes than other media. In 2002, Ximena Bedregal, founder of the feminist website/journal Creatividad Feminista (Feminist Creativity), reflected on the political differences between publishing on- and offline. She argued that her site did not play the same role of building groupalidad (groupness) as La Correa Feminista, the print magazine she edited previously. That magazine had what she called a "concrete role within the feminist movement." Its solidaristic distribution to radical, autonomous feminists across the region made it into "a fundamental, important reference for the construction of one feminist position." In contrast, the web had a more diffuse and unpredictable effect. As she explained, "It is a medium that allows you to introduce a series of ideas that you simply don't have any way of knowing where they circulate, nor how they circulate. It's like casting bottles into the sea. You know that they go to some place. Someone sees them, someone reads them." She knew she was circulating messages, but had little control over what would be done with them: "What you don't know is what they are going to do with this, how to build with this, how to generate the opportunities for change that I want. That I need as a human being in this world."[44] For the next six years, Bedregal nevertheless poured a great deal of time, energy, and her own resources into a site. She claimed it was "a pioneer among women's sites and their first multimedia site (with sound, video, image and text)."[45] Among other resources, it provided a database of feminist texts, chiefly focused on Latin American radical feminism. Its relevance was indicated by its five hundred thousand visits a year.[46] But it was not clear how the thousands more who used the website than read the very limited press runs of *La Correa Feminista* were in community. Instead, Bedregal acknowledged that most users had a more "instrumental necessity . . . some specific article for their academic or political work."[47] Creatividad Feminista became a community reference, but for a community with very diffuse boundaries.

The internet's (relative) affordability contributed to making it a "democratic tool" for community development. In a region characterized by economic inequality, it is no surprise that interviewees frequently cited the low cost of going online as a central benefit. Although many found the internet, like other technologies, to be out of reach, counterpublic organizations were thrilled about their enhanced opportunity for communication. Twenty-six of the fifty-six groups that answered the question about costs found the internet inexpensive (under 5 percent of their budget). Others indicated that their expenses were from telephone usage or computer purchases rather than direct charges for internet access. Moreover, groups could afford this cost without outside assistance. Those that reported no external funding were resourceful: they went online at cybercafés and used free services such as Yahoo and Google accounts. Although the poorest communities had difficulty accessing the physical layer of the internet, counterpublic organizations that were able to go online found more opportunities to contribute to community exchange.

In a striking illustration of the importance of low-cost communications to Latin American counterpublics, groups were able to stay in touch with their broader communities during a time of severe economic crisis. Traveling to Argentina in October 2001 and then a year later, as Argentina descended into its "Second Great Depression,"[48] I heard about the changes that took place during this period. As poverty spread, several of my interviewees noted that it was harder to rely on the internet.

But most reported using email more during the crisis because it was cheaper than telephone calls or regular mail, whose costs multiplied markedly. Alicia Soldevilla of Cordoba's Servicio a la Acción Popular (Popular Action Service), a community organization that focused on the needs of poor women and youth, particularly single mothers, through women's groups, sex education, and welfare advocacy, described how they had operated for a year with no funding whatsoever. This resulted in the disconnection of one telephone line and the obsolescence of one computer, as well as making all but local travel prohibitively expensive. But even if they could no longer afford to go to provincial or national meetings, they could participate via email, depending on it to let people know that they were "still surviving."[49] Email also helped them take part in the regional Red de Educación Popular entre Mujeres de Latinoamérica y el Caribe (Network of Popular Education among Women of Latin America and the Caribbean). As she explained, while the internet enabled connection and information within the network, it was not the reason for its development, since this network was established in 1981. Adriana Rossi of Rosario's Acción Sur (Southern Action), a group that carries out research on the drug economy's exploitation of poor women and children, said they tried hard to limit their telephone costs. But they could not possibly do without the internet. "To be honest, it would be like exiling ourselves," she exclaimed. "To be honest—no, no, no!"[50] These Argentine organizations relied on email to refuse economic exile.

The technology's potential to ease organizations' dependence on external financing, if not liberate them from the demands of funders, mattered in an environment where external funding was an ongoing, often debilitating, source of competition and controversy. But the provision of online resources complicated relations among national groups that found themselves dependent on external support. Members of the Argentine Madres Lesbianas Feministas Autonomas (Autonomous Lesbian Feminist Mothers) warned that the web could provide "false" identities. They talked about groups that were known "in Holland" (that is, by Dutch funders) "that aren't known here. They exist online but don't know people in the next block. [It's] a fantasy image. They can use the web, they can use English, write projects, but they don't exist as group. Except it exists on the web so it exists for the rest of the world."[51] Funders sometimes strain to understand national political reality. By disguising or overrepresenting the contributions of groups who perform better online, web use introduced new inequalities and new tensions in local and national counterpublics. In 2002, more institutionalized organizations depended on European or U.S. funding sources for websites, as for their other work, whereas smaller and, often, more grassroots-oriented groups patched together volunteers' labor. The Madres Lesbianas, for example, were among the first groups to get online through Wamani, the Buenos Aires–based civil server. They had an email account going back to 1994, and designed their first website in 1997. However, because they had no outside sources of support and were self-taught, their site had a handmade appearance. Even as they wielded aspects of the internet deftly, the technology became implicated in preexisting community tensions over resources rather than solving them, again demonstrating how bound up the technology was with its context.

Another illustration of an internet benefit at the logical layer that also challenges community accountability is the ability to interact anonymously. Anonymity allowed those not yet ready or able to claim their feminist ideals, or their sexual or gender identity, to learn and interact. Again, the Madres Lesbianas commented that for some lesbians, it was difficult to use regular mail—writing from a home address and asking information to be sent back there—if they weren't ready to be public about their sexuality. With email, they could ask for information without revealing who they were. But this same option could also obscure community responsibility. Bedregal, founder of Creatividad Feminista, was deeply invested in expanding the perspectives available online. Nevertheless, she believed that anonymous comments on web pages were at cross purposes with feminist goals, claiming that "one of the problems with patriarchal femininity is expressing yourself, claiming what you think and feel. To own what you think with all of the risks that implies. And [online] you don't have to claim your thoughts autonomously." Instead of "introducing yourself into the world," the technology enabled people to say "whatever stupid thing" because "you don't have to show yourself."[52] This kind of participation without accountability was far from helpful in community construction. The Indeso Mujer staff agreed that "the internet also facilitates anonymity and other things. Messages that come and one cannot understand them; people who don't want to show their face and say things for which they do not take responsibility."[53] Though advocates relied on the internet to establish fora for exchange and community building, its openness paradoxically supplied a place to hide and a means for avoiding commitment. Thus, in a seemingly counterintuitive finding, multiple forms of communication exacerbated problems within counterpublics in the early days of internet usage. Technology did not cause these problems, but neither could they be automatically solved by it.

Possibly the most difficult challenge to community building was, ironically, how to integrate the flood of community-building contacts and valuable information that came through the new technology. Even as they rejoiced over the opportunities to widen their circles and send and resend the ideas, declarations, research, and news that wove together their counterpublics, activists were clear how difficult it was to manage these new flows. Groups from Tepoztlán, Mexico, to Buenos Aires, Argentina, underscored the pressure they felt to maintain an email correspondence that was far beyond the capacity of their organizations. Liliana Rainero, the coordinator of the Red Mujer y Hábitat de América Latina (Women and Habitat Network of Latin America) and women's studies group director in the well-institutionalized Centro de Intercambio y Servicios Cono Sur Argentina (Southern Cone/Argentine Center for Research and Services), sat me down in front of her inbox to show me the organization's enormous volume of email. As we scrolled through, she described the internet as being Janus-faced. Besides its beneficial contributions, the "other face . . . is it's overwhelming, there's a saturation . . . this tool means time! Time from your life! That can go against communication itself! It makes things possible and at the same time poses obstacles. You pass over things—you can't deal with all the demands in a timely manner."[54] Even as groups were grateful and excited about their new contacts and the impressive increase in materials they received, they felt unable to keep up with the constant barrage.

The problems associated with incorporating a new volume of information into preexisting communication structures are not unique to these communities' early experiences, as any of us struggling to deal with our email inboxes (let alone texts and Facebook feeds) can attest. But they are acute in counterpublics in which organizational design reflects political commitments. To cope with the workload increase brought about by the advent of the internet, organizations tended toward ad-hoc solutions, with everyone from executive directors to interns put in charge. Marisa Sanamatsu, an independent website editor, reported that at a 2002 regional meeting on gender and internet technology, participants discussed the difficulty of adapting their human resource profiles to the increased work that came with internet usage.[55] As Rainero put it, the internet, and computing in general, generated its own "work ethic": "it ends up being the reference . . . that makes and obliges [us] to look for different ways of managing our work."[56] Some groups downloaded email once or twice a day, then expected all staff members to browse through it for communications of interest. Such solutions quickly became a source of tension, with those more comfortable with the technology ending up with increased responsibility as the keystone species regardless of their other duties. Bezerra de Souza of Cunhã Coletivo Feminista explained that the internet was marvelous for finding new contacts and information—but very difficult to fully incorporate into daily practices; it "changed our dynamic, and our understanding of time and the potential of information, of communication. But . . . it's a process that is going on without us getting to reflect on it."[57] Both the near-instant speed of communication and the rapid pace of technological change left some groups laboring to catch up— and strained their often carefully considered methods for distributing work equitably.

In the flush of early technological adoption, the internet also contributed to a breakdown of communications among or within the organizations undergirding counterpublic community. In some cases, groups aired difficult internal debates with a wider audience, exacerbating local tensions. Several lesbian groups in Mexico described how a national debate over the representational legitimacy of a lesbian who won a seat in the lower house of Congress became known throughout Latin American lesbian feminist networks. When some organizations felt shut out of the representative's nomination process, they circulated an email message around the region declaring that they did not consider this woman their representative. Another group responded via an email message, also aired regionally, denouncing what they believed was a personal attack against the woman, who had a long history of activism. A second acute disagreement between Mexican activists over the ownership of a set of archives achieved regional notoriety after one side posted its claims on a web page. Although the other side saw this page as defamatory, they were unable to persuade the service provider to take it down. Fierce national debates reached regional audiences prior to the use of email and websites, but the transmission was slower and narrower. Rapid regional spread could have serious national fallout; for example, the exchange over the Mexican representative had such negative repercussions within the Mexican lesbian feminist community that at least one organization swore off using the web politically for a time. Still, there is no denying the communicative power that websites give to voices that might otherwise lack a platform: they can offer whole websites, blogs, or other media communicating their positions.

For some, the internet posed an obstacle to internal development. Regina Vargas, the administrative coordinator of the Porto Alegre, Brazil-based Themis Assessoria Jurídica e Estudos de Gênero (Themis Legal Consulting and Gender Studies) center, speculated that their move to high-speed access contributed to, if not caused, a decline in direct interactions among center staff. As she explained, "The time that before we dedicated to exchanging ideas about the work in progress of each team, to informing [each other] about what we were doing and to listening to suggestions, today is dedicated to web searches, to reading and replying to messages and redistributing others, with an evident loss of contributions from colleagues to the work of each person."[58] As organizations such as Themis dedicated themselves to nurturing an information-rich community, they had less time and energy for internal collaboration— the kind upon which feminist engagement is predicated.

To counteract such outcomes, as well as the problems with anonymous participation, many groups insisted on maintaining face-to-face gatherings, unwilling to let the internet completely transform their community building. One of the founders of Madres Lesbianas in Buenos Aires affirmed emphatically that "we continue to believe in meetings. In debating ideas, meeting face to face. It generates commitment. Looks generate it. The internet is impersonal . . . there is the gesture, face, voice, all this internet doesn't give."[59] Monique Altchul, founder and president of Fundación Mujeres en Igualdad (Women's Equality Foundation), also located in Buenos Aires, agreed that "the energy that circulates is different when you meet and one builds on the idea of another much faster."[60] The members of Las Juanas y Las Otras (The Juanas and the Others), a fledgling feminist group in Mendoza, Argentina, initially tried an online discussion list as a forum for serious debate among members. They found, however, that it impeded communication, because "language is not transparent" according to member Alejandra Ciriza. Another member, Josefina Brown, added that it was hard to read the tone of messages, which led to problems with misunderstandings, and longer and longer "email chains" of clarification. The group decided to save discussion for their meetings, and employ email for organizational tasks.[61] Internet-based communication was not always the answer to improved community building

As interfaces changed with the advent of social media, feminist organizations continued to seek arenas for diverse expression of community. Earlier in the decade, there was frequent mention of how much money the internet saved chronically underfunded feminist organizations in their search to distribute distinct perspectives and communicate with one another. The theme of savings surfaced strongly again in postcrisis Argentina. In 2009, groups testified that they were now making publications available on their websites to save printing and mailing costs (or at least using compact discs to collect and distribute lengthy publications more cheaply; I received three in my travels). With the advent of Skype's free service, even more efficiencies were possible. Videoconferences allowed for periodic online meetings, saving on travel and phone costs. Capitalizing on these advantages, both the Red Internacional de Género y Comercio (International Gender and Trade Network) in Buenos Aires and Indeso Mujer began distance-learning seminars.[62]

For a younger generation who "cannot imagine" their lives without internet, it had become the inexpensive digital foundation of their arenas of action. Elige's Vázquez expressed that the internet was "everything" to the Red de Jóvenes por los Derechos Sexuales y Reproductivos (Network of Youth for Sexual and Reproductive Rights; REDLAC); they used it "to maintain communication, to debate, to participate, to construct . . . together—it's everything, right?" Without it, they would not exist, she explained, because REDLAC was largely made up of collectives without much money. She credited its decade of existence to the (updated) internet, "by discussions on Skype, by discussions on chat, by messenger, by being able to construct things now with googledocs, debates, exchanges of experiences."[63] The transformation of the logical layer proved transformative to young people's politics.

Here again, activist political commitments, as reflected in organization design, directed their integration of the internet's new applications—in this case, to help build a network of feminist collectives. Vázquez offered a concrete example of how it helped not only to create but also to sustain regional prochoice counterpublics. In Ecuador, a confidential, prochoice hotline offers referrals and information on medical abortion.[64] The young operators shared their experiences with supporters in other countries. Those supporters replicated the hotline elsewhere, as well as offering urgent email actions, telephone calls, and letters to public authorities when the lines are threatened with legal sanction. This kind of rapidly replicated, deeply networked volunteer-based activism would not be possible without the internet.[65] Young feminists continued to build their regional communities with ever more internet options.

While counterpublic organizations and networks absorbed social media tools to continue their conversations and community building, the new applications, like the first generation, made it difficult for organizations to keep up. Moreover, in the transition older applications seemed to be fading away. Between 2002 and 2014, between one-third and one-half of the original websites disappeared. The Mexican groups seemed to have been much more dependent on their civil server, LaNeta, which closed in 2011. Some sites were still online, but no longer updated, such as Mulheres Negras: Do Umbigo para o Mundo (Black Women: From the Navel for the World), the well-organized information site on Afro-Brazilian women run by founder Eliane Borges. Modemmujer's page was also, in the words of Cavazos, "a little abandoned" for lack of time to devote to it.[66] The fact that some of these sites were among the more attractive and well-designed in the early 2000s shows that the internet did not enhance stability, at least in this dimension. One telling Brazilian example is MAMA, Movimento Articulado de Mulheres da Amazonia (Articulated Movement of Women from the Amazon). In the early years, funding from Ford, UNIFEM, and governmental institutions underwrote what was then a sophisticated and engaging site, but it has since vanished. External funding boosted the integration of digital resources; but external dependence was shaky ground for sustainable development. Some organizations turned to low-cost options, replacing early attempts with blogspot blogs, free website design programs like WIX, or Facebook pages. Frequently the social media transition had stalled out: consider the poignant fate of Grupo Origem, which had bravely proclaimed that it published "the first blog of Brazilian NGOs"—which, as of 2016, has gone without an update since 2006. Older and newer generations of applications alike have proved to be a fragile foundation for community building.

The precariousness of alternative media outlets and other sources of information is not a new counterpublic challenge. Shifts in resources, attention, political orientation, and personal relationships often lead to the exhaustion of specific communication strategies. Access to the internet alone is not enough to resolve these problems. The very real, but too often ignored, labor on shifting digital platforms has to be taken into account in any analysis of internet effectiveness.

INTERNET AND COUNTERPUBLIC IMPACT

Latin American feminists have learned that integrating the internet into counterpublic work is a matter of ethics as much as efficacy. To successfully expand community and weave it together, they have had to address issues of inequality, exclusion, and accountability. Or, put another way, they have had to imbue the layers of internet with their own values, as difficult as that can be. This challenge remains true for the final task of counterpublics: strategizing to have an impact on wider publics. Long experience taught Erika Smith, the Mexico-based APC Women's Rights Programme associate, that technology in itself will not lead to effective political campaigns. As she explained, "The first thing that you have to be aware of in online campaigning is don't be seduced by the tools. Just because you have the tools and the ability to use them, you shouldn't be saying 'Cool! Let's go online!'" It matters what you do with the cool tools, to the answers to questions such as, "Who do you want to reach? What do you want to say? Does it even make sense?"[67] This section focuses on how feminists, mainly in Brazil and Mexico, figured out what they wanted to say, how, and to whom, in order to make strategic sense through the internet.

By the early 2000s, feminist politics had become intertwined with internet technology. Feminist counterpublics in the region had long organized into coalition-type networks, called *articulação* in Brazilian Portuguese. Given the region's diverse feminisms and feminists, coalitions have played a key role in articulating broadly shared political demands without full alignment of all aspects of identity and activism. By the time the internet took off in Latin America, these networks were active at local, national, and international levels. They quickly turned the internet into their principal platform for strategic planning by relying on it to circulate and discuss documents, ideas, and declarations. While such enhanced information diffusion and communications proved to be an enormous support for their actions in wider publics, the internet was far from a guarantee of efficacy. When uncertain information circulated rapidly, even well-meaning reliance on the internet could be detrimental at the local level. Although counterpublics benefited from the influx of new information and the enlarged capacity to communicate with their allies, the politics behind the technology ultimately determined its effectiveness.

Jacira Melo, the former communications coordinator for the Rede Nacional Feminista da Saúde, offered a detailed illustration of the way in which Brazilian feminist activists deployed the internet to integrate the perspectives of thousands of women from across the country into a national feminist platform to influence candidates in the 2002 elections.[68] The Articulação de Mulheres de Brasil (Brazilian Women's Articulation; AMB), the national network of feminist and women's organizations founded in 1994, held meetings in every Brazilian state to discuss the draft platform, which was circulated by email as well as available on a website managed by Cfemea, the Brasília-based feminist policy NGO that served as AMB headquarters at that time. In the less-developed northern states, the few people with email accounts used a chains-of-access approach, downloading the document, copying it, and sending it out through the regular mail. Then they held face-to-face discussions of the platform. Vilma Reis described how organizers in Bahia, the fourth largest state in Brazil, used "all sorts of communications" to bring together the nearly three hundred participants of their meeting, one of the largest in the country. There, they broke into five different groups to read and discuss the preparatory document. Even the small, remote Amazonian state of Amapá held a meeting with 280 women. Each state meeting sent its feedback to Cfemea via email. Staff immediately uploaded it to the website, sharing with all participants what feminists and women's movement activists across the country were formulating. Melo described the way the internet facilitated this country-wide collaboration as "really incredible, because it wasn't just an information instrument, but it allowed this work for this articulation, and at the same time it allowed that this information came so quickly that it was an incentive to others."[69] After three short months, after five thousand women had participated in state-level meetings and sent in their conclusions, a draft final document was pulled together. Based on this document, the thousand attendees of the 2002 Conferência Nacional de Mulheres Brasileiras (National Conference of Brazilian Women) finalized the Plataforma Política Feminista (Feminist Political Platform), which brought together proposals for building "a more equitable society on the basis of the principles of a non-racist, non-homophobic, and anti-capitalist feminism."[70] The platform was then used to lobby candidates for state and national elections that year. Moreover, this model inspired the next presidential administrations to carry out a more participatory form of policy development: over three hundred thousand women took part in preparatory processes for each of three national conferences on public policies for women.[71] Through the judicious integration of internet options, and their connection to other communications media, well-networked Brazilian women built an inspirational and effective model for widespread participation on women's issues.

Black Brazilian feminists also deployed the internet to enhance the strategic skills of their counterpublic, with a focus on a different target: the 2001 UN World Conference against Racism, Racial Discrimination, Xenophobia, and Related Intolerance, known as WCAR or Durban for city where it took place. Given the overlapping inequalities based on

FIGURE 13. Feminist Political
Platform, National Conference
of Brazilian Women (2002).
Reprinted from Comissão
Organizadora da Conferência
Nacional de Mulheres Brasileiras.
Design by Eduardo Meneses.

race, class, and gender in Brazil, the majority of black women did not
have full access to the internet when the conference was being planned.
Lucia Javier and Jurema Werneck, coordinators of Criola, explained the
digital landscape for black women.[72] Like other organizations working
with marginalized populations, their organizing was done in person. In
the *favelas,* or urban ghettos, of Rio de Janeiro, there were very few
computers, and the ones in the community centers were dominated by
men and boys. Many black women were thus dependent on chains of
access. Some could receive email at work, but not at home. Others had
to go to cybercafés. This was a population for whom the internet was
far from a cheap and available resource.

This was the context in which black women's organizations were presented with the mobilizational opportunity of a lifetime: the preparatory
process for WCAR. To ensure that their issues would be included, a group
of organizations led by Criola, Geledés in São Paulo, and Maria Mulher in
Rio Grande do Sul created their own coalition, the Articulação de Mulheres Negras Brasileiras (Articulation of Black Brazilian Women; the
AMNB). The AMNB then coordinated a process through which black
women could develop their own agenda, which was concretized in the

document "Nós, Mulheres Negras: Análise e Propostas" (We, Black Women: Analysis and Proposals). In this manifesto, signed by thirty organizations, the AMNB presented data demonstrating the extent of discrimination black women faced and then addressed their difficulties with specific policy proposals. They published it in three languages and distributed it to both official and nongovernmental representatives from all the countries represented at Durban.[73] Based on this tremendous effort, Edna Roland, the executive director of Fala Preta!—an Afro-Brazilian women's group from São Paulo—was appointed WCAR's speaker, the second-highest position at the conference. She also served as the rapporteur for Brazil, from which position she saw the impact of black women's organizing on the final document: it incorporated both race and gender in its understanding of the distinct ways that racism is experienced by men and women. The conference proved to be a "watershed event" for this counterpublic because it displayed black women's articulation of demands based on race and gender and their pressure on the Brazilian government "to expose and reject its widely held myth of racial democracy."[74] But just as important, the preparation process solidified the black women's counterpublic through the opportunity to engage in discussion and debate from the local to the regional level. Organizing was propelled by the "motivation and excitement" generated by becoming more cognizant of the community's needs and more able to formulate ways to address them.[75]

The multilevel achievements based on WCAR organizing were built on digital foundations, most centrally a distribution list. Nilza Iraci of Geledés explained that, at the time Durban preparations were getting underway, many black women were unfamiliar with the UN conference processes, particularly the ways in which NGOs could attempt to influence official deliberations and the final document. So the AMNB needed to distribute materials explaining how the processes worked and how to organize around them. She and others looked to Eliane Borges, the founder of the Mulheres Negras: Do Umbigo para o Mundo website, who stepped up to put together a distribution list for the AMNB. Borges noted that although the interface was at that point supposedly "free and available," this element of the logical layer was not, in fact, accessible to most black women in Brazil: besides the fact that the majority of them were not online regularly, list directions were in English.[76] Once she agreed to construct and moderate it, the AMNB crafted the list into a powerful engine for black women's counterpublic communications. Javier and Werneck noted that the AMNB only had two face-to-face meetings prior to WCAR; all the rest of the negotiations were carried out through the list, which connected organizations across the country.[77] "It was central in the pre-Durban organizing," attested Lucila Beato, Geledés's coordinator for economic and social research and international relations.[78] Its impact reached beyond its original audience. Iraci called it a "key reference point" for black and other social movements in Brazil and across the region that were preparing for the conference. It was so effective, she believed, because it circulated timely, high-quality information about the conference, from preparation to aftermath.[79] When I talked to Borges in 2002, she explained that she was still moderating it.[80] The AMNB turned a distribution list into a potent vehicle for black Brazilian women's counterpublic development and their impact on international discussions about race and gender.

In another arena of transnational activism, Latin American feminist and women's activists have long relied on a global community of supporters to pressure regional governments to respond to violations of women's (and men's) human rights. Traveling by mail, fax, and phone, urgent action communiqués alerted a wide range of people to individual and systematic violations of human rights. Counterpublic organizations exploited new technological options to improve the reach of this strategy. In 2002, interviewees mentioned petitions focused on local (6), national (17), and international (12) issues, generating support for causes ranging from reproductive rights and health to economic justice. Such petitions, along with urgent action email-writing campaigns, were an extension of an older strategy through a new platform. But this extension in itself was not enough to produce successful outcomes.

In San Cristobal de las Casas, Chiapas, an area of southern Mexico made famous throughout the world by the Zapatista rebellion of 1994 and its subsequent repression by the army and paramilitary forces, I heard how vital such international pressure could be. Marta Figueroa, the public policy and legislation point person for the Grupo de Mujeres de San Cristobal de las Casas (Women's Group of San Cristobal de las Casas), told me that in the mid-1990s, her group and others working with the Zapatistas to demand better conditions for indigenous women and men often sought international solidarity, and received it. Such campaigns had a decisive impact: "Without the internet many of the urgent actions were impossible. Thanks to it, the big groups, like the international ones, immediately became aware of what was going on . . . .The urgent actions, I don't think it's exaggerating [to say] that they have saved lives."[81] Her testimony reflected what many observers have found about the way in which internet-based solidarity helped to publicize both the demands of the Zapatistas and their struggles against state repression.[82] While email was not wholly responsible, its use by a wide network of supporters had the most concrete of results.

But Latin Americans did not only reach out for transnational support through the internet. They also sought to provide it. Mary Martínez, the president of the Fundación Siglo 21 (21st Century Foundation) development organization, located in Jujuy, Argentina, noted that before the internet, it was difficult to demonstrate support for far-flung causes. But now, "you can support something and sign on and there it is. Like in the case of the [Nigerian] Muslim woman who was going to be killed for adultery. . . . To express your opinion . . . it's important." This newfound ability, she felt, had been quickly, and deeply integrated into her life: "What happens is that suddenly it's become like part of us, something so daily that we perceive it like something normal, that always was there."[83] Activists expanded their sense of who was part of their counterpublics, and the responsibility they had toward its members, as the internet shrank the distance between northern Argentina and northern Nigeria—and beyond; she was not alone in mentioning this campaign, which also came up in Brazilian interviews. It demonstrated the potential of definitive, even life-saving impact by galvanizing international responses to local violations of women's rights.

Even with the best of intentions, this expansion of activist horizons sometimes suffered from the mistranslation that rapid transmission can replicate exponentially. In both May and August 2003, Nigerian activists tried to halt the very petition that Martínez referred to. Along with a host of similar efforts, this petition demanded urgent international solidarity to pressure the Nigerian government so that Amina Lawal, who was found guilty of adultery and sentenced to be stoned to death, would be pardoned by the Supreme Court. In an open letter that they circulated across the internet, the organization representing Lawal, BAOBAB for Women's Human Rights, insisted that the petition was both inaccurate and potentially dangerous. They explained that Lawal's case was still far from the Supreme Court, and that she was in the midst of a complex appeal process with a good chance of success. But international intervention threatened their carefully negotiated local strategies and had the potential to create a backlash against what local authorities might well perceive to be external meddling. They mentioned such a case, when the governor of Zamfara State had defied "these letters from infidels" by having a young woman flogged for adultery before BAOBAB could bring her case through the appeal process. Instead of participating in letter-writing campaigns and petitions in cases where local defenders were attempting to use their own legal systems, they entreated international allies to "please check the accuracy of the information with local activists, before further circulating petitions or responding to them." Their goal, they explained, was to rely on local institutions, since that approach "often carries greater legitimacy than 'outside' pressure," and, moreover, "strengthens local counter-discourses."[84] BAOBAB's letter to the eager supporters of Nigerian women's rights asked them to respect the work of local counterpublics in formulating their own strategies to confront their own realities. This was a different situation than Figueroa described in Chiapas, where local groups actively sought international support to save lives. The internet was only as good as the relations behind it.

The advent of social-media applications enabled feminist organizations to further expand their audiences and continue to broadcast their ideas and activities, even as the better-resourced groups among them had more facility in this area. Building on their past experiences, veteran advocates augmented their long-term strategies through social media. Networks old and new used social media to bring even the most regionally controversial of feminist counterpublic demands, the right to reproductive autonomy, to ever-widening publics.

Mexican sexual and reproductive rights movements, galvanized by the conservative backlash to Mexico City's abortion liberalization, integrated social media and older applications to foster a national response. Mexico City's Legislative Assembly, in a 2007 landmark decision, decriminalized abortion in the first trimester of gestation and reduced penalties for abortions later in pregnancy in the cases of rape, incest, or threat to the life or health of the woman. In reaction, over the next two years half of the states in Mexico's federal system changed their constitutions to protect life from the moment of conception. Faced with an onslaught of conservative legal action, Mexican feminists and other supporters of the right to decide came together in a series of networks and mobilizational actions.[85] Leticia Cuevas explained how the imperative to be active across state lines led to an online campaign. They realized that they could not do all their work in person, given the rapidity with which conservative politicians were changing state constitutions: "We can't go to protest in Guanajuato, we can't be there because also it was state after state, state after state, state after state!" Instead, as Cuevas described, they were galvanized to use technology in a new way, deciding, "Let's do it now, now is the moment in which it can also help so that we might mobilize in the whole country! If it's happening in Tlaxcala [a state in central Mexico], let's do something because everyone wants to do something, because it was so outrageous how the whole tidal wave came, that we said let's do something with a click, right?" They used several approaches to ensure dissemination to a wide audience of supporters beyond the core group, "the feminists, who will always sign on."[86] Thus they were able to both organize more inclusively and expand their base while taking a stand on this contentious issue.

To build an organizational network capable of responding to national and local developments in abortion policy, the Campaña Nacional por el Derecho a Decidir (National Campaign for the Right to Decide) built on the content layer laid down by feminist alternative news sources as they leveraged older and newer applications at the logical layer. Begun in 2008, their website offered a database featuring the current state of legislation across the country and opportunities for activism, including an online petition affirming a woman's right to decide. To knit this thirty-organization, hundred-person network together, staff member Lesley Ramírez got up early each morning to scan the websites of major Mexican news outlets and regional feminist information services, such as CIMACnoticias in Mexico and Artemisa Noticias in Argentina, and construct a daily press synthesis and action update. Then she sent this via email to members, many whom resent it to their networks.[87] Coordinator Elsa Conde argued that Ramírez's work was "fundamental for communication. . . . it's allowed us to have a daily daily daily daily presence!"[88] As she explained, when the Campaña asked for national action on an issue in the morning, groups across the country could take part in it by the same afternoon. The group augmented their daily presence with social networking for even wider reach. Ramírez uploaded information to Facebook and Twitter, and started a blog. Moreover, coordinators across the country participated in an online discussion group to be in touch between monthly face-to-face meetings. There, they were able to ensure the representation of women who could not travel to the headquarters in Mexico City, by incorporating another application: they participated over Skype. The Campaña integrated distinct applications and information to construct an inclusive and well-informed network to advance the goals of the Mexican sexual and reproductive rights counterpublic.

To widen the audience for their strategies through online activism, the TuPuedesSalvarTuVida (You Can Save Your Life) portal for women's right to decide, sponsored by Equidad de Género: Ciudadania, Trabajo, y Familia (Gender Equity: Citizenship, Work, and Family) and the Red por los Derechos Sexuales y Reproductivos, built on feminist foundations. Cuevas and four other veteran organizers established Equidad de Género in 1996 to influence public policy and promote women's leadership and participation. The Red por los Derechos Sexuales y Reproductivos, founded in 2003, is a ten-state, 120-person network aimed at influencing policy and promoting activism. Under the political leadership of Leticia Cuevas and with the technological know-how of Carlos Morales, who managed electronic communications, the portal expanded to offer a combination of online strategies.[89] Like the Campaña Nacional, they maintained a database and used Facebook, Twitter, a blog, a YouTube channel, and online surveys. But a main tool of work was their Action Alerts. Through these, they aimed to mobilize people across Mexico to take part in both virtual and physical protest. They also sent out news on the legalization of abortion throughout the region. Some of their activism was primarily online, including petition campaigns to demand the release of women who have been imprisoned for aborting their fetuses (whether spontaneously or not) or protest conservative legal actions in nine different states. And they publicized offline events, such as the late-August 2010 appeal to turn out participants for the commemoration of two years of decriminalized abortion services in Mexico City, involving the symbolic representation of the fifty thousand women who "made a decision over their bodies," as well as next-day posting of the public pronouncement read at the event and pictures from it.

Their outreach to wider publics was effective. They gathered over five thousand signatures through an electronic petition on behalf of seven women who were serving twenty-five-plus-year sentences for "homicide involving a relative" in Guanajuato. One woman, who had been in jail for more than six years, claimed that she had a miscarriage; two others, that their pregnancies were the result of rape, one of the few cases in which abortion is legal under most Mexican law. The TuPuedes campaign, working in conjunction with actions around the country such as those circulated through the Campaña Nacional, succeed in having the seven women released from prison in early September 2010. As with the mobilizations around Chiapas, these were well informed by those working directly on the issue. Such activism used internet-based technology to deepen and broaden their historical struggles for reproductive rights.

As new strategic integrations of the internet went forward, they were still in a context of uneven distribution of material resources. For groups whose priorities aligned with those of international foundations, the availability of resources were a boon for their social media work. For example, one of the MacArthur Foundation's priorities in Mexico was population and reproductive health, including maternal mortality and "abortion-related maternal death,"[90] and several organizations attested that the foundation's support underwrote their online, as well as offline, projects. Salud Integral para la Mujer used foundation support for a wholesale overhaul of their website. Elige also redesigned their website in addition to providing training for staff to manage social media resources. MacArthur underwrote CIMAC's website focusing on maternal mortality, "The Face of Maternal Mortality in Mexico." Foundation recognition of the importance of digital communication was crucial to the revitalization of organizations' image and the potential of their online activism.

But such support also exacerbated the division that has characterized feminist communities in Latin America, between those who can count on outside sources of support and those who cannot. The professionalization of NGOs in alignment with foundation priorities continued apace as they reached out for donors and to steer traffic to their pages with Facebook (if not Google) ads, while other groups offered their more obviously handmade contributions. These look less sophisticated, which could have an impact on how they are perceived by potential allies, funders, and political decision makers. Thus organizations dependent on volunteer labor or less secure funding sources were falling behind online, given their need to focus on the other work they have to carry out to maintain their organizations.[91]

CONCLUSION

Rejecting the "untenable binaries" of on- and offline,[92] this chapter has shown how Latin American feminist, and some queer, organizations have integrated a range of internet applications to confront even the most powerful forces standing in the way of their lives and rights. Whether directly helped by the keystone species of progressive technology-oriented consultants linked to APC and its Women's Programme, or figuring things out on their own, these counterpublic construction workers have sought to expand their communities; coordinate virtual and real demonstrations; and weave coalitions together with fiber optic thread, creating a fabric that sustains their endeavors from the local to the global levels.

In a region as divided by structural inequalities as this one, it would be ludicrous to suggest that everyone working to subvert the gender order has easy access to internet resources. Many do not, even in 2016. But feminists whose political commitments focus on inclusion have insisted on extending access to the various layers of the internet, whether making computers, training, or information available to communities where they are in scarce supply. In a "world of disgraceful contrasts," they cannot rely solely on the internet, but instead link it to other media in chains that resemble the counterpublic strategies at the end of the twentieth century. The most innovative feminist counterpublic organizations were not satisfied with access chains. Instead, they pushed beyond, demonstrating the need to make the physical and logical layers of the internet relevant to marginalized communities.

To build community, feminist counterpublic organizations took advantage of each layer of the early internet to improve on the work that was already well underway. As with its other "affordances," the low cost and widespread availability of physical access of the internet did not directly translate into enhanced opportunities for community building. Instead, organizations created opportunities because they understood how vital access to alternative information and communication was to their survival and success in often hostile environments. For organizations that have difficulty obtaining such information, "when there is such an opportunity, the majority of us launched ourselves" onto the internet, explained Lea Fletcher, the founder and director of Feminaria press in Buenos Aires.[93] Networks old and new thus used the basics of the early logical layer, email and distribution lists, to make their work easier and more inclusive. The relatively low-cost interface meant they could keep in touch during times of crisis.

But the integration of the internet did not only reflect feminist values; it also exacerbated the organizational and material challenges embedded in these counterpublics. Even as they helped to expand and enrich communities, these new resources introduced new tensions around workload within organizations, and reinforced long-standing problems with resource inequities between more established and less professionalized groups. The turn to social media, with its proliferation of free applications, such as blogging platforms, Facebook, and Twitter, did not solve these issues. While the introduction of social media helped younger activists build community within and across national borders, it also illuminated fragile foundations. The social-media era finds a trail of broken or missing links within counterpublics where the bright promise of websites had dimmed, and more recent online projects have often stalled out.

In strategizing to have an impact on the larger national and international contexts in which their counterpublics are embedded, feminist groups reinterpreted the internet to create highly consultative processes.

To integrate the perspectives of communities differently positioned within hierarchies of race and class, they stretched internet chains of access to connect women in northern and southern Brazil, or from the Lacondon forest in Chiapas, Mexico, to Europe and the United States. They then incorporated their ideas and energy to articulate shared demands on candidates for higher office, or engage in human rights campaigns at home or in international venues. Although they benefited from new resources and the enlarged capacity to build coalitions, successful efforts depended on an understanding of the politics behind the interface. Goodwill and an email account were not enough to make an effective impact.

The short case studies in this chapter show activists developing contextual affordances of the internet. Not every application at the logical layer was useful for every organization, and organizations often struggled to keep up with the burgeoning array. But one that stands out is the distribution list. To lobby for their distinct demands, black Brazilian women and feminist health activists in Brazil and Mexico depended on lists run by just a few people, attesting to the power of the keystone species and list membership to expand and enrich Latin American feminist networks. Because this has long been a region where activists confront their shared and separate sources of oppression by building national and regional community, this fairly simple application proved to be a primary asset. The next chapter tightens its focus on the list in order to magnify how one feminist community reconfigured it to provide an online counterpublic: RIMA, the Red Informativa de Mujeres de Argentina.

CHAPTER 4

La Red Informativa de Mujeres de Argentina

Constructing a Counterpublic

In 2011, Dafne Sabanes Plou, the Latin American and Caribbean coordinator for the APC Women's Programme, participated in a panel at the fifty-fifth session of the United Nations' Commission on the Status of Women. In "Take Back the Tech! Reclaiming Technology for Women's Rights," staff members shared the results of a twelve-country study that examined how the internet had been used to commit violence against women, and how women could resist. Among other recommendations, the Women's Programme staff suggested building on their success at the 1995 Beijing Fourth World Conference on Women, where their and others' lobbying resulted in the incorporation of feminist demands in section J of the Beijing *Platform for Action,* "Women and the Media." Over fifteen years later, the Women's Programme was still teaching feminists from around the world how to strengthen their counterpublics.

At the "Take Back the Tech" panel, Plou shared an inspiring model from her home country of Argentina: a "huge distribution list" that embodied all three elements of a counterpublic. For one thing, it was inclusive. As she described, "almost all feminists are there, and almost all activists in the women's movement are there, and especially many deputies and many council members, and also women in government who come out of the women's movement." Beyond the diversity of its membership, an achievement in itself, the list created space for the second element of a counterpublic, the development of community through exchange and debate. Plou described how they were able "to discuss

FIGURE 14. RIMA logo. Courtesy of Irene
Ocampo, RIMA founder. Mariel Bianco,
designer, based on an idea from Irene
Ocampo.

issues that really have to do with our rights. And this has helped us to
also change our mentality and say OK, we can be there, present, discuss
things openly and also come to conclusions." That fruitful discussion
helped activists toward the final goal of a counterpublic, to "bring these
issues up to our authorities and those that make decisions," formulating
strategies to have an impact on wider publics. Plou explained that the
list enabled the development of all three parts of a counterpublic because
it "changes also the political culture and it helps us to open new spaces
for participation and . . . to be really serious about what we are doing."[1]
In Argentina, feminists transformed the basic application of the distribution list into a vibrant counterpublic.

To read through the list Plou described—the Red Informativa de
Mujeres de Argentina (Women's Information Network of Argentina;
RIMA)—is to dive into a swirling vortex of feminist activism. Founded
in 2000, sixteen years later RIMA is among the longest-lasting national
feminist electronic distribution lists in Latin America. "Rimeras" come
from many walks of life: homemakers and professional politicians; lawyers, academics, and activists; young and old, lesbian and hetero, trans-
and cisgender. From an initial membership of ten, RIMA has boasted up
to fifteen hundred subscribers located in every Argentine province and
South American country, as well as countries outside the region. Rimeras have exchanged tens of thousands of messages, which range from
the practical ("Where is the prochoice meeting tonight?"), to the
anguished ("My husband is threatening to take my kids away!"), to the

solidaristic ("Sign this petition to protest the murder of Natalia Gaitán, killed because she was a lesbian!"), to the controversial ("This list censors political expression!"). RIMA is a place where feminism happens.[2]

Given its long run and exciting contents, RIMA would seem an ideal place to analyze the impact of the logical and content layers of the internet on feminist activism. The list offers a wealth of data to consider how this technology affects this set of social justice concerns. Is it used effectively or ineffectively? Can it bring together women across class, race, ideological, or geographical borders? Does it enhance opportunities for political action, agenda setting, policy change? These are vital questions to answer. But as this book insists, the act of separating technology from society in order to study the former's impact on the latter, while a convenient entry point for study, does not fully capture what is at stake. As illustrated in the previous chapters, far from offering a static materiality, internet-based technology, like all technology, is a social product. Rimeras have transformed the distribution list application to reflect the values and expand the practices of Argentine feminisms.

Although feminist counterpublics are far from the only ones driven by values, feminists consistently work to model the worlds they seek by enacting their values through counterpublic practices. The struggles for inclusion, community building, and impact demonstrate how seriously practice is taken. Consider the feminist slogan "The personal is political," which draws attention to how practices inside of households and relationships reflect the hierarchical relations of power that structure society. This slogan has served as a rallying cry for women confronting domestic violence, their "second shift" as mothers and caretakers, and other intimate reflections of male dominance. Or, as Chilean feminists chanted during the campaign to end the dictatorship of Augusto Pinochet (1974–90), "Queremos democracia en el país y en la casa!" ("We want democracy in the country and in the house!"). Just as these women protested authoritarianism wherever it took place, feminists across Latin America have stood for principled action on the issues most relevant to their personal and political lives.

The list is based on the principled practice of moderators and members, captured in the oft-repeated phrase "among us all we make RIMA." Founders Gabby De Cicco and Irene Ocampo and those who joined the coordination team kept the project going despite shifts in technology—most notably the explosion of social networking—because they adapted this element of the logical layer through crucial, if contested, gatekeeping. At the same time, members pushed the list's meaning and purpose

FIGURE 15. "Democracy in the country . . . and in the house!" Reproduced by permission of Guillo Bastías, artist. Scan by Dan Battle.

beyond the founders' initial intent, as women from across the country and their allies outside of it shifted a focus from reporting to interaction, including debate. Together, these women built upon national and regional feminist foundations in ways that both reflected and expanded their established connections. As a result of their interpretation of the internet, their "online and offline worlds [became] deeply entangled."[3] The names that members use for each other attests to this entanglement. Rimeras roughly translates to "women of RIMA" or "RIMA-ers." *Colisteras* literally means "those on the list together" but also suggests other collaborative and supportive relationships such as *comadre,* a godmother or loyal woman friend. The existence of the internet alone cannot account for what they have accomplished. They have enacted their feminist values through the list interface.

And they are not alone. As the previous chapter suggested, feminists elsewhere have made the logical layer of distribution lists into counterpublic spaces for empowerment, community creation, and democratic relations. From North America, the Canadian feminist list "PAR-L" offers an in-depth example of what this application can mean for feminist community.[4] The moderators' evaluation revealed that subscribers not only used the list to share their views on contemporary politics, but also expanded and deepened their connections to each other. Perhaps their most surprising finding concerned women's individual identities.

Studies of internet-based activism usually measure success in terms of "group, rather than individual, empowerment," and in fostering "social ties." In contrast, the internet is predicted to have a negative impact on individuals, including isolation and depression. However, the PAR-L participants reported "feelings of safety and 'asylum,' the empowerment of having their 'finger on the pulse' of the feminist community, and enhanced 'personal sanity' and groundedness."[5] The deliberate construction of community through the list connected individual feminists to something larger than themselves.

PAR-L has wrestled with difference, dissent, and debate in its counterpublic, because "technology in and of itself does not eliminate power differentials and problems of external and internal exclusion."[6] Subscribers complained of problems in managing the number of messages; they contested the degree and direction of moderation; and some made accusations of elitism. The language politics of this dual-language list also sparked controversy, with some English speakers unhappy about the volume of posts in French—and vice versa. Yet while the internet "does not magically erase social, cultural and economic differences," the list's moderators asserted that "it provides a forum where these differences and their implications for social life can be expressed, debated and acted upon."[7] But this space was not so open that those opposed to open discussion of feminist issues could seek to tear it, or its participants, down. For contemporary feminists, who are ever more aware of the need for deliberation and dissent in their ever more diverse communities, this is a distinct benefit: a safe space for displaying and debating difference as well as for building solidarity.

Because feminist counterpublics, like all counterpublics, rise and fall on the strength of their connections, distribution lists can be made to facilitate their construction and expansion. But list technology does not produce these outcomes on its own. As counterpublic infrastructure, it depends critically on the labor of moderators and the participation of their members. This chapter offers an interpretation of the RIMA experience by first describing the context that shaped the values and practices of the list. It then explores the dynamics of moderation, before turning to the ways in which the RIMA list has nurtured each of the three elements of an online counterpublic tethered to its offline reality. It ends by considering whether the advent of social media has shifted RIMA in a fundamental way.

This interpretation shows how one of the simplest internet applications was converted into a place that both reflected and in some ways went beyond offline reality, becoming, as one participant said, "the place within that doesn't exist outside." RIMA is a means through which Argentine feminists have molded technology to build community, or, as one participant expressed, "RIMA OVERFLOWS THE NET AND CONSTRUCTS NETWORKS." It is more than an arena, a support, a scaffold, or a space. The moderators and participants have appropriated the list application in order to create a new counterpublic, where feminists develop their identities, find solace and challenge in community, and offer support for struggles with heterosexist masculinity and patriarchal politics.

A CONTEXTUAL COUNTERPUBLIC

The women who coordinate and populate the RIMA list constructed a successful counterpublic space because many of them took part in offline counterpublic exchanges that predated the internet and continue today. Argentine feminisms, which reach as far back as those in the rest of the region, began a resurgence in the 1980s when activists sought to participate in their new democracy after the fierce repression of the Dirty War (1976–83).[8] They established the Encuentro Nacional de Mujeres (National Women's Encounter; ENM), the near-yearly national feminist meetings. The ENM became a place for feminists to build their identities, understand the barriers in their way, and strategize responses. They modeled it on the feminist Encuentros described in chapter 1, which many had found an inspirational venue for learning, exchange, and support. According to a history of the ENM, organizers adopted values from the Encuentros including democratic decision making and participation as individuals, rather as representatives of political or civic organizations.[9] As one central illustration, although the forty-five women in the first ENM organizing committee worked in spaces ranging from political parties, to human rights organizations, to housewives' groups, they all identified as participating in their personal, rather than professional or political, capacity.[10] This approach to participation would prove crucial to maintaining the ENM as a space for women's exchange and solidarity within the larger Argentine context of profound politicization. At least in terms of size, their efforts would spark an effort to construct a counterpublic even more successful than the regional inspiration. RIMA has drawn from and given back to this feminist site for collaboration and contestation, building a counterpublic on solid foundations.

Begun in 1986 with a thousand women, the ENM grew to thirty thousand a decade later, bringing together women with a broad range of identities, concerns, and strategies. Organizers made it a priority to move the conference around the country, in order to avoid the dominance of *porteñas,* the residents of Buenos Aires. As Argentina's capital and largest city, it is the undisputed political and cultural capital of the country; feminists wanted move beyond its reach. The striking demographic and political diversity is reflected in the array of issues discussed, from human rights to external debt, abortion to sports, sexuality to indigenous peoples.[11] Even as they constructed their own counterpublic space, Argentine feminists drew connections between gender and other sources of structural inequality.

The primary organizing practice of these meetings is the workshop, which is intended to promote a horizontal, but coordinated, field of counterpublic exchange. Limited to forty women, these spaces allow participants to focus their energy and knowledge on one issue. Which of the myriad issues of feminist interest get addressed is largely up to the local organizing committees, which set the agenda. But ENM participants are free to incorporate other preoccupations. In order to make the workshops participative and fruitful, they rely heavily on coordination. But this kind of coordination is of a very specific sort, according to ENM historians Amanda Alma and Paula Lorenzo: "Coordination does not imply any hierarchy or authoritative voice, those who assume this responsibility must ensure [that the workshops are] horizontal, pluralistic and democratic."[12] Given that the workshops are sites of intense discussion, the job of the coordinator is a challenging one. For example, coordinators have had to oversee angry debates about abortion rights when conservative Catholic women have insisted on airing their views in the midst of liberal and radical feminists' decriminalization strategy sessions. Coordination is vital for the counterpublic goals of the meetings to incorporate more voices and expand feminist strategies.

Besides the focused workshops—whose conclusions are brought together on the final day—the ENM offers multiple opportunities for participation. Partaking in hallway and dormitory conversations, sharing communal cups of maté in the plazas, marching in the yearly rally, attending cultural activities, and of course dancing at the closing party, "is also the Encuentro."[13] And, similar to the regional Encuentros, the ENM does not stop at the end of this intense immersion, but continues when "each one of us returns to her place (her home, her family, her organization, her party, her union, her movement, her community, her school, her hospital, her neighborhood, and other places) carrying the debates, exchanges, lived experiences." In this way, women model the deeply democratic world they have attempted to create at the ENM: "We can demonstrate ideas, promote horizontal debates and openness to practices where there is no hierarchy whatsoever. We can thus contribute to the construction of a society in which there is no kind of oppression."[14] The feminist practices honed in the counterpublic space of the ENM have contributed to feminist social change in arenas dedicated to women's rights and beyond.

In addition to the complex management of the diverse interests and physical needs of the thousands of women who attend the ENM, local organizers contend with often overtly hostile local authorities and residents, including elected officials, media outlets, and local Catholic hierarchies, in order to hold the meetings. Such opposition has been vicious. At the 2004 meeting in conservative Mendoza province, for example, the twenty thousand participants encountered open aggression instigated in part by antiabortion groups. This aggression included antifeminist graffiti; verbal and physical threats; and even a homemade bomb in the event space. As Claudia Anzorena of the organizing committee remembered, those participants who had not directly experienced the repression of the Dirty War now realized that "the enemy is not only symbolic, but it is real and there are people who are ready to not let you stand up for your rights."[15] But the following year, the ENM in Mar de Plata welcomed thirty thousand women.[16] Argentine feminists were not deterred by even the most aggressive of opponents in their determination to maintain and expand their vital counterpublic space.

RIMA's history is directly connected to the ENM. Although the attendees of a national seminar on gender and communication in 2000 created RIMA, its growth was spurred by ENM participation. A steep rise in subscription requests in 2002 was partly in response to an exchange at the ENM, when one politician called for the establishment of a national distribution list for activists, only to be immediately answered by several other high-profile feminists that they already had one—RIMA! At later ENM, workshop participants referenced what they had read on RIMA, piquing others' interest. And with founders, members, and coordinators inevitably somewhere at the event, registration could happen in real time. These face-to-face exchanges mean that many of the members know each other, and carry on their connection and conversation through the list.[17] As one Rimera wrote on the list in response to another's praise and query, "Thank you for your words— I don't know if I am the young Paula with a big smile that you refer to, but yes, I frequent the ENM." Online and offline realities have not been separate, but mutually reinforce what each do to build feminist community.

Like the regional feminist media projects and the regional Encuentros, RIMA kindles the space of the ENM, energizing participants long before they meet in person. Often prior to, but always after an ENM, RIMA circulates debates and impressions from the meeting, whether personal or published in national media. This catalytic role is recognized in the published history of the ENM. When ENM organizers discuss the role of internet "facilitating communications" and "socializing reflections, impressions and experiences that enriched the lived experience of the days of encounter," they reference RIMA's role in diffusion, as the place where "impressions, debates, conclusions, photographs, press clippings, etc. of the encounters circulate."[18] This circulation in turn inspires list reflection and discussion between those who attended and those who did not. Virtual and physical spaces support each other.

But the relationship between off- and online counterpublic spaces transcends mutual support. The value-laden practices honed at ENM, that is, the inclusion of a diverse set of participants and issues and nonhierarchical coordination, also guide the RIMA list. Founder Irene Ocampo testified to the ENM's influence on list moderation: "The Encuentro is really the inspiration for the list . . . the Encuentro has always been our spirit to keep in the list."[19] Ocampo viewed the sometimes contentious, but always stimulating debates of the ENM as the original essence of RIMA's online discussion. And she added, feminist leadership practices and values so central to the meetings also informed the list, explaining that there was "no leadership like 'you have to do this.' It's a leadership that comes from behind. This leadership that is service, service for the others to meet, to communicate."[20] One key parameter of the list—that it is women-only (though not women-born women)—also replicates the values of the ENM. During a debate over whether RIMA was justified in being single-gender, one member defended the policy as linked to the ENM's: "This is a Network of Women. . . . it is like the National Encounter of Women, a space for reflection and reading and information about things that happen to women and for women." The ENM have profoundly influenced RIMA to shape a list that conforms to Argentine feminist practices, values, and parameters.

Argentine feminist counterpublic sites are, of course, broader than either the ENM or RIMA. Among other spaces they incorporate bookstores, such as the Libreria de las Mujeres (Women's Bookstore), for over twenty years a central distribution point for feminist texts and community meetings in Buenos Aires; feminist NGOs and anti–domestic violence shelters across the country; university classrooms where gender and other relations of power form a basic framework for analysis, research, and action; and even local, provincial, and national governmental offices for women, depending on who is in power and what they are doing with it. And, like the RIMA list, these sites are not limited by the physical borders of the country, given the multiple arenas in which activists travel and the roles they take on. Many feminists participate who are not physically located in Argentina, whether they are diasporic or part of the larger community engaged with Latin American issues. RIMA overlaps with and contributes to these other counterpublic spaces as well as the ENM. While its central modality is online, it is deeply grounded in other ways Argentine feminists have created and sustained community.

RIMA'S KEYSTONE SPECIES

While crucial to RIMA's inception and expansion, other counterpublic sites cannot explain the list's staying power. Even the most highly trafficked and important lists come and go . . . mainly go. Indeed, since 2005, many have been superseded by the advent of social networking interfaces, which seem to promise more agile, inclusive, and interactive arenas for distribution and exchange. Yet, as of 2016, RIMA has endured for sixteen years, in large part because of the women who run it. Founders created and sustained the list in its early years, and its continued operation relies on the commitment of its "coordinators," as the moderators prefer to be called. While their activity might be perceived as mainly technical or administrative—managing subscriptions, diffusing "netiquette" (the rules for list participation), receiving submissions, and communicating with the server host—each of these tasks involves decisions of considerable consequence for the list community. Internet theorist Geert Lovink asserts that while lists "create an illusion amongst users of technical freedom without human interference," they are "as socially constructed as anything else."[21] While Lovink argues that "most email lists operate as benign dictatorships sustained by the monopoly power that the list owner wields over the boundaries and content of their group,"[22] RIMA coordinators, unlike authoritarians, have listened, time after time, to the demands of the membership even while they perform essential gatekeeping functions oriented to preserving the list's character and goals. The coordinators and members' commitment to collaboration has translated into the survival of this list as a counterpublic space.

RIMA coordinators act as the keystone species of RIMA's information ecology. Similar to the feminist publishers, Hotline International staff, APC Women's Programme, and technically adept staff of other counterpublic organizations, the presence of this species "is crucial to the survival of the ecology itself" because they perform an outsized task of supporting the adaptation of technology to meet local needs.[23] But, in contrast to the more static idea outlined by Bonnie Nardi and Vicki O'Day, which describes a skilled technician imparting wisdom to others in the ecology, RIMA's coordinators have reshaped the list in response to evolving member practices. RIMA coordinators learn by doing.

RIMA's cofounders, Irene Ocampo and Gabby De Cicco, were feminist communication activists when the internet began to spread across Argentina.[24] The hosts of a feminist radio show, they often found out what was happening in their country, whether in distant Patagonia or their hometown of Rosario, by reading international news sources. This situation convinced them there was a need for a media platform through which Argentine feminists could communicate with each other about the issues that mattered to them most. At the same time, they knew that the internet could provide such a platform from their experiences designing their own pages on Geocities, a free web hosting service. But they had been frustrated by the difficulties they had finding feminist material in Spanish on the web. At a 2000 seminar on gender and communication that brought together feminists from throughout the country, Ocampo and De Cicco proposed the idea of a feminist list through which they could share what they had found online, were receiving through their email, and could be circulated from other women across the country. The attendees eagerly approved. RIMA's founders launched it as a counterpublic project that would incorporate internet technology to boost communication among feminists as well as be a platform for their media production and, eventually, distribution to wider audiences.

In a reflection on RIMA's ten-month anniversary (May 2001), the founders celebrated the "handmade" work of creative "alchemists" who enabled counterpublic exchange by bringing feminists together and inspiring their work. They also referenced the country-wide protests that presaged the full-scale revolt against Argentina's Second Great Depression. "Beautiful season . . . full of changes, of mobilizations . . . as is this network, this email list." They celebrated the increasing membership of the new counterpublic, already at 150, which required a reminder of the netiquettes, or rules of posting, including "new lines so that among us all we can maintain RIMA in order . . . this order of alchemists . . . but after all order." And they extolled the potential of the community they fostered. They declared that "if RIMA calls you to go out together, to write a document, to write a poem, an article for a newspaper. If RIMA is useful to find out about something that by another way you would not find out. If it is useful to wake you up with your morning coffee, tea or maté. . . . If RIMA is useful so that you don't feel alone . . . all our effort has a meaning. And we are a little happier in a country, in a city that is falling into pieces." Ten months in, RIMA promised to make a difference by connecting women during a difficult time and inspiring them to change their world through their words.

As the founders' life circumstances changed, they passed on the responsibilities of everyday moderation to others. This was a crucial transition. Without the willingness of other women to take on the coordination, the list would have crumbled. Ocampo clarified that "I never wanted to own it. I always think that for the list to survive, to live, to be this alive like it is now, it has to pass . . . from the people who started it to other people."[25] But these weren't just any other people; both were devoted Rimeras. Gabriela Adelstein became the principal moderator in 2006, and Claudia Anzorena's collaboration grew in the following years. They knew RIMA was, in the words of Adelstein, "too important to let die." Her skill set—an administrator in a large corporation, she used computing and internet applications on a regular basis—enabled her keystone contributions, but she committed to moderating as part of her feminism: "I have this to say about my activism. I feel I am a very privileged person. And being privileged means you have a lot of responsibility toward human beings and the rest of the world. . . . And this is something that I can do."[26] Technological knowledge combined with feminist values resulted in new leadership for the list. Ocampo noted that the new coordinators maintained a focus similar to the founders, "to talk to the people, and say this is discussion list, or information group, please behave, please respect other's opinions."[27] To help, the keystone species stayed in touch. Sometimes a phone consultation with the founders helped Adelstein decide about what to allow on the list when there was a question. The coordinators' ongoing commitment to moderation made sure the list continued to thrive.

As did their listening to what Rimeras told them, both directly and through their practices. RIMA members' actions ultimately determined what happened on the list. For example, a cherished early goal of the founders was the transformation of subscribers into media creators. They repeatedly sought regional correspondents on the list, "who commit themselves to send with some regularity information with respect to women's situation in their provinces: legal debates, actions, alerts, projects, consultations of whatever kind . . . this way we can know what is going on in the rest of the country and see if we can put together, when the case arises, a larger movement for support." The founders envisaged a correspondent network made up of "lay" journalist-activists who could increase feminist mobilization, even including the idea in the initial netiquettes. Yet although information, reports, and opinions poured in from all over the country (and beyond), this goal was never systematically fulfilled by Rimeras. Instead of producing writing specifically for the list, members were more inclined to recirculate analysis from other venues. This may have been due to the creation of other online Argentine feminist media, including an internet-based network of women journalists, Periodistas de Argentina en Red (Network of Women Journalists of Argentina), and the feminist news portal Artemisa Noticias (Artemisa News). Aware of the growing outlets for original production, Rimeras shifted the direction of the list from what the founders intended.

In doing so, RIMA users made the list into what *they* wanted or needed. This is not to say that moderation was ineffectual; but far from establishing Lovink's "benevolent dictatorship," the initial and subsequent moderators adjusted the list to suit its users' evolving practices. Initially, coordinators rejected the idea of the list as an arena for debate; in late 2002, responding to a series of critical posts over yet another heavily politicized ENM, they wrote: "We are a network of information, not debate—so if you want to discuss what's going on with the ENM do it through some other channel." But the *colisteras* would not stop engaging with each other, and, as discussed in more detail further on, disputes repeatedly flared up over contentious issues, from sexuality to party politics. This counterpublic became a place for debating, sometimes fiercely, what to do about everything from human rights impunity to virulent lesbophobia. Coordinators intervened to channel members' energies and interactions toward the purpose of the list, even as they responded to members' own ideas about what that might be.

The issue of moderation—like many issues on RIMA—has been in flux. Because it requires so much work, both Adelstein and Anzorena contemplated other approaches, such as bringing on more volunteer moderators. But Adelstein clarified that the task of moderation is a delicate one and not easily shared: "I'd love to be able to do it more easily, like being four or five people and then taking one day each . . . [but] then we'd have to open up the team to more people, and then it's which people. They have to be moderately versed in geekness, moderately versed in feminism, right?"[28] As chapter 3 described, this dilemma is a common one: how to make sure that the keystone species is as immersed in the values underlying the integration of the technology as in the technology itself. List members are not insensitive to the burdens of coordination, and in January 2013, Adelstein responded to member proposals to pay the coordinators a monthly quota. But she reiterated that the coordinators were not interested in a salary: "Contracting someone to moderate RIMA is *not* an option that is politically coherent or practically viable for us." List moderation has been an unpaid labor of activist love. There have been no outside pressures to respond to besides those of the members, no changing objectives of financial backers or larger political organizations. Instead, she entreated RIMA members to step up to do some self-moderation, explaining that "the list needs to operate with *fewer* controls, that it must function with *fewer* woman-hours: we are all big girls and we can make ourselves perfectly responsible of our exchanges." In early 2014, Adelstein seemed to have gotten her wish; she enthused, "the thing is working! the *colisteras* are automoderating, the coordinators are resting."[29] Whatever the ultimate destination of autopilot moderation, RIMA coordinators set its initial course.

Beyond orienting the list at the content layer, another coordination task has been the crucial, yet largely invisible, responsibility for selecting and maintaining the logical and physical sites of the list. From RIMA's beginning, coordinators faced the issue of where to house the list—which software would suit their purposes and community, and where it would live. To keep costs down, they first took advantage of the free list service of Yahoo Groups, on Yahoo servers. But soon afterward, they established a relationship with their local civil server, the Association for Progressive Communications' Nodo Tau. So Ocampo and De Cicco migrated the list from Yahoo groups to mailman, a program that Tau supported, on its servers. Following on the general APC philosophy, this mailing list management software was open source, meaning that it was free to use, and its code was free to modify. Despite its progressive pedigree, the RIMA coordinators found that the mailman program had limitations in regards to its display, attachment, and search features, limitations that became even more pronounced with the expanding capacity of the web and social network interfaces. But coordinators continued to use mailman, according to Adelstein, to maintain their original policy of keeping the list "light" with respect to attachments, limiting exposure to the viruses common to commercial endeavors, and avoiding the ads sewn into the fabric of the Yahoo list interface. And, of course, so they could work with Tau. RIMA's counterpublic address was a civil server dedicated to making the internet accessible.

As with other counterpublics and their civil servers, RIMA and Tau had a generally supportive working relationship, founded in a politics of progressive solidarity. Tau originally approached RIMA's founders to offer web-page and list hosting in exchange for developing the gender section of Tau's site. Even after Tau obliterated part of RIMA's history, when staff tried to alleviate their overburdened servers by erasing several years of RIMA messages without warning the coordinators, RIMA continued to rely on Tau's services and hosting. To avoid a similar archival disaster, Adelstein shored up what had turned out to be the fragile physical layer of their counterpublic. She gave Tau a server that her employer was phasing out, on the condition that it would always house RIMA's archives. Even through difficult misunderstandings, RIMA and Tau collaborated.

However, like the rest of the APC network, Nodo Tau found itself existentially challenged by the advent of commercial internet providers, as many users sought cheaper connectivity. Although it held out longer than many other civil servers, in July 2013 Tau staff let the RIMA coordinators know it had to close. The coordinators then began the laborious move back to Yahoo, where many Rimeras still had accounts. During this process, some members fell away. But a more felicitous side effect was to activate old members who had become inactive when the original transition to mailman and Tau happened. Back on the list, several expressed their joy at being reunited with their *colisteras*. Even as the internet and its local purveyors shifted around them, RIMA's coordinators ensured its survival. The practice of deeply committed feminist communicators donating their time, effort, and resources ensured the list's persistence as a digital counterpublic.

ENCOURAGING INCLUSIVITY

Like other Latin American feminist counterpublics and the organizations that support them, RIMA's coordinators and *colisteras* have fostered the first element of a counterpublic: a space where women can explore and strengthen their feminist identity. In contrast to the wider publics around them, which in the Argentine case are not only dominated by wealthy, light-skinned, heterosexual men, but also deeply divided by partisan affiliation, Rimeras have constructed a counterpublic "where we can share, debate and discuss in different terms than those imposed by the ruling heteropatriarchal capitalism." Given the intense political identification of many of the members, the community has established an informal norm that they are free to express themselves "always and when it is not a partisan demand, because we have agreed that in this list partisan politics are excluded." Although the list has not engaged in deliberate outreach to women who face the structural barriers of race and class, such as the chains-of-access approach profiled in chapter 3, the coordinators have been keen to keep it accessible and open to a wide range of feminists. And to insist on its distinctiveness from the male-dominated world they face in everyday life, RIMA has adopted a practice from their inspirational ENM: only self-identified women can participate. These boundaries established an arena where women from different generations, geographical locations, and professions have come together.

The founding and later coordinators have sought to bring their ever-expanding counterpublic space within bounds that would allow wide participation, but focused on their primary themes and goals. Following the general mailing-list practice, in early May 2001 coordinators circulated their first netiquettes. But, rather than being an objective exercise of technical skill, these "rules of courtesy and principles of coexistence" came out of early practice by coordinators and users, or as the former explained, they were "elaborated from use of the mailing list; from the opinions of the subscribers; from trial and error." In discussing the focus on "feminist and gender" issues and the exclusion of chainmail and jokes, they explicitly rejected that their stipulations were somehow "authoritarianism or censorship," but instead "only a way to maintain the Network's profile." Argentine feminists, many of whom had lived through the authoritarianism and censorship of the Dirty War, were at great pains to distance their own practices from those of the repressive government they had survived.

At the beginning of the twenty-first century, easy access to the internet could not be assumed, and RIMA's members received email on all sorts of equipment at all levels of connectivity, from a dedicated line to a pay-per-minute cybercafé. One subscriber from Guatemala pleaded with the list not to send heavy documents: "Many (like me) cannot rely on any type of subsidy (more than own resources) for our activity in Internet, and we want to have access to the information but without that representing large investments in telecommunications." Here she challenged the assumed affordance of the internet as inexpensive; costs were determined by connectivity, computers, and more. Another internationally connected Argentine feminist, referencing her overflowing email in-box, suggested the option of a digest form for the list. That she cited the format of the early Mexican list, Modemmujer, for an example underscores the regional nature of Latin American feminist communications. From the beginning, Rimeras offered ways to make the list easy to use for their whole community.

RIMA's rules sought to ensure synchronicity between process and objectives, while also respecting the ways in which their membership accessed the space. They kept the general list free from specific concerns of individual subscribers by offering an email contact for the coordinators. Moderators encouraged subscribers to send in their own material, ranging from opinion articles to reports on local activist endeavors. However, invitations to events, grants, job listings, and the like were to be sent directly to the coordinators, who initially repackaged them in a separate newsletter to avoid cluttering the list. To make sure everyone could receive the information, including those with uneven or expensive connections, posts were to be kept relatively "light" (in 2001, less than a hundred kilobytes) and attachments sent only to the coordinators or offered for individual exchange. Members could choose how often to receive the list. Finally, the rules indicated active moderation. Coordinators assumed the responsibility of keeping the subscribers accountable to the rules, as they explained that "the moderators have the responsibility to indicate the unfulfillment of these *Netiquettes* to the co-listeras. In the case of repeated unfulfillment of some of them, your sent material will be *moderated.*" Anyone who demonstrated "a lack of respect for the whole complete list" by transgressing the rules repeatedly "will be invited to remove herself from the list." The counterpublic did not have room for those who could not respect its process.

Later versions of the rules sought to facilitate the transmission of information in a counterpublic based on mutual respect. In August 2006, these included avoiding short personal exchanges, using a clear subject line without Spanish characters (which were scrambled by the list software), offering contact people for petition campaigns instead of flooding the list with expressions of solidarity, and rereading messages before sending them to avoid their being sent back for editing. The revised instructions also acknowledged the growing use of the internet to propagate swindles, instructing Rimeras not to forward urgent actions "that require the solidarity of the whole planet. . . . Many times behind these messages. . . . There are people who are only interested in obtaining data for free." To "weave networks, making knowledge grow," the neti- quettes emphasized attribution through a citation policy that recognized the work of the original writer or "distributor." In that way, "one respects the work of the person who navigated, read and sent the mate- rial, or who wrote it and who belongs to that network." Again the coor- dinators reminded members that such prompts were linked to their com- mon goals. As they wrote, "Let us try to continue to create this feminist space, with a certain gaze, with certain objectives." This acknowledg- ment of feminist work for feminist ends was fundamental to construct- ing a counterpublic arena for feminist expression and support.

Beyond the netiquettes, coordinators repeatedly intervened to pre- serve the main focus of the list. This was true even at the height of Argentina's 2001–2 Second Great Depression and accompanying social upheaval, when most Rimeras were actively involved in the protest movements sweeping across the country. In reminding members not to resend all the messages they received about protests, the coordinators recognized that there were other, overlapping counterpublics to which their members belonged, supported by "many networks or groups in which we can channel our other interests." Given their many axes of solidarity against multiple sources of oppression, they had to negotiate boundaries again and again: "Let us take care of the specificity of this network, which has taken so much effort to put together. There aren't many other women's information networks in our country, and our objective is to push it forward as it is." The moderators wanted to make their counterpublic boundaries clear.

Inside those boundaries, one of the most noteworthy axes of inclu- sion was partisan, at least from the center to the left of the political spectrum. Ocampo listed "everything: from the K [supporters of Per- onist presidents Nestor and Cristina Kirchner], to the Radicals [the his- toric opposition party of the Peronists], to the left, to anarcos [anar- chists], everything!"[30] A hugely important—and divisive—element of the national political environment, partisan identification was not banned from the list. But, given how much dominance men exercised in this arena, and the impact that party-based conflict had on women's solidarity, a practice tailored to this specific community was to separate it from party politics, or, in the words of a member, "Our practice is radically different from the desperate (and impotent) homogeneous proclamations of the party hacks." While not explicitly stated in the original rules, over time a norm of not discussing party politics emerged in order to achieve "sisterhood" among Rimeras, many of whom would otherwise find themselves in sharp partisan disagreements. As one long-time member remembered the evolution of this parameter, it was quite organic: "In the 8, 9, 10? . . . years of RIMA (help me, *coordis*,[31] with the dates) we have tacitly adopted a kind of avoidance conduct with respect to certain themes that provoke strong discrepancies, like partisan politics and/or the political sympathies of each one." This evolution has been crucial for RIMA. A Rimera explains that "avoiding it, I consider to be profoundly wise in women who chose feminism as the primordial place for militancy and/or political affiliation and we take care to support the sisterhood of this space." In the Argentine context, where partisan identification is one of the most profound sources of difference, "sisterhood" across partisan lines is a striking achievement. But it has not eliminated strong political debate, as described below.

Given the extreme (party) politicization in Argentina, the moderators have been criticized for their perceived censorship—or promotion—of certain views. As Adelstein exclaimed, "lots of times people say we are Kichneristas or Anti-Kirchneristas.[32] And I'm an anarchist! I couldn't care less! I mean I'm just publishing! And you have to assume responsibility for what you send!" Since everyone gets the netiquettes when they join, she felt they should be able to follow them. But being in RIMA means more than "just publishing." Adelstein described her dilemma as moderator and member, when "there are times when I really can't take it. I'm coordinating the list, but I'm not a machine, I'm a person, and I get pissed off about stuff they write. So every once and a while I write to the list myself from my personal account."[33] Gatekeeper and Rimera, Adelstein is no machine; as Ocampo and De Cicco put it in their reflection on the ten-month anniversary of RIMA, "When there are people, there is blood." The counterpublic communicators most directly interpreting the internet mediate the technology through their heads and their hearts.

In contrast to the evolving norm of nonpartisan communications, a deliberate practice to maintain distinction from the wider publics around RIMA is the single-gender nature of the list. This parallels the single-gender meeting spaces of the Encuentro Nacional de Mujeres, which in so many ways served as inspiration and model for RIMA, an information network "of women," including feminist transwomen. As with much else on the list, this requirement has been subject to periodic scrutiny by members. One debate occurred after a member's colleague publicized feeling discriminated against after his RIMA subscription was rejected. To which another member replied by insisting on respect for the all-female list, "It isn't discrimination, it's intimacy, it is a demarcation of a space. . . . I WANT MY SPACE AND I ALSO WANT IT RESPECTED!!!" Another argued that, for those marginalized from other communicative spaces, gender exclusivity was fundamental for counterpublic deliberations. "I am convinced of the validity of preserving spaces, this list and others, exclusively for women," she said. "Why? Precisely because historically this possibility has been denied to us and we are mistaken if we think that up to here, we have equitably shared the space that we have been 'allowed' to occupy." In this counterpublic space, in contrast, "once and for all we might all learn and from ourselves, this practice of sharing, discussing and finding consensus." Rimeras believed their deliberations could be different in a women-only space, as they were in other, similar spaces.

Early Rimeras had a very specific example of what happened when their space was infiltrated: in August 2000, someone who appeared to be a young man "borrowed" the email address of someone on the list and posted a query about whether women were to blame for men's machismo. Although some members answered him, with greater or lesser degrees of patience, the question incensed others. Again they defended their counterpublic's very clear focus on women, arguing that "this is a network of women. That is the name, there are no tricks or obscurities. And some of us choose this space for that, in spite of that, with that, accepting that . . . and it has worked productively throughout this year. To whoever doesn't like the rules of the house, here is the door." This counterpublic space survived by showing the door to those could not respect the need for a separate space for women in which to hone their feminism.

Ensuring gender "purity" is difficult online. To reinforce their goal of an all-female space, De Cicco and Ocampo initially asked subscribers to provide a brief reference from a "godmother" who was already a *colistera*. When the list expanded, they relaxed that requirement but asked potential subscribers to fill out a questionnaire. Some of its questions could reveal potential "interlopers," given the questions about how they found out about the list; why they wanted to join; and what expertise they could offer the community. Were they feminist lawyers? Teachers? Doctors? Activists? Artists? In attempting to include members on the basis of their gender in their offline lives, Rimeras challenged the much-touted idea that "either ignor[ing] or creat[ing] the body that appears in cyberspace" is the ultimate (dis)embodiment of equality.[34] Ann Travers warns of the hierarchies perpetuated in the "celebration" of disembodiment, since "denial of the body has been a foundation of forms of social and political engineering that have cruelly ignored the concerns of those for whom this denial is not possible: women, children, the elderly, the poor."[35] Instead of ignoring their very real bodies, Rimeras sought to honor embodied experiences through their connection outside of "real" time.

The creation of a "disembodied" space claimed by women who explicitly identify as women may seem like a contradiction; but this is a list that was conceived in order to build connections among a specific community of women. And it has done so in a context of single-gender feminist counterpublics in Latin America and specifically in Argentina. The ENM is a women-only space (again, including transwomen); thus its extension online is also, by design, for women. Given the mutual support between the list and the national feminist meetings, that goal is more realistic than in other online organizing spaces. Encounters in real time can and do happen. Even beyond the opportunities of the ENM, Rimeras have come together, as described below. The list's use reflects community boundaries.

The creation of a space that was relatively easy to access, cut across a salient divide, and was reserved for women led to a highly inclusive counterpublic, which would hit a high of around 1,500 members by 2010. Already by 2002, its 350 subscribers were between the ages of twenty and seventy, from Argentina, Latin America, and Europe, and included "lawyers, journalists, psychologists, doctors, office workers, academics, writers, photographers, [national] representatives, [city] council members, artists, theologians, philosophers, anthropologists, health workers, communication specialists, sociologists, students, housewives, editors, unionists, filmmakers and political party activists . . . and non-governmental organizations."[36] Some of the top theorists, most prominent activists, and legislators from different political parties joined, along with women from every Argentine province and many countries inside and outside of Latin America. That the membership crossed provincial lines is also remarkable, given the predominance of Buenos Aires in politics and the economy, and the wide range of political cultures and economic development levels across Argentina's twenty-three provinces. Without minimizing other sources of exclusion, this diversity meant that RIMA was quite representative of Argentine feminists.

While this impressive inclusivity does not mean that everyone writes on a regular basis—in 2009 founder Ocampo estimated that 10 percent did; in 2012, coordinator Adelstein thought more like 15—the frequent confession of "I don't write but I read," opening an infrequent poster's contribution, attests to an attentive membership. Different members contribute distinct ideas, perspectives, and formats, from poetry, to news, to the latest academic theory, to calls for local or international solidarity. A 2002 discussion about Eve Ensler's *Vagina Monologues*, for example, involved participants ranging from an anarchist feminist to a women's ministry staff member. A social worker wrote in to say how wonderful it was that the monologues were turning into dialogues. A lesbian feminist theorist shared her experience of the performance in her conservative province. Although a proposed RIMA outing to see the show foundered over ticket prices, the discussion of the show included women who normally would find it difficult to be in such direct touch. Large numbers of members have allowed the list to survive significant clashes, "because almost everyone knows that there are people who think differently, but all participate anyway."[37]

BUILDING COMMUNITY ONLINE

RIMA's inclusion has created a space for community building that encompasses personal and professional solidarity. But the list is not only a place of consensus. Feminist counterpublics are a space for community building, but not on the basis of preexisting agreement over what feminists issues are or how they should be addressed. Like the Encuentros and ENM, this feminist counterpublic enables the expression and contestation of different perspectives. However, alongside debate has come the constant reminders to respect those on the other side of the screen, much as if the exchange were taking place face-to-face. As one Rimera explained, "this isn't about rules of politeness but real respect, not about tolerance (*I support you even if you are different or think differently*). This is about speaking with each other taking into account that we are speaking with each other." Rimeras entreat each other over and again to remember that they are in community. Like the subscription questionnaire, the requests for citation, and the gender exclusivity, this is a reminder of the people behind the digital interface.

In an anniversary celebration, Diana Coblier, a founding member, expressed how much RIMA's counterpublic had "changed our lives," nurturing both personal and community growth: "It has made us strong and powerful. It has assured us that each smile, complaint, sob, thought, task that we do has a reply. It helps us to think in terms of ourselves. And also of the others." While not an explicit goal of the early list, the practice of personal exchange helped to establish a nurturing space for such growth. The early list was welcoming and *cariñosa* or affectionate:

women were given nicknames, sent in their poetry, drank toasts to the list, and celebrated "Friends' Day." Though the closeness was due in part to many members' preexisting relationships, the list quickly evolved beyond those initial bonds. An early tribute from Julia Ardón from Costa Rica, for whom the list "filled an enormous vacuum" and helped members "to learn, share, and grow collectively,"[38] underscored the personal nature of the exchange in one early post: "I am fascinated by the little rays of friendship and humanity that have entered lately in the list, I am delighted to hear us speaking one to another, commenting on things from a more personal perspective and not only retransmitting cold documents, but instead speaking from and for the heart." Reinforcing this connection, members sought help for their individual needs and those of their neighbors, friends, daughters, mothers, and coworkers. Subscribers requested and received the names of lawyers and therapists and even suggestions of where to get free guitars for survivors of sexual assault; feminist support flowed freely. One member—but far from the only one—who asked for legal advice, in this case from a remote location during a difficult divorce, expressed her gratitude and sense of connection: "Thank you. I ask you please to reply directly to me so as to not hinder the list. And apologies if I don't answer quickly, the connection at the top of a mountain is slow and difficult. Kisses. I have you always with me. I have the list always with me." Such exchange also resulted in one-to-one communications, escaping the netiquettes' prohibitions on such exchange: after one woman apologized for missing a book launch because her mother-in-law fell and needed medical attention, the book's author wrote back "no worries (is your mother-in-law OK?)—we kept a copy for you." Rimeras built community through personal connection.

Particularly during times of list reflection, like anniversary celebrations, members referenced how RIMA helped them to grow as feminists, providing "cybertherapy" that nurtures them "like the bread of every day" in their "daily life, which is definitely where the great theories are put to the test"; "How difficult our everyday path would be without you!" One contributor affirmed the safety of the list for expressing her anger: "The truth is I chose this medium to show my ire because here I feel strongly understood and above all identified." Another one linked professional and personal support: "There you were when I needed data, when I started a campaign . . . , when I got to know fantastic women with whom I [attended] seminars, when they were preoccupied with the sickness of [my partner], when they were happy for his recuperation, when they accompanied the growth of [my son] . . . that is to say always, in different planes of life." The list accompanies women growing into their feminism at home and at work.

Personal growth is tied to community growth. From Mexico, Alma Luz Vazquez wrote: "The closeness that I feel with everyone, nurtures my spirit, clarifies ideas, makes me feel part of the community of women." From RIMA's inception, the founders sought to create community, given their goals to connect feminists across Argentina and beyond much like they had connected in face-to-face counterpublic sites. They asked early members to introduce themselves, "to know with whom we are sharing the cyberspace." While these introductions dropped off as the list expanded, the coordinators still asked for members' occupations and expertise, "to know to whom to direct ourselves when a *colistera* or a person outside of RIMA consults us on a particular issue." Long-time member Susana Bartolomé celebrated the many faces of RIMA that, together, constructed a counterpublic that is more than its online presence: "RIMA IS SO MUCH, SO VERY MUCH, that it is hard to define it, BUT IT IS 'HER,' it is the NETWORK, and RIMA 'OVERFLOWS,' overflows with opinions, discussions, mail, assistance, help, reflections, theorizations, marches, brainstorming, solidarity. RIMA OVERFLOWS THE NET AND CONSTRUCTS NETWORKS." With so many resources so easily available for circulation and discussion, the list built community.

This network has not been bound by screens; community is periodically nurtured by in-person encounters. As described above, RIMA and the ENM are interwoven. But members have also deliberately created opportunities to reinforce their connection. One such opportunity was an *aquelarre,* literally a witch's coven, in the form of a potluck held in September 2012 at the Casa del Encuentro in Buenos Aires. The tangibility of meeting was expressed afterward in the list, which lit up with praises for the food (and a recipe exchange) and the opportunity to be together. Several women wrote about how meaningful it was to put names and faces together, to meet those they knew through their words: "To see the faces . . . the written name [on a nametag] makes one go click! This name has a face, a voice, a gesture and something to say. It's been a long time since I have had such a good time in a meeting of so many known-not-seen, real virtuals, all with a history that we build daily. . . . Today I felt that I liked being in RIMA more." The hosts signed off "until the next coven dear witches." On- and offline, Rimeras have built a community of shared solidarity with other women.

But Rimeras have not only exchanged solidaristic support through the list. They have also used it as an arena for expression of serious disagreements. One contributor testified to the list's counterpublic capacity to allow the expression of diverse viewpoints since it was "a space of debate, of sharing, of informing ourselves. . . . And above all of amplitude, since diverse tendencies coexist, sometimes with polemics, sometimes with celebrations, but fundamentally, with the consciousness of having their own space." At times the list resembles Chantal Mouffe's "agonistic pluralism," glossed by communications theorist Zizi Papacharissi as "a 'vibrant clash of democratic political positions,' guided by unpredictability, and more receptive to the plurality of voices that develop within contemporary pluralist societies."[39] To respect and nurture the value of democracy amid diversity, Rimeras have a practice of open discussion and debate, which they find to enrich their understandings of what they stand for.

Differences often become fraught. A recommended reading on domestic violence sparked a debate over how to approach perpetrators: criminalization or mediation? The overlapping nature of counterpublics was revealed in an urgent appeal to rescue animals released from a shelter without protection. It both generated replies of support ("I was wondering when this list was going to pay attention to animal rights"), and reminders of the nature of the list ("All of us who participate in 'animal rights' lists don't give warnings about kidnapped women in those 'animal rights' lists"). Prominent feminists, including academic and politician Diana Maffía and psychoanalyst and author Eva Giberti weigh in; others timidly or boldly engage with them. While the debates are numerous, two areas are worth highlighting for their centrality to this counterpublic: partisan politics and sexuality.

Although the informal norm of leaving partisan politics at the door has been largely followed, list participants have distinct perspectives on when partisan or other political beliefs should be brought into their carefully nurtured space. As one member wrote, the day there is a partisan "litmus test," "I'm gone. Because precisely what attracts me to the network, is that it unites us beyond the differences to support an objective." But while she herself was not interested in sharing her party position, "neither am I going to criticize someone for demonstrating hers." Rimeras know from direct experience how damaging extreme partisan conflict can be; but they have deeply held beliefs besides their feminism.

As moderator Adelstein confirmed, around election time exchanges can get quite heated. Presidential statements also provoke intense disagreement. In early 2010, directly after a discussion about how best to respond to a national newspaper's photoshopped image of President Cristina

Fernandez de Kirchner as physically battered by the opposition—a portrayal which list members felt was completely inappropriate—a debate broke out over whether she should have used the term "disappeared" with regard to anyone besides those who were kidnapped and never seen again during the Dirty War. Another set of exchanges parsed whether her government's extension of child protection benefits to include maternal care in the second trimester of pregnancy left an opening for first trimester abortion decriminalization—or supported the Catholic Church's view of life beginning before birth. Members disagreed about a strategy of shouting slogans for abortion decriminalization during solemn presidential speeches: terribly disrespectful? But: "Revolution doesn't respect protocol"!

Partisan differences were in stark relief in October 2010, following the killing of a Trotskyite student supporter of the left-wing union confederation during an open fight with its opposition, the government-supported union confederation. One member was disturbed that the moderators seemed to be blocking posts about the incident. The moderators defended their actions as protecting the nature of the list rather than censoring political views: "We deplore and repudiate the assassination of *compañero* Mariano Ferreyra. . . . [But] for this kind of message there are many other mailing lists where the calls to action and expressions of repudiation are circulating. We are going to publish all the personal expressions, but we are NOT going to be a vehicle for partisan communications." Some members appreciated this response. Although acknowledging their shared concern about "cases so brutal and which put so much in evidence the inhumane system in which we live," one *colistera* felt it was important to maintain the focus of RIMA, given that there were other arenas for counterpublic expression online: "Personally I am grateful. . . . When I want to know about gender I enter RIMA, if not I look elsewhere, and that helps me to manage my time and my connection to internet." But others did not accept the moderation; the original poster argued, "Gender perspective is not equivalent to 'women's issues,' nor human rights to repression during the dictatorship." Another Rimera recognized the value of what the moderators do even as she wanted exceptions for cases which unmask the brutal results of class and gender relations of power: "I very much value . . . their effort to maintain the character of the list, but I sincerely believe that in situations like this one—that break with the most essential that we have, which is life, it is necessary to recognize the possibility of making exceptions, and allowing us to think about the many ways that capital and patriarchy have to kill us." But yet another member reminded the list of why a distinct gender perspective was crucial, writing in about the lack of response to news about a young woman from northern Argentina who was savagely raped: "One more time, the country is not paralyzed by a case like this. How much violence, *compañeras*, of so many colors." Constructing a space of free expression without devolving into partisan conflict is a delicate balancing act, and it is not the only one RIMA attempts.

Sexuality is another key axis of difference on the list. Distinct perspectives on the expression of sexual identities are proffered by women who may well have not encountered each other in such "close" proximity before. This is manifest in the kind of complex negotiations that happen inside counterpublics around how to confront ignorance—and worse—in wider publics.

In March 2010, the list exploded with rage and anguish following the death of Natalia "Pepa" Gaitán, a lesbian who was murdered by her lover's stepfather. As Rimeras shared ways they were responding, a representative of a lesbian group circulated a slogan for protest marches: "If together we shout *DYKE* we end fear, death and silence." In response, a Rimera suggested they might be better off using the term "lesbian pride" like the "gay pride marches" instead of something "denigrating." This reply generated a strong reaction by some lesbian members. Adelstein quoted the Argentine lesbian feminist theorist valeria flores: "This hyperidentitarian strategy makes visible a sexual identity historically pushed into the space of abjection or compulsive silencing. And for the moment, as long as the heterosexual pact or contract stays current, it is an efficient manner of fighting the heterosexual presumption." Adelstein went on to remind the list that the word *queer* had also been resignified by those of nonnormative sexuality—and that lesbians' political processes and strategies were distinct from those of gay men. To which the original poster responded in loud capital letters, "QUEER MEANS STRANGE, GAY MEANS HAPPY, STRAIGHT [*DERECHO*] MEANS RIGHT (IT IS USED FOR HETERO). IN THE END . . . WHY DID I GET INVOLVED IN THIS? I WANTED TO HELP AND IT IS AS IF I WERE CHALLENGING YOU. . . . BETTER NOT TO OPINE." Adelstein replied: "I don't feel that we are confronting each other: the word 'dyke' startled you, and we took the educational [opportunity]. And may it be welcome. . . . It is good that you have given your opinion, it is good that we expressed ourselves." Feminist author and activist Yuderkis Espinosa wondered why only lesbians should have "the memory of the lesbian movement within feminism." Another member made clear that such memory was available to all *colisteras*, when she

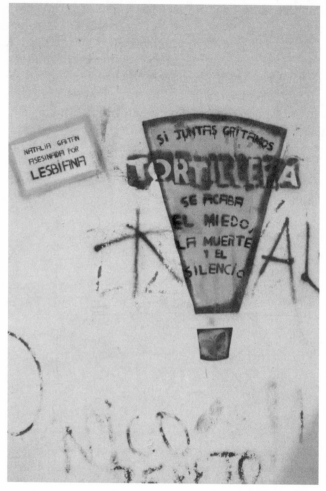

FIGURE 16. "Natalia Gaitán, assassinated for being a lesbian"; "If together we scream DYKE, fear, death, and silence will end." Courtesy of Malas Como Las Arañas, Coletiva Lesbica Feminista, La Plata Argentina.

suggested that members could do a little research in RIMA's archives ("on the list") before weighing in on someone else's organizing strategy.

Although the suggestion to read on the list indicated that RIMA was a central repository of feminist knowledge, it sparked unhappy reactions by those who felt it was somehow chastising discussion participants. Finally, someone wondered if the list might return "to more substantial issues of discussion." But what could be more substantial, responded another Rimera, than saying "one and a thousand times, that Natalia Gaitán (one more time, I name her) was shot for being a lesbian. Not for being poor, not for being a woman, not for being a social activist. She was shot for being a lesbian." In this vibrant counterpublic space full of distinct perspectives and commitments, not all can be resolved. But much can be aired.

Debates in RIMA resonated across Argentine counterpublic arenas. To continue education among equals on this topic in another dimension of the counterpublic, Diana Maffía proposed an intergenerational forum for the next ENM. In doing so she recognized another axis of difference intersecting that of sexuality, age, and the need for some of this fraught exchange to be done in person. This sparked a "coming out" of Rimeras about their age, revealing interlocutors from thirty-three to seventy-five.

The practice of allowing debate reflects the value of horizontal pluralism. In this counterpublic, participation from diverse locations, particularly (but not limited to) partisan and sexual identity, can result in fraught yet fruitful exchanges. As Maffía expressed in a celebratory anniversary post, everyone had a chance to learn—and teach—from their wide range of subject positions:

> In these years the daring learned a little more about these tools, the youth taught us, the lesbians helped us to root out the heterosexism surviving in feminism, the solidaristic professionals come and go off on tangents and move forward, the academics put their wisdom at our disposition, and also the wisdom that they find here to share, the grassroots fighters help us to root out the classism surviving in feminism, the romantics help us express our feelings from time to time contrary to all logic, the afrodescendents and the indigenous help us to root out the racism surviving (yes) in feminism, the women in prostitution challenge us defining themselves in different ways, and thus thus thus pass the years.

This degree of representation and exchange, so vividly summarized by Maffía, is not the inevitable result of the technology of a distribution list. The political commitments of this diverse population have made this interface into one where significant teaching and learning can take place.

To keep that education going, the coordinators began to archive the more significant debates on RIMA's webpage. On March 8, 2001, to celebrate International Women's Day, De Cicco and Ocampo published the first RIMA website, RIMAweb, as "an archive of our feminist movements" (May 2, 2001). Their poetic goal was to have it function as "an active and vital reservoir of our memories of women fighters, thinkers, desirers." From the beginning, this "active reservoir" was intimately linked to the list: their plan was to provide a more stable place for the documents of interest exchanged by the colisteras. The dynamic list revealed a new source for the archives: the more spontaneous discussions and debates enabled by the list interactions. After a rich debate, coordinators might ask whether the exchanges could be published there.

Whether through building each other up, or challenging each other's deeply held beliefs, Rimeras made the list embody the feminist value of horizontal, democratic exchange. Through its long-distance links, women have broadened their personal relationships. By reading and responding, women who might not choose to be in the same room can passionately debate what it means to make change on issues of gender and sexuality. Whether or not they stay in contact as individuals, they have constructed a community of feminist readers and writers.

ADDRESSING LARGER PUBLICS

Buenos Aires city councilwoman Maria Elena Naddeo believed RIMA's diverse, sometimes contentious counterpublic built something bigger than the list itself: a powerful force for change. As she explained, "It links us in time and ideology, even with all the differences of this diverse world that we share, even if we don't personally know many *colisteras,* we have become somehow participants and constituent of a strong and potent collective." She saw Rimeras, nurtured as individuals and a community, influencing both alternative and institutional political arenas: "This list is of enormous value for the diffusion of feminist ideas, for discussion about public policies, about current legislation." Through the diverse organizing practices facilitated by the list, women engaged in the feminist goal of social transformation. In particular, the list has become part of the architecture undergirding activist coalitions. It has enabled such activism by creating the conditions for organizing—the community building—and the organizing itself.

As for so many counterpublics, RIMA's distribution of alternative news is the community's bedrock. This circulation enables feminists to take part in a host of actions, from petitions, to lobbying, to street protests. Early subjects on the list ranged from debt negotiations to the suspected link between breast cancer and antiperspirants. With the list's maturation, regular subjects ranged from reproductive rights and health, to the politics of the Catholic Church, to queer theory. In 2010 Malú

Moreno, the director of the Comisión Mujer, Infancia, Adolescencia y Juventud (Commission for Women, Children, Adolescents and Youth) of the Buenos Aires legislature, alerted the list to an open meeting for the Health Commission where they were going to discuss legislation concerning comprehensive care for women who have had legal abortions.[40] Afterward, she thanked those who made an appearance. Her call on the list was effective at turning out supporters. As psychologist and board member of the Permanent Assembly for Human Rights Leonor Núñez expressed it, RIMA became an information source without peer: "for real women on this side of the planet, RIMA has become the most important virtual newspaper!!! It is almost as if what we don't read in RIMA, doesn't exist!!!" Like the feminist alternative media outlets before it, RIMA has provided the counterpublic with news that they can rely on in taking direct action.

Besides promoting action, the "virtual newspaper" has also performed a key element of counterpublic influence: the circulation of its discourses to the wider world. Feminist journalists on the list have been the conduit for this practice. Mariana Carbajal of the national daily *Página/12* attested: "RIMA occupies an irreplaceable place, permanent source of information, of intellectual enrichment, for the intelligent discussions that circulate there . . . , nexus of essential communication, with acquaintances and others whom I have gotten to know through their messages." Sandra Chaher and Sonia Santoro, founders of the feminist information portal Artemisa Noticias, praised the list as well. They were grateful for *colisteras'* input: "Without the work that you gals do, ours would be much more complicated. Thanks Gabby and Irene for sustaining Rima! Thanks to the *colisteras* who always help us with commentary, telephone numbers or suggestions! And thanks, many thanks, to those who discuss and open our minds!" Feminist journalists recognized how much the *colisteras* helped them hone the stories and perspectives they shared in wider publics.

The impact of the counterpublic in developing and then sharing strategies for change is evident in the ways in which RIMA-based campaigns have been publicized by *colisteras* such as Carbajal. Some actions are entirely created on the list, such as the 2010 campaign to protest fliers advertising prostitution in Buenos Aires. Building on several women's spontaneous efforts to rip them down whenever they found them, the campaign eventually lead to the production of slogans and stickers. Then Carbajal covered it in the national newspaper *Página/12*, where she publicized the initiative and offered a means for participation: "People who want to join the proposal can download and print from the campaniaa-bolicionista.blogspot.com a series of phrases to post in the places where they rip down the flyers with sexual offers [such as]: 'We were not born to be prostituted.'"[41] She took part in a similar process for the "I had an abortion" campaign, which shared personal testimonies to raise awareness about abortion in Argentina and the many different ways it affects the women who choose it. A February 2005 article by Carbajal summarized the trajectory of the campaign: Adelstein, mobilized by the march for abortion depenalization at the ENM and a visit by the Dutch abortion rights organization Women on Waves, posted her "visceral reaction" to RIMA. She testified that she had had an abortion, but, as a middle-class woman, could count on good medical attention and social support; she knew these conditions were far from the norm for women with fewer resources. Her testimony "opened the space for many others to share their experiences or those of family members."[42] In Carbajal's article, RIMA founder Ocampo described how this exchange on RIMA led to the next step in a public campaign. "As the testimonies were coming together," she explained, "we began to ask if it were possible and necessary to make them public. There were *colisteras* that from this [experience] spoke for the first time in their family or with their partner about the issue. And finally, two weeks ago, it was agreed to publish the campaign in RIMA's website."[43] Carbajal's article went on to describe the historical precedents, both foreign and domestic, to this initiative. These campaigns illustrate how Rimeras's exchange on the list enabled each element of their counterpublic on the way to making a public impact. First, it helped individuals to understand their own experiences. Second, they had the opportunity to develop a collective understanding of the problems they faced. Finally, they developed a strategy for change.

Other grassroots campaigns have also developed inside the counterpublic space of RIMA. Responding to the murder of Natalia Gaitán, *colisteras* devised both on- and offline protests. On the list, they debated strategies for the most effective use of Facebook, and, as discussed above, which chants to call out in street protests. In response to *colisteras'* concern over whether their signatures had been added to an online petition to demand justice in the case, an organizer replied that it might take some digging to find a name, since some parts of the list were alphabetized and others were not. But that was in line with the different use of technology by the volunteers coordinating the action: "It is a group of various women who have taken it upon ourselves to keep the blog up to date with the signatures and other interesting contributions that we receive, and each one has a different way of relating with the computer, with internet and with the world." Through their online and offline entanglements, Rimeras brought their individual perspectives and skills to demanding justice for lesbian femicide.

Because Argentine feminist counterpublics overlap considerably with those of other Latin American countries, RIMA also distributes requests from outside the country. For example, in July 2001, the coordinators sent around an urgent action plea from a domestic workers' organization in Lima, Peru, which had been attacked during a protest march against the bloody repression of Alberto Fujimori's government. The coordinators asked Rimeras to distribute the information across their solidarity networks because "we know that this humble Network that is in the midst of the process of growing can offer this information to many women who are in the rest of Latinamerica and in Europe, so from this point we appreciate what you can do for the Peruvian *compañeras.*" In 2009, Honduran feminists described and condemned that year's coup (including links to other websites and YouTube videos). The outrage among *colisteras* culminated in a quickly organized (and jointly drafted) "Pronouncement of Argentine Feminists against the Military Coup in Honduras," posted on RIMA's blog and signed by hundreds, as well as the circulation of videos of Argentine feminists protesting in front of the Honduran and U.S. embassies. The reach of RIMA has spilled over national borders to help in transnational demands for justice.

RELATION TO SOCIAL MEDIA: "WE CAN'T
NEGLECT HAVING A PRESENCE HERE"

RIMA coordinators have been eager to offer their community other opportunities for online interaction, from a website to social media. While these other technologies have been assimilated into the counterpublic with their own distinct dynamics, they have enhanced rather than replaced the core of RIMA, the distribution list. Specifically, RIMA's Facebook page does not seem to have cut off the list. The page does not offer an inherently "social" benefit; instead, the practices of use have determined what Facebook is good for. Overall, the counterpublic benefits the list offers—personal growth, community development, and real-time action—are not yet achieved to the same extent through social networking tools.

With the growth of Facebook, the other social networking tools RIMA incorporated declined in importance, and in any case never offered many of the list's benefits. While a blog was active from 2004 to 2011, it mainly reposted articles from the list, and had its ups and downs in terms of use (from a high of 57 posts in 2005 to a low of 2 in 2007, and a total of 213 posts in seven years).[44] The public nature of the blog meant that anyone could read and comment, which may have expanded the RIMA readership. But commentary there never approached the traffic, nor the depth, of participation on the list. Moreover, posters often used pseudonyms or remained anonymous, whereas all list contributions are sent from personal email addresses, and can be responded to as such (and at the very least, all subscribers' basic profiles are known to the coordinators). A YouTube channel opened in 2006, had seven clips, all from the same event, a Rosario rally to support abortion rights in May 2006; this "video blog" hasn't been used since.[45] It may be that video hosting has been less relevant for the list, given that most of what is exchanged on RIMA is not produced for it. Neither the blog nor YouTube channel proved to be a replacement for the list.

In RIMA's January 31, 2009, Facebook launch, De Cicco offered an explanation of their turn to social media: "We can't neglect having a presence here and see in what way Facebook can be used to dynamize our communication and make it more participative."[46] Through Facebook, "which seems to expect the forms of communication" and "the spaces for exchange," they hoped that members would be active, and those not subscribed to the list could join. "May it be experimentation, play, creativity, communication, art, activism and commitment!" she enthusiastically wrote. To be sure, RIMA's Facebook page offers the possibility of more active participation by more people. Although coordinators need to approve those who seek access, they have opened it to men; moderation mainly takes the form reposting RIMA's mission statement and purpose. And there are many more "subscribers" than *colisteras;* by 2016 the page had magnified RIMA's reach hundred-fold, with nearly 11,550 compared to the approximately 1,200 on the list. In some ways, Facebook use overlaps with the list, since people inform about events, publications, actions, and articles published elsewhere. The overwhelming majority of posts advertise events, from fundraisers to talks, increasingly with catchy infographics and posters; this is also a place to share news, history, and other feminist production through hyperlinks and uploads.[47]

As Facebook became incorporated into RIMA's information ecology— and that of other Argentine feminist counterpublics—RIMA developed a Facebook policy. In response to the frequent messages focused on inappropriate, insulting, or outrageous Facebook pages or posts, the moderators added a new netiquette: any complaints about Facebook should circulate in that arena, and not on RIMA. Adelstein posted to the list that since they had no way to check the information's veracity, they could not publish them. While the list and Facebook might offer similar information, their distinct ways of engaging participation have meant that coordinators were careful to protect their hard-won arena for interaction from the less controlled environment of Facebook.

While it may offer "communication, art, and activism," the Facebook page does not seem to have enabled "experimentation, play, creativity" and the same kind of "commitment" enabled by the list. A study in 2014 revealed much less substantial exchange facilitated on Facebook, and certainly nothing of the kind of in-depth discussions or individual support developed through RIMA. Overall, most of the posts had little to no direct response, with group members "liking" posts more than offering commentary.[48] Although the future balance of RIMA's platforms is uncertain, it is difficult to imagine a full appropriation of the more public, commercial, and visual application as a similar space for identity construction and exchange as the list. But users can alter platforms to serve their own goals through their own practices, and the determination of Rimeras to wield their values on the world may yet translate over to more public applications.

RIMA, "THE PLACE WITHIN THAT
DOESN'T EXIST OUTSIDE"

Esther Andrade, an early Rimera, offered a summary of all that RIMA has offered to her and the others on the list: "[It] is for me the space of encounter, of relief, of critique, of understanding, of embrace. The place of the articulation of actions, the place of complaint. A place that does not exclude either the disagreement or the dissent, because it is the place of trust. Rima is the place within that doesn't exist outside." Through the practices that the coordinators have jointly developed with the membership, RIMA has enabled a complex, value-driven interpretation of the logical layer of the internet that reflects their historical counterpublic experiences. RIMA did not come out of nowhere: its membership boasted long experience with feminist collaboration across difference, and was nurtured by the national women's meetings.

In her ninth anniversary reflection, RIMA cofounder Ocampo wrote that the list's survival has been based on the coincidences between the technology and the principles of feminist communication. This "horizontal communication media" has enabled individual women to express views that reflect a host of distinct positions, "as a spokesperson for her group, community, neighborhood, locality, [who] can count on this space in the web." Not only individual expression, but also feminist community is fostered by the "possibility of counting on a form of communication [that is] non-hegemonic, plural, respectful of different points of view, of the diverse identities and necessities."[49] And, as Ocampo and RIMA cofounder De Cicco affirmed, RIMA's digital counterpublic has contributed to social change as "the daughter of the Argentine feminist movement, and . . . the sister of the popular struggle, of the resistance against bloody and patriarchal capitalism, the expression of voices of women who think, who resist, who come together, opine, and make change daily." But while the coincidences that Ocampo and De Cicco note between activism and technology are real, this chapter argues that they are not a given. RIMA has been able to count on a "non-hegemonic, plural, respectful" internet to enable "the expression of voices of women who think . . . and make change daily," precisely because among all of them—the coordinators and their *colisteras*—they have made a distribution list into what they needed.

The brief trip into RIMA's experience with social media reveals the sociomaterial conclusion that not all applications are equally apt for counterpublic construction. At least at this writing, the more open venue of Facebook enabled more information distribution and less interactivity. The former is an important contribution, and the much larger numbers of people who belong to the page than the list shows that there is an eager audience for RIMA's content. But with fewer boundaries on who is there and what can be shared, RIMA's integration of Facebook has been an extension of, but no replacement for, the list.

Of course, RIMA is no panacea; although it does not exist "outside," it depends on outside for the making of meaning. This is vividly described by Noemi Chiarotti of the decades-old feminist organization Indeso Mujer. While attesting to the extent to which RIMA was able to model "feminist process" online, she affirmed the need to complement online with face-to-face discussion. "It is difficult to digest, metabolize" everything circulating at such a rapid pace via the internet; "it's like you are storing it in your brain on different diskettes," rather than really processing it.[50] She herself liked to download the list for concentrated perusal, and insisted that, for the profound changes demanded by feminism, some reflection and exchange had to be done in person. The symbiotic relationship between RIMA and the ENM, and other opportunities for Rimeras to gather, have enabled such exchange in community.

For a younger generation, the sheer volume of information available in places like RIMA can prove overwhelming, as they were for members of the Canadian PAR-L list. As one member attested, "I have tried to read all that I have succeeded in finding and what has been published in RIMA and I find myself jumping from the creation of the movement and equality feminism to Judith Butler without any intermediate clarification!!!! One might imagine the mental disorder." Plunging into the vast waters that constitute contemporary feminism online today may well cause "mental disorder." But in Argentina, the asset of the RIMA list complements other arenas for exchange.

As "the place within that doesn't exist outside," RIMA's considerable contribution to Argentine feminist counterpublics is a space that cannot be replicated offline. Vividly exemplified by the national meetings, it is a difficult endeavor to provide a place of comfort and challenge for an ever-diversifying population of women. And although those meetings offer significant opportunities for solidarity, they also bring with them deep political divisions, accusations of co-optation, and often direct confrontations with right-wing activists, the Catholic Church, and others. While RIMA does not paper over real divisions, it provides an avenue for encounter that can be accessed according to members' wishes, when and where they want to be comforted, challenged, or championed. Conflict is an integral part of counterpublics; as sociologist Deborah Gould writes about social movements, "[They] are typically filled with contentiousness: conflict and debate are a primary means by which movements analyze the political terrain and figure out what to do."[51] What RIMA shows is how counterpublics can provide room for such constructive conflict on a regular basis. Unlike offline opportunities, the list comes every day.

As this chapter makes clear, the keystone species of founders and coordinators has been crucial to the creation and maintenance of the list. As with such species in the natural environment, they have had an outsized impact on their information ecology. This impact has not been limited to RIMA. The next chapter follows them, as well as other committed activists, to lesbian feminist counterpublics. There, several internet applications have transformed and been transformed by communities looking for both privacy and visibility.

CHAPTER 5

From Privacy to Lesbian Visibility

*Latin American Lesbian Feminist
Internet Practices*

In 2005, a self-identified "faithful visitor" of the Chilean lesbian feminist website Rompiendo el Silencio (Breaking the Silence) posted her story to a page where readers could report acts of discrimination. She affirmed the central importance of the internet in her affective life, since she had met "the most beautiful person in the world" through an online chat. But offline, their lives were terrible. As she wrote in anguish, "my family, my work and friends . . . have humiliated us, they have singled us out . . . they are threatening to take my son away, we've been beaten, we've been threatened with death." Yet even in the face of violent lesbophobia, she stayed true to her "forbidden love," publicly claiming her devotion: "I love you, *negra*, my greatest joy was meeting you . . . if loving you is a sin I want to die sinning, I will endure the beatings for you only for you."

By going online, this woman found a place for a love daring to speak its name despite traumatic rejection. Her personal testimony served as a potential spur for others to express anger over similar abuse, or at the very least reassured readers that that they were part of a larger community standing up to societal sanction. Given such sanction, this level of contact and community, of visibility for lesbian reality, would have been impossible in Latin America without the internet. But the internet in itself has not made such things possible. They are happening because lesbian feminist organizations have recognized how crucial internet-based resources are to meeting their communities' needs.

FIGURE 17. "7 March, Lesbian Visibility Day"; "Commemorating the lesbicide of Natalia Gaitán and repudiating the reiterated censoring of the mural." (This commemorative mural had been repeatedly painted over; it was rendered as a more permanent mosaic in 2016.) Courtesy of Las Safinas.

In Latin America, lesbian feminist counterpublics' internet practices reflect two pressing priorities: their search for privacy and their demands for visibility. Lesbians need privacy because repudiation and, sometimes, violence, threatens their well-being if not their very survival, significant advances in their legal status notwithstanding. Yet they also need visibility to challenge their exclusion, bringing the fact of their existence and demands for recognition to larger publics. Historically discriminated against by gay men on the one hand and feminists on the other, and "practically inconceivable" by society at large,[1] lesbians have organized under the banner of *visibilidad lésbica,* lesbian visibility. They have interpreted internet-based technology through their counterpublic organizations in order to set and reset the boundaries between private and public life.

As RIMA demonstrates, other communities construct counterpublics to achieve both private and public goals. But these goals have a distinct relevance for lesbian and other queer communities. LGBT people need safe places to explore fundamental aspects of their identity, including their sexuality and gender, and to find friends, lovers, and partners.

While that might seem like a private affair, exploring, accepting, and making visible nonnormative sexuality and gender identities are also public issues. As social theorist Michael Warner writes of sex- and gender-based counterpublics, they "are testing our understanding of how private life can be publicly relevant. And they are elaborating not only new shared worlds and critical languages but also new privacies, new individuals, new bodies, new intimacies, and new citizenships."[2] Through their counterpublics, lesbians and other queers develop their private selves and figure out how and when to put them on display. Because so many social and political arenas are closed to their desires, the internet seems to be a crucial place for queer life.

Similar to the cyberfeminists of an earlier generation, who saw the internet as ideally suited to women's expression and feminist organizing, some observers have claimed that there is an inherent link between internet benefits, such as users' abilities to create new identities online, and queer existence: "There's the disembodied performativity of cyberspace, the place where no one knows you're a dog, or whatever you choose to present yourself as. Queer folk are past masters at this game, as nearly every one of us went through the training program during childhood."[3] While this idea suggests an ideal match between queer folk and online performance, I submit that the internet is no more inherently queer than it is inherently feminist. But while it may not be inherently queer, it has been productively queered by queers. For example, feminist technology analysts Manjima Bhattacharjya and Maya Indira Ganesh claim that queer groups may have been the first in India to turn internet applications into spaces for social networking, even before the spread of social media platforms. As they write, "These email lists and online spaces were how queer, marginalized groups (at that time also illegal in India) with access to technology networked, organised, socialised and lived out their 'queer' lives."[4] The incorporation of technology into queer communities in India had everything to do with an offline reality that made it dangerous to connect in other ways, and desirable to connect as much as possible. Because around the world queer folk need places where they can be themselves (or find out who they are), and information ecologies through which they can talk about their own desires, they have turned the internet into a vital support for their communities.

As this chapter shows, in Latin America, lesbian feminists have relied on the ever-developing repertoire of internet applications to improve their private and public lives, addressing long-standing problems of social isolation and resource restriction. Using email, websites, and discussion lists, organizations have helped women find each other and spread the news about their lives and demands to wider publics. As with feminist organizations, lesbian feminist organizations have struggled to make their counterpublics stable using digital means. But they too have transformed the applications to make them serve their own ends, principally around public visibility. Rimeras have been behind one of the most innovative revisioning of the logical layer, the conversion of a blog into an archive of lesbian visibility.

In order to analyze the ways in which lesbian feminist organizations have deployed the logical layer of the internet to support their counterpublics, this chapter uses a framework that maps the private and public goals of these communities onto the three constituent parts of counterpublics: individual incorporation, community building, and strategizing to have an impact on wider publics. In doing so, it also references experiences from other communities, particularly in the Global South, where queers have engaged the internet for counterpublic development. Like most dichotomies, the distinction between the private and public functions of lesbian feminist and other queer counterpublics will not hold up under scrutiny. As this chapter shows, there is no bright line dividing private issues, desires, and presentations from public ones; they are arrayed on a continuum. At one end is the individual identity exploration that enables private engagement on public issues; at the other, the contestation of domination that helps to articulate private issues for public consumption. Between these two poles sits the deliberation through which participants build community. Lesbian feminist organizations have used the internet to underwrite the entire continuum. As APC Women's Rights Programme manager Jac sm Kee enthused, the "wonderful thing" about the internet is that "it occupies several spaces simultaneously: it's private, it's privatized, it's public, it's a kind of public, and you can be everything at the same time."[5] Through the internet, lesbian feminist counterpublics simultaneously occupy private and public space.

The research for this chapter again draws on original interviews and online evidence from Argentina, Brazil, and Mexico, with the addition of websites from Chile and Peru. Besides carrying out interviews with members of lesbian feminist counterpublic organizations in Argentina, Brazil, and Mexico to hear their stories, I have looked at the faces they present to the public, including the most prominent lesbian feminist websites from the early 2000s and more recent social media in Mexico (LeSVOZ, or LeS[bian] VOICE); Chile (Rompiendo el Silencio); Argentina (Safo Piensa, or Sappho Thinks, and Potencia Tortillera, or Dyke

Power); Peru (Grupo de Activistas Lesbianas Feministas [GALF], or Lesbian Feminist Activists Group); and Brazil (Um *Outro* Olhar, or An *Other* Look). Before analyzing how this evidence illustrates the ways in which counterpublic organizations affect and are affected by the internet, I offer a brief overview of Latin American lesbian feminist organizing. This context sets the stage for their online engagement.

A SHIFTING CONTEXT OF CHALLENGES

The contexts lesbians face in Latin America are shifting. Their legal situation, as well as that of gay men and transgender people, has improved, in some cases dramatically, over the last twenty years. Some countries now legally recognize homosexual relationships. Equal marriage rights for gays and lesbians have been legislated in Mexico City, Argentina, and Uruguay; recognized by state or national courts in Brazil and Colombia; and the Ecuadorian constitution recognizes civil unions. Twelve countries—Bolivia, Mexico, Chile, Colombia, Costa Rica, Ecuador, El Salvador, Guatemala, Nicaragua, Peru, Uruguay, and Venezuela—have outlawed discrimination on the basis of sexual orientation. Additionally, seven countries and one major city—Bolivia, Brazil, Chile, Colombia, Cuba, Ecuador, Uruguay, and Mexico City—have laws or constitutional interpretations that ban discrimination on the basis of gender expression or identity. Argentina, Bolivia, Brazil, Colombia, Ecuador, and Uruguay allow transgender people to legally change their gender or name, although Brazil requires gender-reassignment surgery. And same-sex sexual activity is legal across the region.[6] Latin American is ahead of other world regions with respect to some LGBT rights.

This vanguard development extends to regional institutions. Responding to demands of regional LGBT organizations, the Organization of American States (OAS) Inter-American Commission on Human Rights created an LGBTI "Rights Unit" in November 2011, the first of its kind in any regional organization. In February 2012, the OAS's Inter-American Court of Human Rights determined that sexual orientation and gender identity are protected by the American Convention on Human Rights, in a ruling against the Chilean Supreme Court for depriving a lesbian judge, Karen Atala, of custody of her children because of her sexual orientation. Queers have fought for and won opportunities for exerting regional pressure on national governments to uphold their rights.

Besides legal advances, in many urban centers in Latin America it has become easier to publicly claim LGBT identity. Like Judge Atala, other, out gays and lesbians, as well as a few transwomen and men, have served in public positions, including being elected to municipal, and even national, office. Saõ Paulo, Brazil, boasts the world's largest LGBT pride parade, a social phenomenon that has spread from Mexico to Uruguay. Gay neighborhoods, cafés, clubs, bars, and beaches flourish in cities such as Buenos Aires, Argentina, Rio de Janeiro, Brazil, and Bogotá, Colombia. Gay and lesbian characters now appear in popular Spanish-language *telenovelas* (soap operas). In a soccer-obsessed region, lesbians have the opportunity to participate in their own indoor soccer tournament in Mexico City or the *fulbito* games in Lima, Peru. Queer life has become ever more visible in Latin America.

But despite these gains, many obstacles remain. Several countries—El Salvador, Honduras, the Dominican Republic, and even Ecuador—have enacted constitutional prohibitions against same-sex marriage. In most countries, less than half of the population expresses high tolerance for the political rights of LGBT people or approves of same-sex marriage.[7] Police violence against queers, especially those who do not conform to gender norms, is widely reported. Transgender people are singled out for harassment and much worse; the Inter-American Commission on Human Rights found that hundreds of transgender women were murdered over a fifteen-month period starting in early 2013.[8] That is in addition to the difficulty they face in obtaining legal recognition of their chosen gender, appropriate medical care, and education and employment opportunities. The multiple axes of oppression many Latin Americans face along the lines of sexuality, gender, race/ethnicity, and class means that many LGBT people cannot even claim the legal rights to which they are entitled.[9]

As Atala's court case suggests, lesbians have been deeply involved in the ongoing campaigns for legal and social recognition and acceptance. Through decades of organizing, they have developed their communities and reached out to wider publics. Although some of this has taken place within wider counterpublics, lesbians, and particularly lesbian feminists, have also found it imperative to build their own. The emergence of independent lesbian feminist activism can be traced to the influences of both larger political dynamics and interactions with the potential allies of gay men and straight feminist women.

LGBT organizing has been marked by the tumultuous political history of the Latin American region, including long periods of authoritarian repression and drawn-out democratization processes.[10] Many of the first lesbian activists cut their political teeth in communist, socialist, or anarchist parties or movements, through which they fought for national (socialist) and sexual liberation. While some smaller left parties and movements were open to their queer cadre, larger ones often rejected homosexuality. Until the 1990s, the Castro government in Cuba promoted gay "reeducation" and quarantined people living with AIDS; thousands fled to the United States during the 1980 Mariel boatlift. On the right, some repressive regimes actively targeted sexual minorities.[11] Lesbians found both right- and left-leaning regimes inhospitable, if not repressive.

Although political liberalization in the 1980s allowed more room for LGBT activism and advocacy,[12] democratic politics have been no guarantee for LGBT public expression. In one notorious incident, during the preparations for a 1990 regional lesbian Encuentro in democratic Costa Rica, a major newspaper published the names of the organizers and the themes for discussion. In response, the Costa Rican secretary of state announced that border police would investigate whether single women headed into Costa Rica might be attendees and that all Costa Rican consulates were to deny visas to single women during the meeting dates. Threatened and frightened, the organizers found a secret location for the meeting, at which they assembled all the attendees who managed to arrive. With a regular "patrol" outside, the meeting took place over the next four days without incident, until the last night when drunken men attacked the site, shouting obscenities, hammering on the doors, and throwing rocks. Only in the early morning hours could the women "evacuate."[13] The difficult political contexts lesbians have faced have made their organizing more complex, but have also stimulated it.

To confront the hostility and rejection of the wider political milieu, lesbian activists initially joined in mixed gay/lesbian and/or women's liberation organizations. The former were slowed by political repression, but grew clandestinely and with increasing inspiration, and sometimes direct support, from the United States and Europe. Women joined men in the early groups, but often became disillusioned by the predominance of male leadership and gay issues. Meanwhile, both the international and regional development of feminist and women's organizations attracted lesbian participants. Throughout the 1970s, many politically active lesbians fought for reproductive rights and an end to violence against women, while supporting grassroots organizing for better working and welfare conditions. But straight feminists ignored or rejected lesbian-specific issues for fear of realizing society's suspicions that feminism was indeed the work of "man haters." It would take years before the feminist demand for women's control over their bodies and the lesbian demand for women's control over their sexuality would become part of the same struggle.

In response to misogyny from gay men and homophobia from straight feminists, in the early 1980s lesbians founded autonomous groups to strengthen their identities, communities, and political effectiveness. The counterpublic space of the regional Encuentros played a role in bringing lesbians together: several credit a "miniworkshop" on lesbianism that drew an audience of three hundred at the 1982 Encuentro as the inspiration to form groups back home.[14] Eventually they would also come together at the regional level. By building an autonomous movement—one with its own marches and meetings—lesbians explored new forms of expression and new arenas for encounter and organizing.[15] Organizing on their own, lesbian feminist activists could focus more directly on their interests without having to subordinate them to the gay or (straight) feminist agenda.

Independent lesbian activists created counterpublics to support their private lives and seek greater visibility in wider publics. Lesbian-only spaces offered women the opportunity to meet others for friendship or intimate relationship as well as political solidarity. There they also discussed how to respond politically to the challenges that confronted them, whether those were internal, such as the acceptance of trans-women, or external, including rejection and repression in wider publics.

These counterpublics faced substantial obstacles. Like other queers, lesbians were often isolated from each other, and faced rejection from their families and communities. Learning about their identity or finding out about local gatherings relied on word-of-mouth. Some groups published their own alternative media, such as newsletters or journals, in order to share political, literary, and artistic work, but the publications had limited circulation. In the 1980s, for example, the Peruvian Grupo de Activistas Lesbianas Feministas distributed their handmade bulletin, *Al Margen* (On the Margin) in discoteques and in women's centers.[16] Moreover, groups found it difficult to maintain physical counterpublic spaces: GALF lost its meeting place when a local café closed. Having a permanent space helped another group in Mexico to attract supporters, but its upkeep fell to a few people with little money and it too closed down.[17] Meeting together at the ninth Encuentro Feminista (1999), lesbians from across the region shared story after story of bars, cafés, and other meeting spaces that had shut their doors. Providing ways to connect and build community has been difficult in the face of limited information and places for encounter.

The rest of this chapter portrays how the integration of internet-based technology has helped Latin American lesbian counterpublics confront such obstacles, while bringing its own set of complications. The internet acts as a "virtual lifeline,"[18] as online interaction mitigates isolation for Latin American lesbians in their private life and web presence eases resource restrictions for organizations. In the face of widespread rejection, lesbians can go online to speak their own vernacular of courting and connection, and make common cause. In their visible life, they can express their ideas, broadcast news, and mobilize.

ENHANCING PRIVATE LIFE: FINDING EACH OTHER ONLINE

How can a website be a place for privacy? When it helps people "to understand who they are," in the words of a founder of the Argentine Madres Lesbianas Feministas Autonomas (Autonomous Lesbian Feminist Mothers) back in 2001. When I asked her, "Why have a website?" she answered, "To show that a group of lesbian mothers exists here in Argentina. In the interior [of the country] there are women who are mothers who have feelings for other women . . . how are they going to know who they are?"[19] Although physically based in Buenos Aires, they reached out, "not only in our country, but also to countries such as Paraguay, Mexico—to women who don't belong to a group, but are lesbian mothers."[20] Those who were wary of revealing their identities could learn about lesbian motherhood in this space. Websites and other applications expanded the opportunities for lesbian identity construction, the fundamental building block of counterpublics.

Affirming the importance of the content and logical layers of the internet for lesbians and other queers, legal scholar Edward Stein argues that, in sharp contrast to mainstream society, the internet is "an ideal environment."[21] Its anonymity and vastness enables exploration of things "that are difficult or taboo offline," from developing an awareness of sexual or gender identity to finding partners. As APC Women's Rights Programme senior project coordinator Jan Moolman argues, it allows those still exploring their sexuality or gender identity "the chance to immerse themselves in aspects of the virtual culture, the language and practices, attitudes and beliefs, and to try them out, so to speak, in the relatively safe environment of the internet before coming out."[22] One comparison of LGBT websites in the United States, Germany, China, and Japan claimed that "there is no other forum in which so many people of so many different backgrounds have safely disclosed, and felt comfortable disclosing, their sexual identities."[23] With the spread of the internet, younger people have been able to access information or support that helped them come to terms with their sexual orientation, to the point where many are coming out online before they do so offline.[24] In Latin America, a survey of Chilean queer youth found that they "do not understand how they would have made their lives" without the internet.[25] The virtual closet can have an open door.

The role of the internet in alleviating the isolation of lesbians is undeniable, so much so that the same Chilean study claims lesbians were the most adept at using the internet to connect for self-help and mutual support.[26] The nonterritorial nature of the community and the threat of violence individuals face makes online exchange critical, however it takes place. Because Latin American lesbian organizations concentrate in the major cities, and rural areas tend to be much more traditional, women living outside of those cities depend on the internet to make contact. But even in large cities, those who cannot easily attend meetings and may not be interested in a bar scene have found refuge online.

In the early days of the internet, email and websites were the primary resources for breaking through isolation. In 2002, Martha Patricia Cuevas Armas, the co-coordinator of the Mexico City–based Nueva Generación de Jóvenes Lesbianas (New Generation of Lesbian Youth), reported regularly receiving email messages from lesbians across the country seeking groups near them.[27] According to Mariana Pérez Ocaña, founder and editor of the LeSVOZ lesbian website and magazine, also based in the capital, there was not much to tell them: "We get a lot of email from women from the provinces because in the provinces there is nothing! No magazines, nowhere to go."[28] RIMA founders Gabby De Cicco and Irene Ocampo, who also established the lesbian feminist distribution list Safo Piensa, noted that in Argentina, the internet quickly became "quite a resource for women who have trouble finding each other"[29]—wherever they lived. The safe space provided by websites was at once local, national, and regional, revealed by posts to Safo Piensa's "guest book" from the early 2000s.[30] A Buenos Aires woman reflected on the importance of the website for learning more about her community: "It seems really important to have a place to go when we are eager for information. Society is tough and makes an effort to make difficult a life that . . . I think is beautiful. In this way I can learn, socialize, try to change situations and share moments and ideas. Simply for that, THANK YOU." An Argentine woman outside the capital city affirmed this appreciation:

"Thank you very much for existing and helping us, I live in a city where we don't have any help like you offer." Another woman wrote in because there was nowhere to turn with her coming-out process in her home country of the Dominican Republic: "Two years ago I realized I am a lesbian it affected me a lot but I didn't accept it now I need help I don't know if it's alright." While this area of the webpage may not have been the most effective place to find in-person support, that a Dominican woman posted her distress on an Argentine site illustrates how Safo Piensa enabled valuable connections across vast distances.

Beyond their assistance at the content layer in distributing information, lesbian feminist organizations also enabled users to get in touch with each other. Personal contacts were fostered by four of the websites from the mid-2000s, and were in high demand. Personal ads have since migrated, but in the early days of lesbian websites, the provision of ads was an integral part of creating community.[31] Although seemingly peripheral to creating social change, this web-based service was a direct affirmation of lesbian identity; just reading them could foster a sense of belonging. The realization that others are "out" there is significant to women who are struggling to accept their own identity in a hostile environment. LeSVOZ accepted personal ads via email (which were then printed in their print magazine). Um *Outro* Olhar had about five hundred personals listed. Safo Piensa ran a discussion list of seventy lesbian, lesbian feminist, and bisexual women. Rompiendo el Silencio hosted thirteen different discussion fora, the largest of which (with nearly thirty-five hundred messages) was for "contacts," and provided a chat service for instant interaction. It also offered online psychological counseling, a boon for women unable to discuss their sexuality elsewhere. To move from the articulation of identity to community exchange, discussion lists and fora were important early on.

Given their need for safe, private spaces, it is not surprising that Latin American lesbian groups have been eager to maintain control over their online counterpublic services, setting boundaries for participation. This is a global phenomenon. The founder of Desi Dykes, a transnational discussion list for queer South Asian women, used phone screening to ensure those who joined were what they claimed to be; this screening, along with the ability of members to remain anonymous, was crucial in enabling women to "feel secure when their offline realities are not."[32] Meem, a Lebanese lesbian organization built online because it could not safely exist offline, put a premium on confidentiality among their members: "We trust you to maintain the privacy of Meem and all its members if you join the group. We are very strict about this. Meem is not a lesbian or trans zoo. We do not exist to provide you with a display of women of different sexualities or persons of a variety of genders for your university project or TV program or sexual fantasies."[33] Returning to Latin America, one study shared that "insiders" allied with research initiatives on sexuality and the internet could not convince the moderators of a Brazilian lesbian online space to respond to their queries, revealing the "particular (and gendered) concerns that lesbians might have over online interaction and community building, and the strategies necessary to maintain the safety of their spaces."[34] This desire to protect members' privacy may seem difficult to implement, given the general problems with maintaining privacy online. But even if aspirational, these policies attest to counterpublic organizations' desire to incorporate internet affordances based on their own priorities: to establish a space for their community that is not on display for curious or prurient outsiders.

As they had with RIMA, the moderators of Safo Piensa's distribution list attempted to transform this element of the logical layer into what its members wanted, in this case a safe and private space for meaningful discussion. They responded to some subscribers' anger at being "observed" by other subscribers who "wouldn't show their 'faces'" (i.e., never wrote in, only read) by instituting a more inquisitive registration process.[35] They asked potential subscribers to provide their names; how they heard about the list; why they wanted to subscribe to a list of lesbian feminists; how they self-identified; what they thought the list would offer them—or what they could offer the list; and whether they were interested in face-to-face meetings. Through this process, Ocampo and De Cicco sought to infuse their online community with some of the relations and responsibility offline communities can more easily provide.

However, like those offline communities, Safo Piensa encountered difficulties managing discussion around controversial issues. By 2006, the list fell apart over the intense, region-wide debates about whether to accept transwomen as part of the community or insist on a woman-born-woman lesbian feminist identity. One founder explained that, rather than this event destroying the community, much of it moved over to RIMA, migrating their issues and voices into this overlapping counterpublic.[36] Where, to be sure, debates continued apace, over things such as whether or not to use the term *dyke* during marches protesting the assassination of Natalia Gaitán. But in this case, entering into a wider community was a benefit, as RIMA's larger, more diverse membership and a wider focus could more robustly withstand polemics.

With the expansion of applications, there has been considerable shifting among platforms. Discussion lists, guest books, and websites have disappeared. At the same time, Um *Outro* Olhar and Rompiendo el Silencio, now based on blog technology, include Twitter, Facebook, and video accounts. While these do not provide the same kind of private exchange hidden in a discussion list or behind a personal ad, the spread of smart phones no doubt has enabled many to move their more intimate exchanges into even more intimate spaces. And newer media also offer counterpublic organizations other opportunities for visibility in wider publics.

MOVING TOWARD LESBIAN VISIBILITY

In the mid-2000s, websites were a window of visibility into lesbian life, as they presented material to publicly build community and display lesbian existence and demands to wider publics. Across the different sites, the ever-present double women's symbols—rainbow hued, golden, rotating—and erotic stories and pictures invoked a common identity daring to speak its name. The websites' full names evoked this identity: "An *Other* Look"; "Sappho Thinks: Network of Lesbian Feminists"; "Breaking the Silence: Lesbian Online Magazine"; "LeS(bian) VOICE: Lesbian Feminist Culture"; and "Lesbian Feminist Activists Group." Distinct kinds of information—political, social, even artistic—promoted community. News about LGBT politics reminded lesbians that they face common problems along with other GBT people and offered ways to get involved; scholarly articles enabled deeper reflection on what it meant to be a lesbian; and interviews, reviews, and artistic presentations reflected other facets of lesbian life. These images and ideas were available to women far from cosmopolitan centers, an opportunity almost unimaginable prior to the internet.

Building on their identity development, activists demanding gender or sexual citizenship, where they can participate in wider publics without denying their nonnormative sexual or gender identity,[37] have used the internet to formulate and then speak their truths to a broad audience. Online, communities can articulate and negotiate "public issues that are barred, tabooed, restricted, or subject to regulation offline."[38] In the Global South, queer counterpublics have been eager to appropriate the internet given the problems accessing offline spaces. In India, the queer community first "appropriated" ideas from North America and Europe that were disseminated online, then turned to the challenges of their own organizing. That organizing was facilitated by the internet because of the real obstacles for offline organizing, "at a time when offline or real contact between Indian queers for nonsexual purposes was deemed largely unimaginable."[39] In China, state repression of LGBT organizing has made digital counterpublics "the most significant venue for the gay"; where they have "dramatically extend[ed] traditional queer public spaces."[40] In Lebanon, "the current visibility and dynamism of its queer activism was directly attributed to the emergence and availability of the internet in the country."[41] The imbrication of technology and activism there was indicated by the fact that the registration of "GayLebanon.com" was seen as "one of the manifestations of the beginning of an organised LGBT movement."[42] Similar to India and China, the lack of physical spaces for encounter led to heavy use of the web, including mailing lists and websites.

While Latin American queer communities do not experience repression at the levels found in many other southern regions, the inexpensive online platforms for expression and exchange comparatively free from censorship address ongoing problems with counterpublic spaces for organizing and visibility. But they do not guarantee sustainability, as the three examples below illustrate.

When the members of the Peruvian organization Grupo de Activistas Lesbianas Feministas (GALF) launched their website, which featured an electronic journal and a database of articles, they continued in the tradition of promoting regional, if not global, alternative media for counterpublic construction. According to the first issue of their electronic journal *La Revista Labia* from 2001, they wanted "to reach the greatest number of lesbians, whether already organized or not, of the Americas region and, if it is possible lesbians of the whole world." They sought a high level of interaction for their ambitious plans of counterpublic communication and impact: "to communicate, discuss and develop regional/ global strategies that contribute to raising consciousness with respect to the interrelation and universality of the diverse forms of discrimination and intolerance and that advocate for the recognition of the rights of lesbians as components of human rights."[43] Their regional projection was reinforced by their hyperlinked resources, which included Peruvian and other Latin America groups, as well as those from Spain and Puerto Rico. Although the majority of the links were to lesbian organizations, there were many others focused more generally on the LGBT community, as well as some progressive and human rights organizations. GALF believed that the internet would be a conduit for convincing wider publics that lesbian rights were human rights.

Besides distributing their own publication, GALF's major contribution to lesbian visibility included an impressive virtual documentation center. Their full-text database offered a plethora of analytic and provocative articles from Latin America and elsewhere, when needed in Spanish translation. In a context in which lesbian feminist theory and related writing is difficult to find, this free library of Spanish resources held extraordinary potential for the community of readers, whether members of lesbian feminist counterpublics or not. The website built on GALF's more than twenty years of political and social activism in Peru—its founders were the first in the country to speak publically about lesbian feminism—to offer a regional resource for reflection on the lesbian condition. But with the demise of GALF as an organization in 2007, the website, along with all of its valuable materials, disappeared. Integrating the internet into their organization did not solve the entrenched problem of sustainable spaces for counterpublic work.

Other lesbian feminist organizations offer other approaches to approximating sustainability through internet applications. In Mexico, the LeSVOZ website and magazine have lasted through technological shifts by combining old and new media. In 2002, founder Mariana Pérez Ocaña explained that the website and distribution list, at that point with nine hundred subscribers, offered a wider reach than the relatively small print run of the magazine. While it was hard to convince magazine stands to carry the LeSVOZ magazine and many lesbians could not afford a subscription, the website had a very different life. Through it, far more people heard about them, because it was easily accessible: "It's a communications media that everyone can access, that is very economical, whereas other media are very expensive, or even blocked. [And] it's always there!" This was a wonderful development for an organization dedicated to making lesbian lives visible. For them, "it's magnificent, and we can put whatever we want."[44] Ocaña had found the internet to be an effective extension of the alternative media goals of her organization. But, as GALF's experience above illustrates, the "always there" website had to be actively maintained. Ocaña and her volunteer staff sustained their online resources, even through the complexities of the social media transition. In 2010 she explained that, through "a lot more work," they managed keep up with the learning curve on new technologies like a blog platform for their website and a Facebook page without leaving behind email communication.[45] And at the center of their mission, they maintained their print magazine.

FIGURE 18. "History does not write itself . . . we write it ourselves." LeSVOZ banner with pictures of magazine covers. Reproduced by permission of Mariana Pérez Ocaña, designer.

I was surprised to see the unflagging commitment, throughout this period of rapid cycling through internet applications, to producing a print magazine; while visiting in 2010 I was introduced to the machine used for handmade assembly. Ocaña explained that a lot of their readers still did not have their own computers, and would have to go to a cybercafé to read *LeSVOZ* if it were only available online—an option that might compromise their privacy or safety, depending on who was sitting next to them. But the physical copy had other advantages: "If the magazine's in print they can go to a store and buy it, and have it in their house, or under their mattress."[46] Given the realities of Mexican lesbians' existence, the digital counterpublic has had a paper trail.

LeSVOZ's offline life notwithstanding, the growing inseparability of the internet and lesbian feminist counterpublics was made clear to me when I revisited organizations in 2010 and beyond. In 2013, I spoke with Alejandra Novoa, who had helped to establish the "Lesbian March" that, every two years, brings thousands of women to wind their way, loud, proud, and purple-clad, through the historical center of Mexico City. As a documentary filmmaker, she was unhappy that so few of the March documentaries were on the constantly reformulated website. "The webpage is always new! Why?" she exclaimed. "It could have all the work from the beginning, it could have the videos. It's not fleeting, disposable like 'Face.' It's like an archive. It can be maintained, like a virtual library . . . the page could have everything stored! But that rich history is lost!"[47] Her unhappiness about this missed opportunity for a more permanent website demonstrated how seriously she took the digital space. The web offered something lesbian feminists long sought: a place that, unlike so many of its physical counterparts, did not have to be fleeting but could be maintained, could offer their stories to newer generations, could strengthen community efforts and display them to anyone, to the world. Migration to Facebook ("Face") was not the answer for Novoa: not all platforms were equally useful for her lesbian feminist ends, even as they were thwarted.

Her call has been answered in another country. Potencia Tortillera (Dyke Power), a digital archive of lesbian activism in Argentina, instantiates the desire for a more permanent space of national lesbian visibility, in its vast diversity. The organizers wanted to show lesbians' history, since it "does not figure in books and magazines adequately or directly is not recorded."[48] Invisibility is not limited to the larger public, but sometimes happens within overlapping counterpublics; Safo Piensa founder Ocampo reflected that "when we're together, all the dykes together, we say: we do the work for the feminists and we are invisible! We go there, we shout in the march, we paint the signs—OK. [On Potencia Tortillera] we can show that we do, and we did, a lot. For ourselves."[49] Potencia Tortillera demonstrates the power of dykes to creatively repurpose the logical layer of a blog application to make their history known.

The blog was started by five lesbian feminist activists from different Argentine provinces who were well aware of the difficulties of finding time and space for real-time encounters, above all those that included the diverse members of their counterpublic. But, as with RIMA, they were motivated by face-to-face counterpublic opportunities, particularly those that brought together younger activists from across the country. At one such meeting, in the lesbian cultural space Casa Brandon in Buenos Aires, they heard an inspiring presentation by a Spanish activist and author. She realized the importance of writing a Spanish lesbian history when an older activist entrusted her with a suitcase full of ephemeral documents. This resonated loudly for the Argentine groups, one of which had tragically lost its own archives in a shipping mishap. The five founders of the blog—RIMA coordinator Gabriela Adelstein, valeria flores, Canela Gabrila, María Luisa Peralta, and Fabi Tron—decided to explore how new technology could preserve old documents and current contributions.

Their project is not only meant to make lesbian history visible to those outside of the community; it is also intended to create "collective memory" within the counterpublic, with a focus on younger generations. It is a resource for individuals making their "own story," as the founders explain: "This archive socializes documents and memories of the diversity of the movement, so that each person might make her own story and construct her own personal and political history." Its display of dyke history is also intended to support organizing. Instead of feeling as if they have to start from zero again and again, activists "can turn [to the materials], to take them, leave them, complicate them, but [know what was] tried already by other lesbians." This piece of the logical layer socializes knowledge through sharing content.

Attempting to represent the range of Argentine lesbian organizing and cultural production, the founders have been sweeping in their archival acquisition. Among them, they started with quite a cache, which was quickly augmented by donations from throughout Argentina and materials they found online. Given the weight of Buenos Aires in most counterpublic spaces, they focused on the visibility of groups outside of the capital, and those that were dependent on their own labor rather than state or other funding. According to Adelstein, "This is a space for groups which otherwise will get lost." But whatever their perspectives and size, lesbian feminist organizations have a place to be seen. Adelstein contended: "We're not choosing or taking sides. Also we're not giving our opinions—this is an archive. Like when you go to a library, there are all these books and you have to make a decision about what's good and what's bad."[50] The archive's contribution to the counterpublic is to make as much lesbian activism as possible visible.

Although blog technology is designed to highlight new "logs" or entries, as well as be a place for interactivity through a comments function, the founders of Potencia Tortillera translated this application into one that would suit their needs for the historical record of a diverse community. They set the blog's date range to go all the way back to the 1970s, at the inception of lesbian feminist activism. They post archival materials in the year they were created, assembling text, graphics, photography, video, and audio from different generations, geographical locations, and political positions. And the archive displays the span of lesbian activism. For example, in November 2014, pictures from Pride marches taking place across the country, several of which commemorated Natalia "Pepa" Gaitán, the lesbian murdered by her lover's step-father in 2009, made their actions, and their mourning, visible to all who cared to look. This interpretation has transformed an application designed for tracking and talking about recent ideas or impressions into one that reflects the depth of counterpublic history and activism.

Unlike the repurposing of internet applications to enhance counter-public privacy, this archive trades privacy for visibility. Adelstein justi-fied that lesbians' appearance on the blog isn't a danger to them because "everybody here is public."[51] The isolated example she could think of when someone objected to her name being associated with one of the groups was easily addressed by removing that name from the descrip-tion. For the most part, groups seeking to exhibit their activism have been eager to be included.

Potencia Tortillera addressed the long-standing problem of resource restrictions in lesbian feminist communities—and the kinds of conflict generated by the search for and use of external support. The blog found-ers deliberately chose not to seek external funding. Instead, volunteers carry out the archival blogging. Adelstein sees that to be a fundamental reason the project has worked as well as it has, with little in-fighting, "because there was no money" about which to come into conflict. The posting of archival material gathered from many activists to a blog by volunteers made this possible: "The material is donated, blogger is free, and the time and dedication is activism!"[52] As long as that activism continues, Argentine lesbian feminist history has a home online.[53]

CONCLUSION

Argentine lesbian feminist activist and Potencia Tortillera cofounder Fabi Tron explained that, through online spaces, "the idea is to try to construct another imaginary, in which gay, lesbian, travesti people would not be seen as monsters, but more as other ways of being peo-ple."[54] Like feminists, lesbians and other queer activists have interpreted the internet into their own vernacular, through their own imaginaries, as a space where they can be who they decide they are. This is a means through which they can write their histories and distribute their current realities—not because of the inherent properties of the technology, but because of how activists have transformed it reflect their desire(s).

Latin American lesbian feminists have integrated the internet into their counterpublics to enhance both their private and visible lives. Confronted by a world in which they cannot count on social acceptance or legal recognition, lesbians need places for personal and political interaction and from which they can engage wider publics. Lesbians who have experienced isolation because of their sexual identity learn more about their identities and find each other online. Websites, blogs, and Facebook offer inexpensive platforms for socializing and activism, and all have been used to distribute sources of alternative information, crucial for communities ignored or criticized in the mass media. Most strikingly, lesbian feminists in Argentina have brought their history into the light by redirecting the purpose of blog technology to underwrite their own archive.

Yet, although internet access is cheaper than the rent for a physical meeting space, digital spaces can be similarly precarious. They are dependent on the dynamics of organizations, funding options, and the ever-shifting landscape of technological possibility. As with feminist counterpublic organizations, here again politics determines the feasibility of those possibilities. For lesbians online, representing their own desire is a work of permanent construction.

As they have attempted to both meet private needs and offer public interventions, lesbian feminist counterpublic organizations blur the line between private and public life, as well as on- and offline life. Communications theorist Zizi Papacharissi argues that all individuals under advanced capitalism rely on the internet to "constantly and personally" redraw the boundaries between private and public. They establish the "private public": "an interactive form of communication that enables attentiveness and responsibility toward other participants in a shared *social* space, understanding by the emphasis on *social* that such spaces do not reduce to the conventionally physical spaces within which bodies move."[55] Given their history of ostracism and the (often literal) policing of their intimate lives, lesbian feminists are past masters at creating "social space." Through their insistence on telling their stories of love (and lust), they have constantly transgressed the public/private boundaries established in part to normalize private life as heterosexual and nuclear-family based, and to restrict public life as the province of patriarchs. It is no wonder, thus, that lesbian feminist online interaction has magnified the transgressive propensity of this community. Through the internet, they have created a social space where they can engage attentively with each other, display their past, and debate their future.

Conclusion

Making the Internet Make Sense

In 2014, the communications team of the thirteenth Latin American and Caribbean Feminist Encuentro incorporated a range of internet applications to expand and amplify a flourishing regional counterpublic. The website boasted a history section, podcasts, and reports from the meeting in addition to basic orientation materials such as the meeting location and program. Organizers also relied on Facebook and made an effort to raise conference funding through the Indiegogo fundraising site.[1] Through these applications, even those unable to attend the Encuentro in Lima, Peru could refresh their memories of past meetings, follow current debates, and offer support. Given the central argument of this book—that the internet gains its relevance through the way people use it in their own contexts—the Encuentros illustrate how communities on the front lines of social transformation have interpreted the internet.

As with every meeting since 1981, the 2014 Encuentro facilitated learning, debate, and solidarity among the participants, but the website significantly extended its resources. There, readers could pore over a meeting program that offered opportunities to discuss "communitarian," "intercultural," and "decolonial" feminisms. Due to the saliency of ethnic identity in Peru, its intersections with gender reflected national concerns, but were also compelling to others across the multiethnic region. Website viewers could also follow conference deliberations over the full incorporation of transgender people. Although transgender women have openly taken part in Encuentros for nearly a decade, transmasculine participants in 2014 questioned the gender binary the Encuentros uphold, since the conference welcomes only those who identify as women. Informing and mobilizing feminist sympathizers about the region's most pressing issues, meeting organizers also posted the final demands from the four days of discussion: liberty for the seventeen women imprisoned under El Salvador's total abortion ban; justice for the forty-three students murdered in Ayotzinapa, Mexico, in September 2014; an end to governmental complicity with feminicide and the abuse of human rights defenders; and respect for the rights and movements of sex workers, migrant women, women with disabilities, and indigenous women. Nearly fifteen hundred women attended the Encuentro in 2014, but anyone with internet access could continue to read, view, and even listen to the contestations and consensus of the Encuentro long after the conference had ended. A feminist politics of communication translated the internet into a platform for a connected regional counterpublic, broadening and deepening access beyond those who could be physically present.

Of course, the internet did not launch this expectation for widespread access. Encuentro communications committees have always assumed that their responsibilities extended far beyond distributing registration forms and program details. The circulation of Encuentro documents, debates, and personal stories have fortified feminist identities and organizations across the region from the very beginning of the meetings. But with the internet, the numbers of people who can experience them nearly in real time, or access their conclusions for contemplation, is potentially limitless. Encuentro organizers took advantage of many internet applications to build on and expand their regional counterpublic.

Not all the methods aimed at broadening their audience and fortifying their counterpublic seemed to be effective. While the most recent communications strategy offered a range of resources for engaging with feminist ideas, many of them went unused. Few readers took advantage of the website articles' comment areas—aptly labeled "controversy"—to continue lively Encuentro discussions. Similarly, Facebook responses came mainly in the form of "likes," rather than commentary and replies. A mere 19 percent of the $15,000 Indiegogo goal was raised before the campaign closed. And a decade-old idea to organize an ongoing "Network of Encuentro Communication" and a website to replace the usually short-lived Encuentro page with "www.encuentrosfeministas.org" did not come to fruition.[2] Organizers had bigger hopes for their own communications innovations than their users proved willing to try. But those innovations did not include a communications infrastructure to serve the regional counterpublic going forward. Without a permanent network and website, the wonderful assets of the most recent one continue to depend on the labor, funds, and commitment of the most recent coordinating team, making the current efforts as potentially ephemeral as many web-based resources on which Latin American feminists rely—including past Encuentro websites, all of which seem to have disappeared. The internet offered no magic bullet for generating robust counterpublic discussions or a lasting archive.

Looked at another way, however, these limits to technological benefits make sense, at least for this counterpublic. Public websites and Facebook pages are not the most appropriate places to engage with controversies that can be difficult to manage even within the dynamic face-to-face opportunities of the Encuentros. The long-desired goal of Encuentro self-financing cannot be accomplished in a single cycle on an Indiegogo fundraising platform not yet available in Spanish and Portuguese, and distributed in a region in which donation-based organizational support is not typical. Finally, websites do not publish, update, or finance themselves. The much-delayed feat of ongoing communications coordination through a centralized website would be a difficult task for the unpaid Encuentro organizers. At a deeper level, any attempt to systematize information and communication that shifts according to the perspectives, goals, and abilities of each new coordinating team would have significant political implications. Sometimes intentionally—and sometimes by accident—the latest team and the many members of the regional counterpublic have interpreted the internet in ways that reflect the complexities of their regional reality.

Like the Encuentros, many of the feminist and queer organizations profiled in this book were already thriving before the internet. Since its inception, they have woven one application after another into their alternative media-fueled counterpublics. Despite ongoing struggles with inequality and resources, they have incorporated the internet in order to enhance each of the three elements of their counterpublics: developing members' identities, constructing community, and negotiating strategies to influence wider publics. But, perhaps even more remarkably, their engagement with the physical, content, and logical layers of the internet show how a diverse set of activists have interpreted the internet into their own vernacular, reorienting the technology to reflect their goals and values. This sociomaterial perspective again demonstrates that technology and society must be analyzed as an integrated whole.

In terms of their members' identities, counterpublic organizations have used the internet to expand who is included in their communities. Some, though by no means all, feminist and queer groups have directly confronted structural inequalities, using multiple media resources to improve inclusivity, creating, for example, chains of access so that Afro-Brazilian, indigenous, and poor urban women could also benefit from internet resources. Lesbian feminist websites nurtured lesbians' identity development through informative websites and internet applications for personal connection. With the inception of social media and its wider array of options, established groups have reached out to younger populations, and a new generation of leaders are finding their own ways online.

At the strategy level, feminist and queer groups have seized one digital option after another to develop ever-broader national and international campaigns. In Brazil, preexisting networks have improved their mobilizational reach, incorporating the energies and opinions of thousands of women across vast geographical distances to lobby national decision makers and have an impact on UN conferences. In Mexico, local activists have reached out for urgent transnational support to protect the human rights of indigenous peoples, while national organizations have built cyberactivist coalitions to defend reproductive rights against a tidal wave of conservative legislation.

Although both identity and strategy are key elements of any counterpublic, ultimately community building is the lynchpin. And that crucial component has also in many ways been improved with the integration of the internet. Community has to exist in order to encourage new members to join. And as organizations have circulated information, uploaded their videos and pictures, hosted personal ads, opened chatrooms, and moderated discussion lists, they have provided more opportunities to help members develop their identities, and more places where they can go to do so. Likewise, they have facilitated both the solidaristic exchanges and tension-filled debates that allow counterpublic members to grapple with the who, what, where, and how of their strategizing for social change.

But even widespread, low-cost applications cannot solve the continuing conundrum of how to manage the real labor behind the screens of counterpublic organizations. Free websites, email accounts, social media applications, and even free wifi are wonderful resources, but they still require people to design, write, send, moderate, and manage, quite often through unpaid and largely unnoticed work. As the trail of abandoned digital projects shows, community spaces are only as secure as the efforts behind them, regardless of which generation of applications is at issue. External funding is one potential solution, but, as always, it can exacerbate divisions between those whose missions have been recognized by outside audiences, and those who rely on volunteers. And when money runs out, the promising sites often go dark. The inequalities and dependencies that characterize counterpublics are also apparent in their digital dimensions. The transformative work of social justice counterpublics depends on many aspects of their information ecologies beyond the internet.

Despite these challenges, some of the organizations profiled in this book have not only used the internet to transform their counterpublics; they have also had an impact on the technology itself. This has happened at all three layers of the internet: physical, content, and logical. From the internet's inception, activists who formed the all-important keystone species extended the not-so-invisible physical anchors of the invisible web to ever-wider horizons. In the mid 1970s, U.S. women's rights supporters developed Hotline International, a computer-based transnational communications project focused on negotiations at the United Nations 1975 World Conference of the International Women's Year. Though limited in reach, it established the potential for "applying technology in a new way to enhance communications for global action," to quote its founders.[3] In the following decades, social justice-seekers helped to create and diffuse the internet as we know it today because of their commitment to widespread access. Establishing low-cost civil servers eventually affiliated with the Association for Progressive Communications (APC), they extended the technology to those with little social power. Despite state and commercial gatekeeping, progressive engineers managed to graft their values of global and decentralized participation into internet architecture and into our expectations for access, distribution, and citizen control. Building on this foundation, feminists in APC and many counterpublic organizations worked tirelessly to ensure that women would be included. The potential of the internet for enhancing counterpublic communications and collaboration depends on such deliberate appropriation. However imperfectly, members of the keystone species made sure that this new technology included space for work and ideas that existed outside the commercial and political mainstream.

At the physical layer, counterpublic constructors have taken on the digital divide mapping over deep-seated inequalities such as race, ethnicity, class, and geography. They are not alone here: many are the projects to address the obvious exclusions of physical access. Setting up telecenters in low-income urban areas; giving away laptops or smart phones to poor children and their families; or installing free wifi in rural community centers are presented as the most effective solutions. But these scenarios ignore the ways in which marginalized communities take part in chains of access. The organizations in this book demonstrate valiant efforts to "socialize the email," or deploy older forms of technology to extend the internet's reach, as Indeso Mujer, CIMAC, and so many other organizations have done. Projects focused on physical access alone also assume that technology in itself will somehow solve the problems of deeper structural inequalities. But, as Vilma Reis reminds us, "the technology in itself is nothing fantastic. Fantastic is you putting content in the use of technology."[4] It is not enough to address the physical issues with access without paying attention to what makes that access meaningful.

In many ways the content layer—what is transmitted across the physical layer—makes meaning. At the heart of the internet's capabilities are its transmission of communications and information, so much so that it is also known as the central element of "ICT," or "information and communication technology." The exchange and the information together enable the three parts of counterpublics. Women can learn more about feminism, discrimination, sexuality, and health by reading new sources, like the ones GALF produced and put online. Communities and campaigns are woven together by circulating such sources and trading opinions about them, as the multiple networks of reproductive rights campaigners in Mexico have done. As the most tangible element of what the internet offers, the content merits careful attention; it has undeniably helped to make counterpublics into places where more people can gain more insights.

Their work on the physical and content layers notwithstanding, Latin American feminist and queer counterpublics have offered their most original interpretations, their most dramatic transformations, of the internet at the logical layer. Two applications stand out: the older format of the distribution list, and the newer social media application of the blog. As profiled above, the Rimeras, led by their dedicated keystone species, transformed something that was designed for sharing information into a vibrant arena for all three elements of a counterpublic. Deliberately eschewing the divisive partisan fights of their national context, members have grown into their feminism; shared their experiences and activities in community; deeply debated; and strategized how to challenge injustice in Argentine society. Reflecting the yearly national feminist encounters that continue to inspire RIMA, the list is a place of struggle as well as sisterhood. RIMA's practices of integrating multiple perspectives have strengthened and developed feminisms in ways that enhance offline experiences. This is a space where a broad range of feminists, by following—and contesting—their moderators' rules of engagement, can inform and connect, debate and plan, whenever they choose to read and respond.

Like the Rimeras, feminists across Latin America have incorporated their values into a technology that many see as value-neutral, using it in feminist ways unforeseen by its origins. The Articulação de Mulheres Negras Brasileiras also used a list to bring together a counterpublic focused on making change at home and abroad, not so incidentally solving the enormous problem of how to coordinate communities with very limited resources or opportunities for face-to-face meetings. Again dependent on dedicated women who made up its keystone species, this list became a reference across the region and helped a counterpublic achieve its goal of external impact, in this case bringing the perspectives of black Brazilian women to the United Nations' World Conference on Racism. As it turns out, there was a reason why so many of my interviewees mentioned receiving so many lists. They have been the fiber with which organizations have woven their own version of the web: a place as diverse, widespread, and active as the regional counterpublic itself. This integration of feminist ideals at the logical level of the internet transformed a static technology into a dynamic network of users. And this dynamic network provided a significant innovation: through these lists, national, regional, and international counterpublics interacted and took action in ways inconceivable prior to the inception of the internet.

Counterpublic organizations have also made a more recent element of the logical layer, the blog, serve their own purposes. Designed to highlight the most recent information, idea, or image a blogger offers, blogs keep a chronology of posts that start with the first time the blog was used. They are also equipped with comment functions so that readers can interact with what they see. To use them as a place to showcase lesbian feminist history, however, the founders of Potencia Tortillera adapted the chronology function, establishing their own starting point—the first year of contemporary lesbian activism in Argentina. Each post then corresponded to an action, picture, or publication from a specific month and year going forward from that early date. Although the designers left the comments function active, they either did not intend it to be much used, or its users have not much bothered with it. But in either case, online interactivity was not the primary focus of this archival project. To attempt to provide a stable home for the varied resources demonstrating the length, depth, and diversity of activism, blog founders again modified typical blog practice. While most blog posts link to other elements on the web, the precious primary sources of this archive are uploaded from contributors' hard drives (or live in the cloud). This gives the archive as much stability as those spaces will allow, rather than relying on the often fleeting web. Lesbian feminists have interpreted the internet to advance lesbian visibility.

Latin American feminist and queer counterpublics have transformed the logical layer of the internet to suit their own ends. In a sense, they have hacked the internet's logic. But rather than hacking the computer code underneath this layer, they have hacked the intentions of these applications. They made distribution lists highly interactive and blogs into exhibitions. These were not inherently the right technologies for these communities, but activists disrupted them to shift toward what they needed.

In offering interpretations of internet engagement not only in different places, but also over time, this book refutes the idea that each new generation of internet applications—whether email, distribution lists, websites, or the exploding social media modalities—will transform who we are and what we do. Whether appropriating technology designed to please consumers and reworking it into technologies for social change, such as doing political outreach through Facebook or adapting blog technology as an archive of lesbian visibility, activists weigh internet options according to their own standards. As the work of Latin American feminist and queer activists illustrate, people shift technologies to reflect their dreams and desires, "embracing the skillful task of reconstituting the boundaries of daily life," to quote feminist science and technology studies scholar Donna Haraway. Even if counterpublic members do not count themselves among Haraway's famous feminist cyborgs, they do so "in partial connection with others, in communication with all [their] parts."[5] With consciousness and creativity, feminist and queer counterpublics have shown how to make the internet make sense.

Notes

INTRODUCTION

1. In this book I use the adjective *queer* and the acronym *LGBT*—which stands for lesbian, gay, bisexual, transgender—as synonyms, following increasingly common usage in the United States. Although they have different histories, both reference individuals and communities whose lives in some way challenge heterosexual, cisgender, and patriarchal norms. However, the communities I profile in Latin America use a range of terms to self-identify that are relevant in their own contexts.

2. Wilding and Hernándes, "Situating Cyberfeminisms," 22–23.

3. Carlos Alvarez (founder, Wamani), interview with the author, Buenos Aires, October 2012. Unless otherwise noted, all translations are by author.

4. Van Zoonen, "Gendering the Internet," 20.

5. Latham and Sassen, *Digital Formations.*

6. In Latin America, some women's organizations do not call themselves feminist, particularly if they are not directly focused on altering gender power relations. But because their work on women's behalf implicitly, if not explicitly, addresses gender inequality, and because it is cross-fertilized through activism with explicitly feminist organizations, I include them as part of feminist counterpublics. Whether or not self-defined as feminist, organizations of women often take part in multiple and often overlapping counterpublics.

7. Orlikowski and Scott, "Sociomateriality," 463.

8. Bennett, *Vibrant Matter;* Latour, *Science in Action.*

9. Plant, "The Future Looms"; Sampaio and Aragon, "'To Boldly Go'"; Puente, "From Cyberfeminism to Technofeminism."

10. Grossman, "Woman's Place."

11. E.g., Gurumurthy, *Gender and ICTs.*

12. Brophy, "Developing a Corporeal Cyberfeminism," 942.

13. Sundén, "What Happened to Difference in Cyberspace?" 226–27.

14. Many activists committed to regional exchange communicate with each other in *Portuñol*, a casual combination of Portuguese (*português*) and Spanish (*español*).

15. There are many excellent works on Latin American feminism and women's organizing. Just a sample of the English-language books include Alvarez, *Engendering Democracy in Brazil;* Baldez, *Why Women Protest;* González and Kampwirth, eds., *Radical Women in Latin America;* Jaquette, ed., *Feminist Agendas;* Maier and Lebon, eds., *Women's Activism;* Miller, *Latin American Women;* Molyneux, *Women's Movements;* and Thayer, *Making Transnational Feminism.*

16. Guzman Bouvard, *Revolutionizing Motherhood.*

17. Molyneux, *Women's Movements;* Smith and Padula, *Sex and Revolution.*

18. Mongrovejo, *Un amor que se atrevió a decir su nombre;* Babb, "Out in Nicaragua."

19. Fernández-Kelly, *For We Are Sold;* Bickham Mendez, *From the Revolution to the Maquiladoras.*

20. Schild, "New Subjects of Rights?"

21. Molyneux and Thompson, *CCT Programmes and Women's Empowerment.*

22. Miller, *Latin American Women.*

23. Saporta Sternbach et al., "Feminisms in Latin America."

24. Alvarez et al., "Encountering Latin American and Caribbean Feminisms," 548.

25. Monasterios, "Bolivian Women's Organizations in the MAS Era," 33–34; Alvarez et al., "Encountering Latin American and Caribbean Feminisms," 547; Schild, "New Subjects of Rights?"

26. Alvarez et al., "Encountering Latin American and Caribbean Feminisms," 539.

27. Corrales and Pecheny, eds., *Politics of Sexuality in Latin America.*

28. Mongrovejo, *Un amor que se atrevió a decir su nombre.*

29. Díez, *The Politics of Gay Marriage in Latin America.*

30. "Internet Users in the World," last modified November 2015, www.internetworldstats.com/stats.htm (accessed April 11, 2016).

31. Average is based on single or lower houses of parliament. "Women in National Parliaments: World Average," last modified February 1, 2016, www.ipu.org/wmn-e/world.htm (accessed April 11, 2016). Although the Nordic countries have a higher average at 41 percent, Europe as a whole comes in second to the Americas.

32. Friedman, "Re(gion)alizing Women's Human Rights."

33. Díez, *The Politics of Gay Marriage in Latin America;* Encarnación, *Out in the Periphery;* Friedman, "Constructing 'The Same Rights.'"

34. Habermas, *Structural Transformation.*

35. Saco, *Cybering Democracy,* 29.

36. Ibid., xx.

37. Hubertus Buchstein, as quoted in Dean, "Cybersalons and Civil Society," 246.

38. Shirkey, "Political Power of Social Media."

39. Palfrey, "Four Phases of Internet Regulation," 989.

40. Kidd, "Indymedia.org."

41. Castells, "Network Theory of Power."

42. Sundén, "What Happened to Difference in Cyberspace?" 225.

43. Daniels, "Race and Racism in Internet Studies," 708.

44. Ibid., 696.

45. Nakamura, *Digitizing Race.*

46. Ngai, *Made in China;* Charles Duhigg and David Barbozajan, "In China, Human Costs Are Built into an iPad," *New York Times,* January 25, 2012.

47. Fuchs, "Information and Communication Technologies and Society."

48. Kee, ed., *Erotics,* 13.

49. Corrêa et al., "Internet Regulation and Sexual Politics."

50. Jan Moolman (senior project coordinator, Association for Progressive Communications Women's Rights Programme), Skype interview with the author, August 2012.

51. Responding to the demands of a mobilized user base, Facebook began a process to accept users' chosen identities in late 2015.

52. Michelle Goldberg, "Feminist Writers Are So Besieged by Online Abuse That Some Have Begun to Retire," *Washington Post,* February 20, 2015.

53. "The Top Six Unforgettable Cyberbullying Cases Ever," last modified November 22, 2015, http://nobullying.com/six-unforgettable-cyber-bullying-cases (accessed February 23, 2016).

54. Fraser, "Rethinking the Public Sphere," 67.

55. Ibid.

56. Ibid., 68.

57. Rodríguez, *Citizens' Media against Armed Conflict,* 24.

58. Travers, "Parallel Subaltern Feminist Counterpublics in Cyberspace," 231.

59. Dahlberg, "The Internet, Deliberative Democracy, and Power," 56.

60. Jac sm Kee (manager, Association for Progressive Communications Women's Rights Programme), interview with the author, San Francisco, March 2015.

61. Dahlberg, "Internet Research Tracings."

62. Nardi and O'Day, "Information Ecologies."

63. Ibid.

64. Sassen and Latham, "Digital Formations," 26.

65. Marvin, *When Old Technologies Were New,* 4.

66. Blair, Gajjala, and Tulley, "The Webs We Weave," 17.

67. For example, Geert Lovink's "notion of virtual communities as actual social networks." *Dynamics of Critical Internet Culture,* 19.

68. International Telecommunication Union, "ICT—Free Statistics Home Page," www.itu.int/ITU-D/ict/statistics (accessed June 16, 2003).

69. The percentages add up to more than 100 percent because groups may receive funding from more than one source.

70. Benkler, *The Wealth of Networks,* 392.

71. John Schwartz, "Who Owns the Internet? You and i Do," *New York Times* Week in Review, December 29, 2002.

72. Tony Long, "It's Just the 'internet' Now," *Wired Magazine*, August 16, 2004, http://archive.wired.com/culture/lifestyle/news/2004/08/64596 (accessed July 9, 2016).

CHAPTER 1. CONCEIVING LATIN AMERICAN FEMINIST COUNTERPUBLICS

1. As quoted in Miller, *Latin American Women*, 44.
2. Ibid., 98.
3. Mitchell, "Women's (Community) Radio," 74.
4. Olcott, "Transnational Feminism," 264.
5. Seminar on Women and Culture in Latin America, "Toward a History," 178.
6. Greenberg, "Toward a History," 182.
7. Seminar on Women and Culture in Latin America, "Toward a History," 174.
8. Ibid., 175.
9. Miller, *Latin American Women*, 74.
10. Thayer, *Making Transnational Feminism*, 38.
11. Seminar on Women and Culture in Latin America, "Toward a History."
12. Ibid., 173.
13. Ibid., 175.
14. Hahner, *Empancipating the Female Sex*, 35.
15. Thayer, *Making Transnational Feminism*, 38.
16. Friedman, "Re(gion)alizing Women's," 357; Miller, *Latin American Women*, 95.
17. Thayer, *Making Transnational Feminism*, 41.
18. Greenberg "Toward a History," 182.
19. Miller, *Latin American Women*, 204–5.
20. Urrutia, "Una publicación feminista," 10.
21. Luciak, *After the Revolution*.
22. Biron, "Feminist Periodicals," 154, 162.
23. Olcott, "Empires of Information."
24. Miller, *Latin American Women*, 207.
25. Santa Cruz and Erazo, "La comunicación alternativa," 85.
26. Miller, *Latin American Women*, 207.
27. Ibid.
28. Mata, "Being Women."
29. Biron, "Feminist Periodicals," 162–63.
30. Grammático, "Feminismos en clave latinoamericana."
31. Hodgdon, "*Fem*," 96.
32. Fitch, *Side Dishes*, 68, 101.
33. Biron, "Feminist Periodicals," 155.
34. Hodgdon, "*Fem*," 102.
35. Ibid., 101.
36. As quoted in Grammático, "Feminismos en clave latinoamericana."

37. Santa Cruz, "Fempress," 51.

38. Saporta Sternbach et al., "Feminisms in Latin America," 430.

39. When I was a graduate student, my discovery of the brightly colored back issues of the magazine in my university library precipitated a plunge into the deep end of Latin American feminisms, as I avidly read about Venezuelan women's organizing, Argentine human rights, and Mexican lesbian activism.

40. Santa Cruz, "Fempress," 52.

41. Fraser, "Rethinking the Public Sphere," 67.

42. Santa Cruz, "Fempress," 54.

43. Ibid., 52.

44. Comunicación e Información de la Mujer, "Trayectoria institucional," www.cimac.org.mx (accessed June 3, 2014).

45. Santa Cruz and Erazo, "La comunicación alternativa."

46. Santa Cruz, "Se despide *mujer/Fempress.*"

47. Saporta Sternbach et al, "Feminisms in Latin America," 395.

48. Ibid., 417.

49. Stephen, *Women and Social Movements.*

50. Galvan, "El mundo etnico-racial."

51. Alvarez et al., "Encountering Latin American."

52. Gargallo, "El desencuentro."

53. Adames and Enciso, "El 9° Enceuntro Feminista."

54. León, "Encuentro latinoamericano"; Enciso, "Primer encuentro."

55. Thayer, *Making Transnational Feminism,* 51–52.

56. Gittler, "Mapping Women's Global," 92.

57. Ibid.

58. Winslow, *Women, Politics,* 144.

59. Walker, "The International Women's Tribune Centre," 91.

60. Ibid., 93.

61. Ibid., 94.

62. Kidd, "Talking the Walk," 184.

63. Portugal, "Isis International," 106.

64. Boniol and Calma, as quoted in ibid., 105.

65. Ana Maria Portugal, as quoted in Grammàtico, "Feminismos en clave latinoamericana."

66. Portugal, "Isis International," 106.

67. Ibid.

68. Kidd, "Talking the Walk," 185.

69. Grammático, "Feminismos en clave latinoamericana."

70. Leet and Leet, "Hotline International Operation," June 25, 1975.

71. Leet, "Press Release: Pioneer Communication Project Launched," June 11, 1975, 2.

72. Clark, "Suggestions for Focal Points."n.d., 12.

73. Leet and Leet, "Hotline International Operation."

74. Although their work was sponsored by the North American Committee of NGOs Concerned with the Environment, the Spirit of Stockholm Foundation, and the Community Development Foundation, the Leets had to underwrite

much of the Hotline themselves, and often solicited participants' help in paying for the telephone time to connect computer terminals.

75. Leet, "The N.Y. Current Meeting Is Convened," June 25, 1975, 59; Leet and Leet, "On this historic occassion [*sic*] . . ." June 18, 1975, 27.

76. Clark, "Comments to Buffalo," n.d., 119.

77. Leet and Leet, "Hotline International Report," July 18, 1975.

78. Leet and Leet, "Guidelines for Focal Points," June 11, 1975, 10.

79. Mead, "Message from Margaret Mead," June 10, 1975, 6.

80. Hotline International Mexico Task Force," n.d.

81. Leet and Leet "Hasta Luego Memo," June 9, 1975.

82. Clark, "Message to Mrs. Helvi L. Sipila," June 16, 1975, 15.

83. Dobyns, Phyllis. "IWY Mexico City," June 25, 1975, 79.

84. "Statement from Senator Charles Percy," June 23, 1975, 48.

85. Millie and Glen Leet to Mildred Marcy, International Women's Year Director, July 9, 1975.

86. Clark, "Greetings from Worcester, Mass," 54.

87. As cited in Portugal, "Isis International," 107.

88. Olcott, "Empires of Information," 35.

89. "Press Release IWY Hotline International Women's Year Conferences," June 16, 1975, 7.

90. "Message from Mary Ann Krupsak," June 28, 1975, 73.

91. Olcott, "Transnational Feminism," 264.

92. Olcott, "Empires of Information," 35.

93. "Vancouver Focal Point Meeting of June 24th," June 24, 1975, 86.

94. Ibid.

95. "Statement from Senator Charles Percy," June 23, 1975, 48.

96. "The Senator Had a Packed House," June 23, 1975, 50.

CHAPTER 2. THE CREATION OF "A MODERN WEAVING MACHINE"

1. Beatriz Cavazos (founder and director, Modemmujer), interview with the author, Mexico City, June 2002; Erika Smith (staff member, Association for Progressive Communications Women's Networking Support Programme and LaNeta), interview with the author, Cuernavaca, May 2002.

2. Desai, *Gender and the Politics of Possibilities*, 81.

3. Crack, *Global Communication*, 157.

4. Wajcman, "Feminist Theories," 149.

5. León, Burch, and Tamayo, *Social Movements;* Warkentin, *Reshaping World Politics;* Dilevko, "The Working Life of Southern NGOs"; Norris, *Democratic Phoenix;* Saco, *Cybering Democracy.*

6. Hajnal, "Conclusion."

7. Willetts, "NGOs, Networking," 84.

8. Rosenzweig, "Wizards, Bureaucrats, Warriors," 1545.

9. Willetts, "NGOs, Networking," 97.

10. Ibid., 91.

11. Carvalho, "A trajetória da Internet no Brasil," 113.

12. Willetts, "NGOs, Networking," 111.

13. Sallin, *The Association for Progressive Communications*, 27.

14. I am grateful to César Coria of the Mexico City-based Colectivo de Hombres por Relaciones Igualitarias (Men's Collective for Egalitarian Relations) for suggesting this term during a 2002 interview. Although in English *civil server* gestures to *civil servant* as well as *civil society,* his words in Spanish, *servidor civil,* are much closer to *sociedad civil,* the term for civil society, than *functionario público,* the term for civil servant.

15. Sallin, *The Association for Progressive Communications*, 28.

16. Surman, "Economics of Community Networking," 570.

17. Willetts, "NGOs, Networking," 96.

18. Ibid.

19. Sallin, *The Association for Progressive Communications*, 26–27, 41, 47.

20. Ibid., 42.

21. Surman, "Economics of Community Networking," 571.

22. Sallin, *The Association for Progressive Communications*, 43, 61.

23. Willetts, "NGOs, Networking," 111.

24. Fico, *Ibase,* 59; information about AlterNex's founding is from Carvalho, "A trajetória da Internet no Brasil," 111–14.

25. Ibid., 114.

26. Sallin, *The Association for Progressive Communications*, 51–53.

27. Ibid.

28. "Programa LaNeta," www.laneta.apc.org/nuevaneta/QuienesSomos.htm (accessed June 3, 2004).

29. María Eugenia Chávez (communications coordinator, Salud Integral para la Mujer), interview with the author, Mexico City, June 16, 2002.

30. Annis, "Giving Voice to the Poor," 99.

31. Carlos Alvarez (founder, Wamani), interview with the author, Buenos Aires, October 2012.

32. Noemi Chiarotti, Mabel Gabarra, and Susana Moncalvillo (coordinators, Indeso Mujer [Instituto de Estudios Jurídico Sociales de la Mujer]), interview with the author, Rosario, September 2002.

33. Sandra Infurna (librarian, CEPIA: Cidadania, Estudo, Pesquisa, Informação e Ação), interview with author, August 2002.

34. Tania Robledo Banda (youth project coordinator, APIS—Fundación para la Equidad), interview with author, May 2002.

35. Sallin, *The Association for Progressive Communications*, 68.

36. Ibid., 71.

37. Willetts, "NGOs, Networking," 110.

38. First of May/People's Network, "Communiqué 23 de noviembre de 2011."

39. Ibid.

40. Willetts, "NGOs, Networking," 113.

41. Ibid.

42. Rosenzweig, "Wizards, Bureaucrats, Warriors," 1543; Kidd, "Indymedia.org."

43. "About APC," Association for Progressive Communications website, www.apc.org/en/about (accessed March 29, 2015).

44. Wajcman, *Technofeminism*, 7.

45. Wood, *Putting Beijing Online*, xi.

46. Banks, "APCWNSP: Pioneering Women's," 5.

47. Ibid., 4.

48. Gurumurthy, *Gender and ICTs*, 4–5.

49. Thayer, *Making Transnational Feminism*, 16.

50. Farwell, "Internet links Huairou."

51. Plou, "Latin America and the Carribean," 67.

52. Wood, *Putting Beijing Online*, 61.

53. Stienstra, "Gender, Women's Organizing" 206; Banks, "APCWNSP: Pioneering Women's," 26.

54. Banks, "APCWNSP: Pioneering Women's," 23.

55. Wood, *Putting Beijing Online*, 22.

56. Ibid., 25.

57. United Nations, "Platform for Action," 239 ff.

58. Ibid., 242 b, c.

59. Wood, *Putting Beijing Online*, xv.

60. Gittler, "Mapping Women's Global Communications," 94–95.

61. Wood, *Putting Beijing Online*, 45.

62. Willetts, "NGOs, networking," 93.

63. Plou, "Latin America and the Carribean," 69.

64. Ibid.

65. Banks, "APCWNSP: Pioneering Women's," 5.

66. Cavazos, interview with the author.

67. Plou, "Latin America and the Carribean," 71.

68. Ibid.

69. Walker, *Women's Communications Strategies*, 2.

70. Ibid., 2–3.

71. Association for Progressive Communications, *Progress Report, 2004–2008*, 32.

72. Smith, interview with the author.

73. Ibid.

74. "About the APC Women's Networking Support Programme," Association for Progressive Communications website, www.apcwomen.org/about_wnsp (accessed September 13, 2010).

75. Association for Progressive Communications, *Progress Report 2004–2008*, 42–43.

76. African Gender Institute, "In Conversation with . . . " 92.

77. Friedman, "Gendering the Agenda"; Friedman, "Women's Human Rights."

78. "16 Days of Activism against Gender-Based Violence Campaign," Rutgers University website, http://16dayscwgl.rutgers.edu (accessed January 19, 2016).

79. Smith, interview with the author.

80. Jac sm Kee (Manager, Association for Progressive Communications Women's Rights Programme), interview with the author, San Francisco, March 2015.

81. Kee, "Building a Feminist Internet."

82. Jan Moolman (project coordinator, Association for Progressive Communications Women's Rights Programme), Skype interview with the author, August 2012.

83. Erika Smith, "Telling stories has this amazing power . . . ," www.apc .org/es/blog/telling-stories-has-amazing-power, Association for Progressive Communciations website (accessed February 26, 2016).

84. See figure 11.

85. Kee, interview with the author.

86. Rosenzweig, "Wizards, Bureaucrats, Warriors," 1531.

87. León, Burch, and Tamayo, *Social Movements on the Net*, 7.

88. Diamond, "Liberation Technology."

CHAPTER 3. WEAVING THE "INVISIBLE WEB"

1. Maria de Pilar Delgado (general coordinator of Legal Area, Defensa Jurídica y Educación Para Mujeres S.C. Vereda Themis), interview with the author, Mexico City, August 2010.

2. Ibid.

3. Pudrovska and Ferree, "Global Activism in 'Virtual Space,'" 118.

4. Mariana Pérez Ocaña (founder, editorial and design director, LeSVOZ website and magazine), interview with the author, Mexico City, May 2002.

5. Barassi and Treré, "Does Web 3.0," 6.

6. Noemi Chiarotti, Mabel Gabarra, and Susana Moncalvillo (coordinators, Indeso Mujer), interview with the author, Rosario, September 2002.

7. International Telecommunication Union, "ICT—Free Statistics Home Page," International Telecommunications Union website, www.itu.int/ITU-D /ict/statistics (accessed June 16, 2003).

8. TeleGeography, *Global Internet Geography 2003*.

9. Gloria Carreaga Pérez (consultative council member, El Closet de Sor Juana and academic coordinator, Programa Universitario de Estudios de Género, Universidad Nacional Autónoma de México), interview with author, Mexico City, June 2002.

10. Lucia Javier and Jurema Werneck (coordinators, Criola), interview with the author, Rio de Janeiro, August 2002.

11. Estelizabel Bezerra de Souza (communications coordinator, Cunhã Coletiva Feminista), interview with the author, João Pessoa, September 2002.

12. Nimia Ana Apasa (secretary of law and land, Consejo De Organizaciones Aborígenes De Jujuy), interview with the author, Jujuy, October 2002.

13. Luciana Siqueira Peregrino (communications coordinator, Grupo Origem), interview with the author, Olinda, September 2002; Rosa Marinho (planning coordinator, Grupo de Apoio á Prevenção á Aids), interview with the author, San Salvador de Bahia, August 2002.

14. Javier and Werneck, interview with the author.

15. Chiarotti, Gabarra, and Moncalvillo, interview with the author.

16. Edelmira Diaz (coordinator, Proyecto Mujeres Campesinas y "Trama" Red de Técnicos de la Secretaría de Agricultura), telephone interview with the author, Buenos Aires, October 2001.

17. Elba Muler de Fidel (regional coordinator and National Project Committee president, Asociación Mujeres de Negocio y Profesionales—Argentina), interview with the author, Mendoza, October 2002.

18. Sara Llovera (general coordinator, CIMAC), interview with the author, Mexico City, May 2002.

19. Zildete Dos Santos Pereira (president, Mulheres do Alto das Pombas), interview with the author, San Salvador de Bahia, August 2002.

20. Siqueira Peregrino, interview with the author; Denise Arcoverde (executive coordinator, Grupo Origem), interview with the author, Olinda, September 2002.

21. Nilza Iraci (communications coordinator, Geledés), interview with the author, São Paulo, August 2002.

22. Vilma Reis (sociologist and black women's movement activist), interview with the author, San Salvador de Bahia, August 2002.

23. Perla Vázquez (general coordinator, Elige), interview with the author, Mexico City, August 2010.

24. Edurne Cardenas (coordinator, CLADEM-Argentina), interview with the author, Buenos Aires, June 2009.

25. "Internet Users in the World," last modified November 2013, Miniwatts Marketing Group website, www.internetworldstats.com/stats.htm (accessed December 1, 2013).

26. Cardenas, interview with the author.

27. Noemi Chiarotti (coordinator, Indeso Mujer), interview with the author, Rosario, Argentina, 2009.

28. Beatriz Cavazos (founder and director, Modemmujer), interview with the author, Mexico City, August 2010.

29. Ibid.

30. Mabel Bianco (founder and president, FEIM), interview with the author, Buenos Aires, June 2009.

31. Leticia Cuevas (senior staff member, Equidad de Genero: Ciudadania, Trabajo, y Familia; executive coordinator, Red por los Derechos Sexuales y Reproductivos), interview with the author, Mexico City, August 2010.

32. Mariana Rios (research associate for development and outreach, GIRE), interview with the author, Mexico City, August 2010.

33. Cuevas, interview with the author; Elsa Conde (staff member, Campaña Nacional por el Derecho a Decidir), interview with the author, Mexico City, August 2010.

34. Delgado, interview with the author.

35. Graciela Selaimen (coordinator, NUPEF), interview with the author, Rio de Janeiro, August 2002.

36. Vázquez, interview with the author.

37. Cristina Zurutuza (coordinator, CLADEM-Argentina), interview with the author, Buenos Aires, November 2001.

38. Norma Sanchís (president and founder, Asociación Lola Mora), interview with the author, Buenos Aires, November 2002.

39. José Aguilar (Coordinator, Red DemySex), interview with the author, Mexico City, June 2002.

40. Paula Viana (general coordinator, Curumim), interview with the author, Recife, September 2002.

41. Jacira Melo (founder, Communications Team, Rede Nacional Feminista da Saúde), interview with the author, São Paulo, August 2002.

42. Sonia Corrêa (cochair, Sexuality Policy Watch), interview with the author, Rio de Janeiro, June 2012.

43. Norma Sanchís, interview with the author.

44. Ximena Bedregal (founder, Creatividad Feminista website), interview with the author, Mexico City, May 2002.

45. Ximena Bedregal, "MUERE Creatividadfeminista.org, NACE MamaMetal.com," November 2, 2008, Mujeres en Red. El periódico feminista website, www.mujeresenred.net/spip.php?article1637 (accessed July 4, 2009).

46. Ibid.

47. Ibid.

48. This period came after a decade of unsustainable neoliberal economic reform, and was characterized by widespread unemployment and social and political upheaval, as half of the population, and 70 percent of all children, sank into poverty.

49. Alicia Soldevilla (general coordinator, Servicio a la Acción Popular de Cordoba), interview with the author, Cordoba, October 2002.

50. Adriana Rossi (president, Acción Sur), interview with the author, Rosario, September 2002.

51. Madres Lesbianas Feministas Autonomas (founders), interview with the author, Buenos Aires, October 2001.

52. Ximena Bedregal, interview with the author.

53. Chiarotti, Gabarra, and Moncalvillo, interview with the author.

54. Liliana Rainero (coordinator, Red Mujer y Hábitat de América Latina; women's studies group director, Centro de Intercambio y Servicios Cono Sur Argentina), interview with the author, Cordoba, October 2002.

55. Marisa Sanamatsu (independent website editor), interview with the author, São Paulo, August 2002.

56. Rainero, interview with the author.

57. Bezerra de Souza, interview with the author.

58. Regina Vargas (administrative coordinator, Themis Assessoria Jurídica e Estudos de Gênero), email interview with the author, August 2002.

59. Madres Lesbianas Feministas Autonomas, interview with the author.

60. Monique Altchul (founder and president, Fundación Mujeres en Igualdad), interview with the author, Buenos Aires, October 2001.

61. Claudia Anzorena, Alejandra Ciriza, and Josefina Brown (members, Las Juanas y Las Otras), interview with the author, Mendoza, October 2002.

62. Norma Sanchís (co-coordinator, Latin American Section of the Red Internacional de Género y Comercio), interview with the author, Buenos Aires, June 2009; Noemi Chiarotti, interview with the author.

63. Vázquez, interview with the author.

64. Taking the drug misoprostol to end a pregnancy has become a popular alternative to surgical abortion in Latin America, even in the few places where the latter is legal.

65. Ibid.

66. Cavazos, interview with the author.

67. Erika Smith (staff member, Association for Progressive Communications Women's Programme and LaNeta), interview with the author, Cuernavaca, August 2010.

68. Melo, interview with the author.

69. Ibid.

70. Ana Alice Alcântara and Cecilia Sardenberg, "Brazil: 'State Feminism' at Work," April 18, 2012, openDemocracy website, www.opendemocracy .net/5050/ana-alice-alc%C3%A2ntara-cecilia-sardenberg/brazil-state-feminism-at-work (accessed June 3, 2015).

71. Ibid.

72. Javier and Werneck, interview with the author.

73. Caldwell, "Advocating for Citizenship," 182.

74. Franklin, "Afro-Brazilian Women's," 110.

75. Ibid.

76. Eliane Borges (founder, Mulheres Negras: do Ombigo para o Mundo), interview with the author, Rio de Janeiro, July 2002.

77. Javier and Werneck, interview with the author.

78. Interview Lucila Beato (coordinator, economic and social research and international relations, Geledés), interview with the author, Rio de Janeiro, July 2002.

79. Iraci, interview with the author.

80. Borges, interview with the author.

81. Marta Figueroa (legal representative and coordinator of Public Policy and Legislation Project, Grupo de Mujeres de San Cristobal de las Casas), interview with the author, San Cristobal de las Casas, July 2002.

82. Crack, *Global Communication,* sec. 6.5; Martinez-Torres, "Civil Society."

83. Mary Martínez (president, Fundación Siglo 21), interview with the author, Jujuy, October 2002.

84. BAOBAB for Women's Human Rights, "Nigeria: Summary of Appeal."

85. Conde, interview with the author; Cuevas, interview with the author.

86. Ibid.

87. Lesley Ramírez (staff member, Campaña Nacional por el Derecho a Decidir), interview with the author, Mexico City, August 2010.

88. Conde, interview with the author.

89. Cuevas, interview with the author; Carlos Morales (electronic communications coordinator, Equidad de Género: Ciudadania, Trabajo, y Familia), interview with the author, Mexico City, August 2010.

90. MacArthur Foundation, "Focus Countries: Mexico," www.macfound .org/site/c.lkLXJ8MQKrH/b.981791/k.F6E8/International_Grantmaking__ Focus_Countries__Mexico.htm (accessed August 23, 2010).

91. Mariana Pérez Ocaña (founder, general director, and analyst programmer, LeSVOZ website and magazine), interview with the author, Mexico City, August 2010.

92. Brophy, "Developing a Corporeal Cyberfeminism," 942.

93. Lea Fletcher (founder and director, Feminaria Editora), interview with the author, Buenos Aires, October 2001.

CHAPTER 4. LA RED INFORMATIVA DE MUJERES
DE ARGENTINA

1. Plou, "Take Back the Tech."
2. Unless otherwise specified, the direct quotes in this chapter are from the RIMA list.
3. Brophy, "Developing a Corporeal Cyberfeminism," 935.
4. Ollivier et al., "Feminist Activists On-line."
5. Ibid., 455–56.
6. Ibid., 461.
7. Ibid., 462.
8. During this period, a military council ruled the country and undertook a massive counterinsurgency campaign that led to the torture, death, and disappearance of tens of thousands of people—students, faculty, human rights workers, laborers, clergy, professionals, party leaders, and grassroots activists—accused of subversion.
9. Alma and Lorenzo, *Mujeres que se encuentran,* 35–38.
10. Ibid., 85–86.
11. Ibid., 45.
12. Ibid., 44.
13. Ibid., 48.
14. Ibid., 186–87.
15. As quoted in ibid., 74.
16. Ibid., 73–75.
17. Ocampo and De Cicco, "RIMA: Una experiencia."
18. Alma and Lorenzo, *Mujeres que se encuentran,* 47–48, 195.
19. Irene Ocampo (founder, RIMA), interview with the author, Rosario, Argentina, 2012.
20. Ibid.
21. Lovink, *Dynamics of Critical Internet,* 15.
22. Ibid., 13.
23. Nardi and O'Day, "Information Ecologies."
24. Origins of RIMA are from Irene Ocampo and Gabby De Cicco (founders and coordinators, RIMA), interview with the author, Rosario, Argentina, 2002; and Ocampo and De Cicco, "RIMA: Una experiencia."
25. Ocampo, interview with the author, Rosario, Argentina, 2012.
26. Gabriela Adelstein (coordinator, RIMA), interview with the author, Buenos Aires, June 2012.
27. Ocampo, interview with the author, 2009.
28. Adelstein, interview with the author.
29. Personal communication via email.
30. Irene Ocampo (founder, RIMA), interview with the author, Rosario, Argentina, 2009.
31. *Coordis* is a Spanish-language abbreviation for "coordinators."

32. Supporters of Nestor Kirchner and Cristina Fernandez de Kirchner, the powerful husband and wife presidents in office from 2003 to 2015.

33. Adelstein, interview with the author.

34. Michael Heim, as quoted in Travers, "Parallel Subaltern," 226.

35. Ibid.

36. Ocampo and De Cicco, "RIMA: Una experiencia," 4.

37. Ocampo, interview with the author, Rosario, Argentina, 2012.

38. Julia Ardón (former member, RIMA), interview with the author, via email, August 2012.

39. Papacharissi, *Private Sphere,* 233.

40. Although abortion is generally illegal in Argentina, there are exceptions in the case of danger to the life or health of the pregnant woman, or if the pregnancy has resulted from the rape of a mentally disabled woman. Even in these cases, abortions are difficult to obtain.

41. Carbajal, "A sacar los volantes de prostitucion," *Página/12,* October 22, 2010, www.pagina12.com.ar/diario/sociedad/3–155486–2010–10–22.html (accessed July 31, 2015).

42. Carbajal, "Dar la cara por el aborto," *Página/12,* February 20, 2005, www.pagina12.com.ar/diario/sociedad/3–47532–2005–02–20.html (accessed July 31, 2015).

43. Ibid.

44. RIMA blog, http://mujeresabordo.blogspot.com (accessed July 19, 2016).

45. RIMA YouTube channel, www.youtube.com/user/mujeresabordo (accessed July 19, 2016).

46. RIMA—Red Informativa de Mujeres de Argentina Facebook page, www.facebook.com/groups/RIMAlista (accessed July 19, 2016).

47. This assessment is based on a seven-month review of the Facebook page, from January to August 2014.

48. Ibid.

49. Irene Ocampo, "Rima en primera persona," *Página/12 Rosario/12,* July 7, 2009, www.pagina12.com.ar/diario/suplementos/rosario/14–19240–2009–07–07.html (accessed June 16, 2015).

50. Noemi Chiarotti (coordinator, Indeso Mujer), interview with the author, Rosario, Argentina, 2009.

51. As quoted in Howe, *Intimate Activism,* 124–25.

CHAPTER 5. FROM PRIVACY TO LESBIAN VISIBILITY

1. Sardá, "Avances y retrocesos."

2. Warner, *Publics and Counterpublics,* 62.

3. Larry Gross, as quoted in Mitra and Gajjala, "Queer Blogging in Indian Digital Diasporas," 401.

4. Bhattacharjya and Ganesh, "Negotiating Intimacy and Harm," 88–89.

5. Jac sm Kee (manager, Association for Progressive Communications Women's Rights Programme), interview with the author, San Francisco, March 2015.

6. "LGBT Rights by Country or Territory," last modified July 18, 2016, https://en.wikipedia.org/wiki/LGBT_rights_by_country_or_territory (accessed July 19, 2016).

7. Latin America Public Opinion Project, "Support for Same Sex Marriage in Latin America, 2010," https://sites.google.com/site/samesexmarriagelatinamerica/chart (accessed March 29, 2015).

8. "IACHR Expresses Concern over Pervasiveness of Violence against LGBTI Persons and Lack of Data Collection by OAS Member States," Organization of American States press release, www.oas.org/en/iachr/media_center/PReleases/2014/153.asp (accessed March 29, 2014).

9. Wilkinson, "Who the Rainbow Tide Leaves Out."

10. Mongrovejo, *Un amor que se atrevió*, 63.

11. Brown, "'Con discriminación y represión no hay democracia'"; Mongrovejo, *Un amor que se atrevió*.

12. Green and Babb, "Introduction"; Corrales and Pecheny, eds., *Politics of Sexuality*.

13. Mongrovejo, *Un amor que se atrevió*, 340–44.

14. Jitsuya and Sevilla, "Lesbofobia y sexismo."

15. Mongrovejo, *Un amor que se atrevió*.

16. Ibid., 309; Jitsuya and Sevilla, "Lesbofobia y sexismo."

17. Mongrovejo, *Un amor que se atrevió*.

18. Stein, "Queers Anonymous," 183.

19. With regard to the phrase "interior of the country": the Spanish term *el interior* usually refers to any place outside of the dominant metropolitan centers or capital cities, whether or not those places are literally in countries' interior or in border areas.

20. Madres Lesbianas Feministas Autonomas (founders), interview with the author, Buenos Aires, October 2001.

21. Stein, "Queers Anonymous."

22. Prinsloo, McLean, and Moletsane, "The Internet and Sexual Identities," 139.

23. Heinz et al. "Under the Rainbow Flag," 109.

24. Ibid., 139.

25. "Diversidad sexual, diversidad de redes."

26. Ibid.

27. Martha Patricia Cuevas Armas (founder, Nueva Generación de Jóvenes Lesbianas), interview with the author, Mexico City, May 2002.

28. Mariana Pérez Ocaña (founder, editorial and design director, LeSVOZ website and magazine), interview with the author, Mexico City, May 2002.

29. Irene Ocampo and Gabby De Cicco (founders and coordinators, RIMA), interview with the author, Rosario, Argentina, 2002.

30. "Safo piensa/Lesbianas Feministas en Red," Safo piensa Lesbianas Feministas en Red en la web; RIMAweb, http://anterior.rimaweb.com.ar/safopiensa/index.html (accessed June 3, 2004).

31. Burke, "In Search of Lesbian Community."

32. Bhattacharjya and Ganesh, "Negotiating Intimacy and Harm," 89.

33. Moawad and Qiblaw, "Who's Afraid of the Big Bad Internet?" 111.

34. Kee, *Erotics,* 9.

35. Irene Ocampo and Gabby De Cicco, interview with the author.

36. Personal communication via email with Irene Ocampo, December 2, 2012.

37. Kee, *Erotics,* 7.

38. Corrêa et al., "Internet Regulation," 23.

39. Mitra and Gajjala, "Queer Blogging in Indian Digital Diasporas," 407.

40. Cao and Lu, "Preliminary Exploration of the Gay Movement," 845.

41. Kee, *Erotics,* 13.

42. Ibid.

43. This editorial circulated on the RIMA distribution list on April 18, 2001.

44. Pérez Ocaña, interview with the author, Mexico City, May 2002.

45. Mariana Pérez Ocaña (founder, general director, and analyst programmer, LeSVOZ website and magazine), interview with the author, Mexico City, August 2010.

46. Ibid.

47. Alejandra Novoa (founder and general director, Telemanita), interview with the author, Tepoztlan, Morelos, June 2013.

48. "Sobre este blog," Potencia Tortillera blog, http://potenciatortillera .blogspot.com (accessed July 20, 2016).

49. Irene Ocampo (founder, Safo Piensa and RIMA), interview with the author, Rosario, Argentina, 2009.

50. Gabriela Adelstein (coordinator, RIMA), interview with the author, Buenos Aires, June 2012.

51. Ibid.

52. Ibid.

53. In April, 2016, Potencia Tortillera successfully transitioned from its founders to new curators, eight activists from across Argentina.

54. Fabi Tron (lesbian feminist activist), interview with Red Nacional de Medios Alternativos, "A cinco años del lesbicidio de Natalia Pepa Gaitán," March 2015, www.rnma.org.ar/noticias/18-nacionales/2420-a-cinco-anos-del-lesbicidio-de-natalia-pepa-gaitan (accessed March 29, 2015).

55. Papacharissi, *Private Sphere,* 74.

CONCLUSION

1. See the 13 Encuentro Feminista website, www.13eflac.org; and Facebook page, www.facebook.com/13EFLACPERU/?fref = ts (accessed April 24, 2016).

2. Restrepo and Bustamante, *10 encuentros feministas,* 51

3. Leet, "Press Release: Pioneer Communication Project Launched—Hotline International," June 11, 1975, 2.

4. Vilma Reis (sociologist and black women's movement activist), interview with the author, San Salvador de Bahia, August 2002.

5. Haraway, "Manifesto for Cyborgs," 223.

Bibliography

Adames, Nita, and Rotmi Enciso. "El 9° Encuentro Feminista Latinoamericano y del Caribe: Resistencia activa frente a la globalización neoliberal." *fem* 27, no. 238 (2003): 18–22.

African Gender Institute. "In Conversation with Jennifer Radloff and Jan Moolman on Technology-Related Violence against Women." African Gender Institute website, *Feminist Africa*, 2014, http://agi.ac.za/sites/agi.ac.za/files/in_conversation_jennifer_radloff_with_jan_moolman.pdf (accessed February 22, 2016).

Alma, Amanda, and Paula Lorenzo. *Mujeres que se encuentran: Una recuperación histórica de los Encuentros Nacionales de Mujeres en Argentina (1986–2005)*. Buenos Aires: Feminaria Editora, 2009.

Alvarez, Sonia E. *Engendering Democracy in Brazil: Women's Movements in Transition Politics*. Princeton, NJ: Princeton University Press, 1990.

Alvarez, Sonia E., et al. "Encountering Latin American and Caribbean Feminisms." *Signs: Journal of Women in Culture and Society* 28, no 2 (2002): 537–80.

Annis, Sheldon. "Giving Voice to the Poor." *Foreign Policy*, no. 84 (Autumn 1991): 93–106.

Association for Progressive Communications. *APC Annual Report 2009*. Melville, South Africa: APC, 2009.

———. *Progress Report, 2004–2008*. Melville, South Africa: APC, 2009.

Babb, Florence E. "Out in Nicaragua: Local and Transnational Desires after the Revolution." *Cultural Anthropology* 18, no. 3 (2003): 304–28.

Baldez, Lisa. *Why Women Protest: Women's Movements in Chile*. Cambridge: Cambridge University Press, 2002.

Banks, Karen. "The APCWNSP: Pioneering Women's Electronic Networking." In *Networking for Change: The APCWNSP's First 8 Years, Women in Sync: A*

Toolkit for Electronic Networking, Part II. The Philippines: Association for Progressive Communications Women's Networking Support Programme, 2000. APC website, www.apcwomen.org/netsupport/sync/sync.html (accessed July 7, 2016).

BAOBAB for Women's Human Rights. "Nigeria: Summary of Appeal—Amina Lawal vs. the State USC FT/CRA/1/02, 2003." Women Living under Muslim Laws website, www.wluml.org/node/1025 (accessed July 31, 2016).

Barassi, Veronica, and Emiliano Treré. "Does Web 3.0 Come after Web 2.0? Deconstructing Theoretical Assumptions through Practice." *New Media and Society* (2012): 1–17. Sage Journals website, http://nms.sagepub.com/content /early/2012/06/12/1461444812445878 (accessed July 31, 2016).

Benkler, Yochai. *The Wealth of Networks: How Social Production Transforms Markets and Freedom.* New Haven, CT: Yale University Press, 2007.

Bennett, Jane. *Vibrant Matter: A Political Ecology of Things.* Durham, NC: Duke University Press, 2010.

Bhattacharjya, Manjima, and Maya Indira Ganesh. "Negotiating Intimacy and Harm: Female Internet Users in Mumbai." In *Erotics: Sex, Rights, and the Internet,* edited by Jac sm Kee, 66–108.Association for Progressive Communications, 2011. APC website, www.genderit.org/sites/default/upload/erotics_ finalresearch_apcwnsp.pdf#synthesis (accessed July 31, 2016).

Bickham Mendez, Jennifer. *From the Revolution to the Maquiladoras: Gender, Labor, and Globalization in Nicaragua.* Durham, NC: Duke University Press, 2005.

Biron, Rebecca. "Feminist Periodicals and Political Crisis in Mexico: Fem, Debate Feminista, and La Correa Feminista in the 1990s." *Feminist Studies* 22 (1996): 151–69.

Blair, Kristine, Radhika Gajjala, and Christine Tulley. "The Webs We Weave: Locating the Feminism in Cyberfeminism." In *Webbing Cyberfeminist Practice: Co'mmunities, Pedagogies, and Social Action,* edited by Kristine Blair, Radhika Gajjala, and Christine Tulley, 1–19. Cresskill, NJ: Hampton Press, 2008.

Brophy, Jessica. "Developing a Corporeal Cyberfeminism: Beyond Cyberutopia." *New Media and Society* 12, no. 6 (2010): 929–45.

Brown, Stephen. "'Con discriminación y represión no hay democracia': The Lesbian Gay Movement in Argentina." *Latin American Perspectives* 29, no. 2 (2002): 119–38.

Burke, Susan K. "In Search of Lesbian Community in an Electronic World," *CyberPsychology and Behavior* 3, no. 4 (2000): 591–604.

Caldwell, Kia Lilly. "Advocating for Citizenship and Social Justice: Black Women Activists in Brazil." In *Women's Activism in Latin America and the Caribbean: Engendering Social Justice, Democratizing Citizenship,* edited by Elizabeth Maier and Nathalie Lebon, 175–86. New Brunswick, NJ: Rutgers University Press, 2010.

Cao, Jin, and Xinlei Lu. "A Preliminary Exploration of the Gay Movement in Mainland China: Legacy, Transition, Opportunity, and the New Media." *Signs: Journal of Women in Culture and Society* 39, no. 4 (2014): 840–48.

Carvalho, Marcelo Sávio Revoredo Menezes de. "A trajetória da Internet no Brasil: Do surgimento das redes de computadores à instituição dos mecanismos de governança." M.Sc. diss., Universidade Federal do Rio de Janeiro, 2006. Net History website, www.nethistory.info/Resources/Internet-BR-Dissertacao-Mestrado-MSavio-v1.2.pdf (accessed July 31, 2016).

Castells, Manuel. "A Network Theory of Power." *International Journal of Communications* 5 (2011): 773–87.

Clark, Carl, "Comments to Buffalo." N.d. Folder "Hotline International" hookup to Mexico City / Millie Leet and Glen Leet ("Hotline International"), 119; National Commission on the Observance of International Women's Year (1975) (NCOIWY 1975); 1973–78, Records Relating to the UN IWY World Conference Mexico (IWY Records); Subject File H-M (SF H-M); Box 23; N3-220-78-6 (Box 2 E-5) (Box 23); National Archives and Records Administration (NARA); Record Group 220 (RG 220); Schlesinger Library, Radcliffe Institute, Harvard University, Cambridge, MA (SLR).

———. "Greetings from Worcester, Mass." "Hotline International," n.d., 54; NCOIWY 1975; IWY Records: SF H-M; Box 23; NARA; RG 220; SLR.

———. "Message to Mrs. Helvi L. Sipila." "Hotline International," June 16, 1975, 15; NCOIWY 1975; IWY Records: SF H-M; Box 23; NARA; RG 220; SLR.

———. "Suggestions for Focal Points." "Hotline International," n.d., 12; NCOIWY 1975; IWY Records: SF H-M; Box 23; NARA; RG 220; SLR.

Corrales, Javier, and Mario Pecheny, eds. *The Politics of Sexuality in Latin America: A Reader on Lesbian, Gay, Bisexual, and Transgender Rights.* Pittsburgh: University of Pittsburgh Press, 2010.

Corrêa, Sonia, et al. "Internet Regulation and Sexual Politics in Brazil." In *Erotics: Sex, Rights, and the Internet,* edited by Jac sm Kee, 19–66. Association for Progressive Communications, 2011. APC website, www.genderit.org/sites/default/upload/erotics_finalresearch_apcwnsp.pdf#synthesis (accessed July 31, 2016).

Crack, Angela. *Global Communication and Transnational Public Spheres.* New York: Palgrave MacMillan, 2008.

Dahlberg, Lincoln. "The Internet, Deliberative Democracy, and Power: Radicalizing the Public Sphere." *International Journal of Media and Cultural Politics* 3, no. 1 (2007): 47–64.

———. "Internet Research Tracings: Towards Non-Reductionist Methodology." *Journal of Computer-Mediated Communication,* 9, no. 3 (2004). Wiley Online Library, http://onlinelibrary.wiley.com/doi/10.1111/j.1083–6101.2004.tb00289.x/full (accessed July 31, 2016).

Daniels, Jesse. "Race and Racism in Internet Studies: A Review and Critique." *New Media and Society* 15, no. 5 (2012): 695–719.

Dean, Jodi. "Cybersalons and Civil Society: Rethinking the Public Sphere in Transnational Technoculture." *Public Culture* 13, no. 2 (2001): 243–65.

Desai, Manisha. *Gender and the Politics of Possibilities: Rethinking Globalization.* Lanham, MD: Rowman & Littlefield Publishers, 2009.

Diamond, Larry. "Liberation Technology." *Journal of Democracy* 21, no. 3 (2010): 69–83.

Díez, Jordi. *The Politics of Gay Marriage in Latin America. Argentina, Chile, and Mexico.* Cambridge: Cambridge University Press, 2015.

Dilevko, Juris. "The Working Life of Southern NGOs: Juggling the Promise of Information and Communications Technologies and the Perils of Relationships with International NGOs." In *Civil Society in the Information Age,* edited by Peter I. Hajnal, 67–94. Burlington, VT: Ashgate, 2002.

"Diversidad sexual, diversidad de redes: El impacto de la web 1.0 y 2.0 en la visibilidad de la comunidad homosexual chilena." MS in author's possession.

Dobyns, Phyllis, "IWY Mexico City." "Hotline International," June 25, 1975, 79; NCOIWY 1975; IWY Records: SF H-M; Box 23; NARA; RG 220; SLR.

Encarnación, Omar. *Out in the Periphery: Latin America's Gay Rights Revolution.* New York: Oxford University Press, 2016.

Enciso, Rotmi. "Primer encuentro latinoamericano y del caribe de mujeres negras." *fem* 16, no. 116 (1992): 27–28.

Farwell, Edie. "Internet Links Huairou to the World and Beyond." *Forum '95,* September 4, 1995, 6.

Fernández-Kelly, María Patricia. *For We are Sold, I and My People: Women and Industry in Mexico's Frontier.* Albany: State University of New York Press, 1983.

Fico, Carlos. *Ibase: Usina de Idéias e Cidadania.* Rio de Janeiro: Garamond, 1999.

First of May/People's Network. "Communiqué 23 de noviembre de 2011." Email message in author's possession, 2011.

Fitch, Melissa A. *Side Dishes: Latina American Women, Sex, and Cultural Production.* New Brunswick, NJ: Rutgers University Press, 2009.

Franklin, Jessica. "Afro-Brazilian Women's Identities and Activism: National and Transnational Discourses." In *Latin American Identities after 1980,* edited by Gordana Yovanovich and Amy Huras, 97–116. Waterloo, Ontario: Wilfrid Laurier University Press, 2010.

Fraser, Nancy. "Rethinking the Public Sphere: A Contribution to the Critique of Actually Existing Democracy." *Social Text* 25–26 (1990): 56–80.

Friedman, Elisabeth Jay. "Constructing 'The Same Rights with the Same Names': The Impact of Spanish Norm Diffusion on Marriage Equality in Argentina." *Latin American Politics and Society* 54, no. 4 (2012): 29–59.

———. "Gendering the Agenda: Women's Transnational Organizing at the UN Conferences of the 1990s." *Women's Studies International Forum* 26, no. 4 (2003): 313–31.

———. "Re(gion)alizing Women's Human Rights in Latin America." *Politics and Gender* 5, no. 30 (2009): 349–75.

———. "Women's Human Rights: The Emergence of a Movement." In *Women's Rights, Human Rights: International Feminist Perspectives,* edited by Julie Peters and Andrea Wolper, 18–35. New York: Routledge, 1995.

Fuchs, Christian. "Information and Communication Technologies and Society: A Contribution to the Critique of the Political Economy of the Internet." *European Journal of Communication* 24, no. 1 (2009): 69–87.

Galvan, Sergia. "El mundo etnico-racial dentro del feminismo Latinoamericano." *Fempress*, special issue, *La mujer negra* (1995): 34–36.

Gargallo, Francesca. "El desencuentro de los encuentros feministas." *fem* 17, no. 130 (1993): 37–38.

Gittler, Alice M. "Mapping Women's Global Communications and Networking." In *Women@Internet: Creating New Cultures in Cyberspace*, edited by Wendy Harcourt, 91–101. London: Zed Books; Society for International Development, 1999.

González, Victoria, and Karen Kampwirth, eds. *Radical Women in Latin America: Left and Right*. University Park: Penn State Press, 2001.

Grammático, Karin. "Feminismos en clave latinoamericana: un recorrido sobre Fem, Isis y Fempress." *Mora* (Buenos Aires) online, 17, no. 2 (2011), www.scielo.org.ar/scielo.php?script=sci_arttext&pid=S1853-001X20110002000 02&lng=es&nrm=iso (accessed July 31, 2016).

Green, James N., and Florence E. Babb. "Introduction." *Latin American Perspectives* 29, no. 123 (2002): 3–23.

Greenberg, Janet. "Toward a History of Women's Periodicals in Latin America: A Working Bibliography." In *Women, Culture, and Politics in Latin America*, Seminar on Feminism and Culture in Latin America, 182–231. Berkeley: University of California Press, 1990.

Grossman, Rachel. "Women's Place in the Integrated Circuit." *Radical America* 14, no. 1 (1980): 29–50.

Gurumurthy, Anita. *Gender and ICTs*. Overview, BRIDGE, University of Sussex, Brighton: Institute of Development Studies, 2004.

Guzman Bouvard, Marguerite. *Revolutionizing Motherhood: The Mothers of the Plaza de Mayo*. Lanham, MD: SR Books. 2004.

Habermas, Jürgen. *The Structural Transformation of the Public Sphere: An Inquiry into a Category of Bourgeois Society*. Translated by Thomas Burger, with the assistance of Frederick Lawrence. 1989. Repr., Cambridge: Polity Press, 2011.

Hahner, June. *Emancipating the Female Sex: The Struggle for Women's Rights in Brazil, 1850–1940*. Durham, NC: Duke University Press, 1990.

Hajnal, Peter I. "Conclusion." In *Civil Society in the Information Age*, edited by Peter I. Hajnal, 243–47. Burlington, VT: Ashgate, 2002.

Haraway, Donna. "A Manifesto for Cyborgs: Science, Technology, and Socialist Feminism in the 1980s." In *Feminism/Postmodernism*, edited by Linda Nicholson, 190–233. New York: Routledge, 1990.

Heinz, Bettina, et al. 2002. "Under the Rainbow Flag: Webbing Global Gay Identities." *International Journal of Sexuality and Gender Studies* 7, nos. 2–3 (2002): 107–24.

Hodgdon, Tim. 2000. "*Fem*: A Window onto the Cultural Coalescence of a Mexican Feminist Politics of Sexuality." *Mexican Studies/Estudios Mexicanos* 16, no. 1 (2000): 79–104.

"Hotline International Mexico Task Force." NCOIWY 1975; IWY Records: SF H-M; Box 23; NARA; RG 220; SLR.

Howe, Cymene. *Intimate Activism: The Struggle for Sexual Rights in Postrevolutionary Nicaragua*. Chapel Hill, NC: Duke University Press, 2013.

Jaquette, Jane, ed. *Feminist Agendas and Democracy in Latin America.* Durham, NC: Duke University Press, 2009.

Jitsuya, Nelly, and Rebecca Sevilla. "Lesbofobia y sexismo en el movimiento feminista y el movimiento homosexual." CenDoc LF: Centro de Documentacion Lesbico Feminista, 2004, www.galf.org/cendoc/pdf/JitsuyaSevilla-Movimientos.pdf (accessed June 3, 2006).

Kee, Jac sm. "Building a Feminist Internet." *Ignite: Women Fueling Science and Technology.* Ignite website, http://ignite.globalfundforwomen.org/gallery/building-feminist-internet (accessed March 29, 2015).

———, ed. *Erotics: Sex, Rights, and the Internet.* Association for Progressive Communications, 2011, APC website, www.genderit.org/sites/default/upload/erotics_finalresearch_apcwnsp.pdf#synthesis (accessed July 31, 2016).

Kidd, Dorothy. "Indymedia.org: A New Communications Commons." In *Cyberactivism: Online Activism in Theory and Practice,* edited by Martha McCaughey and Michael D. Ayers, 47–70. New York: Routledge, 2003.

———. "Talking the Walk: The Communication Commons amidst the Media Enclosures." PhD diss., Simon Frasier University, 1998.

Latham, Robert, and Sassen, Saskia, eds. *Digital Formations : IT and New Architectures in the Global Realm.* Princeton, NJ: Princeton University Press, 2005.

Latour, Bruno. *Science in Action: How to Follow Scientists and Engineers through Society.* Cambridge, MA: Harvard University Press, 1987.

Leet, Glen, and Mildred Robbins Leet. "Guidelines for Focal Points." "Hotline International," June 11, 1975, 10; NCOIWY 1975; IWY Records: SF H-M; Box 23; NARA; RG 220; SLR.

———. "Hasta Luego Memo." June 9, 1975; NCOIWY 1975; IWY Records: SF H-M; Box 23; NARA; RG 220; SLR.

———. "Hotline International Report on International Women's Year/Conference." July 18, 1975; NCOIWY 1975; IWY Records: SF H-M; Box 23; NARA; RG 220; SLR.

Leet, Mildred Robbins. "The N.Y. Current Meeting Is Convened." "Hotline International," June 25, 1975, 59; NCOIWY 1975; IWY Records: SF H-M; Box 23; NARA; RG 220; SLR.

———. "Press Release: Pioneer Communication Project Launched." "Hotline International," June 11, 1975, 2; NCOIWY 1975; IWY Records: SF H-M; Box 23; NARA; RG 220; SLR.

Leet, Mildred Robbins, and Glen Leet. "Hotline International Operation." "Hotline International," June 25, 1975; NCOIWY 1975; IWY Records: SF H-M; Box 23; NARA; RG 220; SLR.

———. "On this historic occassion [*sic*] . . . " "Hotline International," June 18, 1975, 27; NCOIWY 1975; IWY Records: SF H-M; Box 23; NARA; RG 220; SLR.

León, I. "Encuentro latinoamericano y del Caribe de lesbianas feministas. *fem* 16, no. 117 (1992): 33–34.

León, Osvaldo, Sally Burch, and Eduardo Tamayo. *Social Movements on the Net.* Quito, Ecuador: Agencia Latinoamericana de Información, 2001.

Lovink, Geert. *Dynamics of Critical Internet Culture*. Amsterdam: Institute of Network Cultures, 2009. Institute of Network Cultures website, http://networkcultures.org/blog/publication/no-01-dynamics-of-critical-internet-culture (accessed July 31, 2016).

Luciak, Ilja A. *After the Revolution: Gender and Democracy in El Salvador, Guatemala and Nicaragua*. Baltimore: Johns Hopkins University Press, 2001.

Maier, Elizabeth, and Nathalie Lebon, eds. *Women's Activism in Latin America and the Caribbean: Engendering Social Justice, Democratizing Citizenship*. New Brunswick, NJ: Rutgers University Press, 2010.

Martinez-Torres, Maria Elena. "Civil Society, the Internet, and the Zapatistas." *Peace Review* 13, no. 3 (2001): 347–55.

Marvin, Carolyn. *When Old Technologies Were New: Thinking about Electric Communication in the Late Nineteenth Century*. London: Oxford University Press, 1990.

Mata, Maria. "Being Women in Latin American Popular Radio." In *Women in Grassroots Communication: Furthering Social Change*, edited by Pilar Riaño, 192–211. Thousand Oaks, CA: Sage Publications, 1994.

Mead, Margaret, "Message from Margaret Mead." "Hotline International," June 10, 1975, 6; NCOIWY 1975; IWY Records: SF H-M; Box 23; NARA; RG 220; SLR.

"Message from Mary Ann Krupsak." "Hotline International," June 28, 1975, 73; NCOIWY 1975; IWY Records: SF H-M; Box 23; NARA; RG 220; SLR.

Miller, Francesca. *Latin American Women and the Search for Social Justice*. Hanover, NH: University Press of New England, 1991.

Millie and Glen Leet to Mildred Marcy, International Women's Year Director. "Hotline International," July 9, 1975; NCOIWY 1975; IWY Records: SF H-M; Box 23; NARA; RG 220; SLR.

Mitchell, Caroline. "Women's (Community) Radio as a Feminist Public Sphere." *The Public* 5, no. 2 (1998): 73–85. European Institute for Communication and Culture website, http://javnost-thepublic.org/article/1998/2/6 (accessed July 31, 2016).

Mitra, Rahul, and Radhika Gajjala. "Queer Blogging in Indian Digital Diasporas: A Dialogic Encounter." *Journal of Communication Inquiry* 32, no. 4 (2008): 400–423.

Moawad, Nadine, and Tamara Qiblaw. "Who's Afraid of the Big Bad Internet?" In *Erotics: Sex, Rights, and the Internet*, edited by Jac sm Kee, 109–34. Association for Progressive Communications, 2011. APC website, www.genderit.org/sites/default/upload/erotics_finalresearch_apcwnsp.pdf#synthesis (accessed July 31, 2016).

Molyneux, Maxine. *Women's Movements in International Perspective: Latin America and Beyond*. 2nd ed. London: Institute of Latin American Studies, 2003.

Molyneux, Maxine, and Marilyn Thompson. *CCT Programmes and Women's Empowerment in Peru, Bolivia and Ecuador*. CARE Policy Paper, 2011. CARE International website, http://insights.careinternational.org.uk/publications/cct-programmes-and-womens-empowerment-in-peru-bolivia-and-ecuador (accessed July 31, 2016).

Monasterios, Karin. "Bolivian Women's Organizations in the MAS Era." *NACLA Report on the Americas* 40 (2007): 33–37.

Mongrovejo, Norma. *Un amor que se atrevió a decir su nombre: La lucha de las lesbianas y su relacion con los movimientos homosexual y feminista en America Latina.* Mexico, D.F.: Plaza y Valdes Editores/CDHAL, 2000.

Nakamura, Lisa. *Digitizing Race: Visual Cultures of the Internet.* Minneapolis: University of Minnesota Press, 2007.

Nardi, Bonnie A., and Vicki L. O'Day. "Information Ecologies: Using Technology with Heart. Chapter 4: Information Ecologies." *First Monday* 4, no. 5 (1999). First Monday website, http://firstmonday.org/ojs/index.php/fm/article/view/672/582 (accessed July 14, 2016).

Ngai, Pun. *Made in China: Women Factory Workers in a Global Workplace.* Durham, NC: Duke University Press, 2005.

Norris, Pippa. *Democratic Phoenix: Reinventing Political Activism.* Cambridge: Cambridge University Press, 2003. Pippa Norris website, https://sites.google.com/site/pippanorris3/publications/books/democratic-phoenix (last accessed July 14, 2016).

Ocampo, Irene, and Gabriela De Cicco. "RIMA: Una experiencia de comunicacion feminsta alternative." Presented at Las Jornadas "Periodistas en red." Santiago de Chile, July 11 and 12, 2002. In author's possession.

Olcott, Jocelyn. "Empires of Information: Media Strategies for the 1975 International Women's Year." *Journal of Women's History* 24, no. 4 (2012): 24–48.

———. "Transnational Feminism: Event, Temporality, and Performance at the 1975 International Women's Year Conference." In *Cultures in Motion,* edited by Daniel T. Rodgers, Bhavani Raman, and Helmut Reimitz, 241–66. Princeton, NJ: Princeton University Press, 2013

Ollivier, Michèle, et al. "Feminist Activists On-line: A Study of the PARL-L Research Network." *Canadian Review of Sociology and Anthropology* 43, no. 4 (2002): 445–63.

Orlikowski, Wanda J., and Susan V. Scott. "Sociomateriality: Challenging the Separation of Technology, Work, and Organization." *Academy of Management Annals* 2, no. 1 (2008): 433–73.

Palfrey, John. "Four Phases of Internet Regulation." *Social Research* 77, no. 3 (2010): 981–96.

Papacharissi, Zizi. *A Private Sphere: Democracy in a Digital Age.* Cambridge: Polity Press, 2010.

Plant, Sadie. "The Future Looms: Weaving Women and Cybernetics." *Body and Society* 1, nos. 3–4 (1995): 45–64.

Plou, Dafne S. "Latin America and the Caribbean: Electronic Networking in the Women's Movement." In *Networking for Change: The APCWNSP's First 8 Years, Women in Sync; A Toolkit for Electronic Networking, Part III.* The Philippines: Association for Progressive Communications Women's Networking Support Programme, 2000. APC Website, www.apcwomen.org/netsupport/sync/sync.html (accessed July 31, 2016).

———. "Take Back the Tech! Q&A Session" Event at the Fifty-fifth Commission on the Status of Women, 2011. Vimeo website, http://vimeo.com/20637971 (accessed July 31, 2016).

Portugal, Ana Maria. "Isis International: A Latin American Perspective." In *Developing Power: How Women Transformed International Development*, edited by Arvonne S. Fraser and Irene Tinker, 103–14. New York: Feminist Press at CUNY, 2004.

"Press Release IWY Hotline International Women's Year Conferences." "Hotline International," June 16, 1975, 7; NCOIWY 1975; IWY Records: SF H-M; Box 23; NARA; RG 220; SLR.

Prinsloo, Jeanne, Nicolene C. McLean, and Relebohile Moletsane. "The Internet and Sexual Identities: Exploring Transgender and Lesbian Use of the Internet in South Africa." In *Erotics: Sex, Rights, and the Internet*, edited by Jac sm Kee, 135–75. Association for Progressive Communications, 2011. APC website, www.genderit.org/sites/default/upload/erotics_finalresearch_apcwnsp.pdf#synthesis (accessed July 31, 2016).

Pudrovska, Tetyana, and Myra Marx Ferree. "Global Activism in 'Virtual Space': The European Women's Lobby in the Network of Transnational Women's NGOs on the Web." *Social Politics* 11, no. 1 (2004): 117–43.

Puente, Sonia Núñez. "From Cyberfeminism to Technofeminism: From an Essentialist Perspective to Social Cyberfeminism in Certain Feminist Practices in Spain." *Women's Studies International Forum* 31, no. 6 (2008): 434–40.

Restrepo, Alejandra, and Ximena Bustamante. *10 encuentros feministas latinoamericanos y del caribe: Apuntes para una historia en movimiento*. Mexico, D.F.: Comité Impulsor XI Encuentro Feminista, 2009. Scribd website, www.scribd.com/doc/19627857/10-ENCUENTROS-FEMINISTAS#scribd (accessed July 31, 2016).

Rodríguez, Clemencia. *Citizens' Media against Armed Conflict: Disrupting Violence in Colombia*. Minneapolis: University of Minnesota Press, 2011.

Rosenzweig, Roy. "Wizards, Bureaucrats, Warriors, and Hackers: Writing the History of the Internet." *American Historical Review* 103, no. 5 (1998): 1530–52.

Saco, Diana. *Cybering Democracy: Public Space and the Internet*. Minneapolis: University of Minnesota Press, 2002.

Sallin, Susanne. *The Association for Progressive Communications: A Cooperative Effort to Meet the Information Needs of Non-Governmental Organizations*, 1–107. Consortium for International Earth Science Information, Harvard University. Cambridge, MA: Havard-CIESIN Project on Global Environmental Change Information Policy, 1994.

Sampaio, Anna, and Janni Aragon. "'To Boldly Go (Where No Man Has Gone Before)': Women and Politics in Cyberspace." *New Political Science* 41–42 (1997): 145–67.

Santa Cruz, Adriana. "Fempress: A Communication Strategy for Women." *Gender and Development* 3, no. 1 (1995): 51–55.

———. "Se despide *mujer/Fempress*," 2000. Cotidiano Mujer website, www.cotidianomujer.org.uy/sitio/index.php/cotidiano-mujer-no-34/100-los-20-anos-de-fempress (accessed March 29, 2015).

Santa Cruz, Adriana, and Viviana Erazo. "La comunicación alternativa de la mujer." *Ciencias Sociales* 25 (1983): 85–90.

Saporta Sternbach, Nancy, et al. "Feminisms in Latin America: From Bogotá to San Bernardo." *Signs: Journal of Women in Culture and Society* 17, no. 2 (1992): 393–434.

Sardá, Alejandra. "Avances y retrocesos en el reconocimiento de los derechos de lesbianas y mujeres bisexuals." *Cuadernos Mujer Salud* 5 (2002): 107–12. Red de Salud de las Mujeres Latinoamericanas y del Caribe website, www .reddesalud.org/espanol/datos/ftp/sarda.pdf (accessed June 3, 2006).

Sassen, Saskia, and Robert Latham. "Digital Formations: Constructing an Object of Study." In *Digital Formations : IT and New Architectures in the Global Realm*, edited by Robert Latham and Saskia Sassen, 1–34. Princeton, NJ: Princeton University Press, 2005.

Schild, Veronica. "New Subjects of Rights? Women's Movements and the Construction of Citizenship in the 'New Democracies.'" In *Cultures of Politics/Politics of Cultures: Latin American Social Movements Revisited*, edited by Sonia E. Alvarez, Evelina Dagnino, and Arturo Escobar, 93–117. Boulder, CO: Westview Press, 1997.

Seminar on Women and Culture in Latin America. "Toward a History of Women's Periodicals in Latin America." Introduction to *Women, Culture, and Politics in Latin America*, by Seminar on Feminism and Culture in Latin America, 173–81. Berkeley: University of California Press, 1990.

"The Senator Had a Packed House." "Hotline International," June 23, 1975, 50; NCOIWY 1975; IWY Records: SF H-M; Box 23; NARA; RG 220; SLR.

Shirkey, Clay. "The Political Power of Social Media: Technology, the Public Sphere, and Political Change." *Foreign Affairs* 90, no. 1 (2011). Foreign Affairs website, www.foreignaffairs.com/articles/2010-12-20/political-power-social-media (accessed July 31, 2016).

Smith, Lois M., and Alfred Padula. *Sex and Revolution: Women in Socialist Cuba.* New York: Oxford University Press, 1996.

"Statement from Senator Charles Percy." "Hotline International," June 23, 1975, 48; NCOIWY 1975; IWY Records: SF H-M; Box 23; NARA; RG 220; SLR.

Stein, Edward. "Queers Anonymous: Lesbians, Gay Men, Free Speech, and Cyberspace." *Harvard Civil Rights-Civil Liberties Law Review* 38, no 1 (2003): 159–213.

Stephen, Lynn. *Women and Social Movements in Latin America: Power from Below.* Austin: University of Texas Press, 1997.

Stienstra, Deborah. "Gender, Women's Organizing, and the Internet." In *Technology, Development, and Democracy: International Conflict and Cooperation in the Information Age*, edited by J.E. Allison, 187–211. Albany: State University of New York Press, 2002.

Sundén, Jenny. "What Happened to Difference in Cyberspace? The (Re)turn of the She-Cyborg." *Feminist Media Studies* 1, no. 2 (2001): 215–32.

Surman, Mark. "The Economics of Community Networking: Case Studies from the Association for Progressive Communications (APC)." In *Community Informatics: Enabling Communities with Information and Communications Technologies*, edited by Michael Gurstein, 568–83. Hershey, PA: IRMA Group Publishing, 2000.

TeleGeography. *Global Internet Geography 2003: International Internet Statistics and Commentary*. Washington, DC: TeleGeography, 2003.

Thayer, Millie. *Making Transnational Feminism*. New York: Routledge, 2010.

Travers, Ann. "Parallel Subaltern Feminist Counterpublics in Cyberspace." *Sociological Perspectives* 46, no. 2 (2003): 223–37.

United Nations. *Platform for Action, Fourth World Conference on Women*. UN Document no. A/CONF.177/20, Annex II (17 October). New York: United Nations, 1995.

Urrutia, Elena. "Una publicación feminista." *fem* 10 (1986–87): 9–11.

van Zoonen, Liesbet. "Gendering the Internet: Claims, Controversies, and Cultures." *European Journal of Communication* 17, no. 1 (2002): 5–23.

"Vancouver Focal Point Meeting of June 24th." "Hotline International," June 24, 1975, 86; NCOIWY 1975; IWY Records: SF H-M; Box 23; NARA; RG 220; SLR.

Wajcman, Judy. "Feminist Theories of Technology." *Cambridge Journal of Economics*: 34, no. 1 (2010): 143–52.

———. *Technofeminism*. Cambridge: Polity Press, 2004.

Walker, Anne. "The International Women's Tribune Centre: Expanding the Struggle for Women's Rights at the UN." In *Developing Power: How Women Transformed International Development,* edited by Arvonne S. Fraser and Irene Tinker, 90–102. New York: Feminist Press at CUNY, 2004.

———. *Women's Communications Strategies: Utilizing ICTs and Strategic Alliances Worldwide,* 2002. UN Women website, www.un.org/womenwatch /daw/egm/media2002/reports/EP9Walker.PDF (access date July 31, 2016).

Warkentin, Craig. *Reshaping World Politics: NGOs, the Internet, and Global Civil Society*. Lanham, MD: Rowman & Littlefield Publishers, 2001.

Warner, Michael. *Publics and Counterpublics*. Cambridge: Zone Books, 2002.

Wilding, Faith, and María Hernández. "Situating Cyberfeminisms." In *Domain Errors: Cyberfeminist Practices!* edited by María Hernández, Faith Wilding, and Michelle M. Wright, 17–28. New York: Autonomedia, 2002.

Wilkinson, Annie. "Who the Rainbow Tide Leaves Out." *NACLA Report on the Americas* 47, no. 4 (2015): 30–32.

Willetts, Peter. "NGOs, Networking, and the Creation of the Internet." In *Non-Governmental Organizations in World Politics: the Construction of Global Governance,* 84–113. Abigdon, Oxon: Routledge, 2011.

Winslow, Anne, ed. *Women, Politics, and the United Nations*. Westport, CN: Greenwood Press, 1995.

Wood, Peregrine. "Putting Beijing Online: Women's Working in Information and Communication Technologies; Experiences from the APC Women's Networking Support Program." In *Networking for Change: The APCWNSP's First 8 Years, Women in Sync: A Toolkit for Electronic Networking, Part I.* The Philippines: Association for Progressive Communications Women's Networking Support Programme, 2000. APC website, www.apcwomen.org /netsupport/sync/sync.html (accessed July 7, 2016).

Index